WRITING AND SELLING YOUR

MYSTERY NOVEL

HALLIE EPHRON

how to knock 'em
DEAD with style

WRITER'S DIGEST BOOKS
Cincinnati, Ohio
www.writersdigest.com

Visit our Web site at www.writersdigest.com for information on more resources for writers.

To receive a free weekly e-mail newsletter delivering tips and updates about writing and about Writer's Digest products, register directly at our Web site at http://newsletters.fwpublications .com.

09 08 07 06 05   5 4 3 2 1

Library of Congress Cataloging-in-Publication Data

Touger, Hallie Ephron.
    Writing and selling your mystery novel : how to knock 'em dead with style / by Hallie Ephron.—1st ed.
        p.   cm.
    Includes index.
    ISBN 1-58297-317-2 (hardcover : alk. paper)—ISBN 1-58297-376-8 (pbk. : alk. paper)
        1. Detective and mystery stories—Authorship. 2. Authorship—Marketing. I. Title.

    PN3377.5.D4T68   2005
    808.3′872—dc22   2005006279
                                                                                             CIP

Edited by Michelle Ruberg
Design by Claudean Wheeler
Cover design by Grace Ring
Cover image by Image Source
Production coordinated by Robin Richie

PERMISSIONS

For Donald Davidoff, to whom I owe this particular version of insanity.

ACKNOWLEDGMENTS

Thanks to the writers who helped me get the advice right without being preachy or bossy, as is my wont: Connie Biewald, Maggie Bucholt, Pat Rathbone, Donna Tramontozzi, Lynn Denley-Bussard, and Didi Foster. Thanks to Molly Touger for her editor's eye.

Thanks to my agent, Gail Hochman, for her support and enthusiasm; to Melanie Rigney and Barb Kuroff for paving the way for me at Writer's Digest Books; and to editor Michelle Ruberg for her on-point suggestions and for ably shepherding this along.

And thanks to the generous mystery writing community of which I'm proud to be part, and to the writers who shared their experiences and thoughts, including Linda Barnes, Lorraine Bodger, Rhys Bowen, Jan Brogan, Lee Child, Kate Flora, Jim Fusilli, Judith Greber, Naomi Rand, Tom Sawyer, Sarah Smith, Jessica Speart, and Carolyn Wheat.

Special thanks to S.J. Rozan, a modern master of the genre, for graciously agreeing to write the foreword to this book and for doing a smashing job.

And loving thanks to my husband Jerry Touger and my daughters Molly and Naomi.

ABOUT THE AUTHOR

Hallie Ephron is co-author of the Dr. Peter Zak mystery series by G.H. Ephron. She reviews crime fiction in a monthly column for *The Boston Globe*. Past president of the New England chapter of Sisters in Crime and a member of Mystery Writers of America, Hallie chaired the 2003 judging committee for the Edgar® award for best short story. She is also a freelance journalist and essayist whose work has appeared in *More*® magazine and on NPR. Hallie grew up in Los Angeles, and her parents, Phoebe and Henry Ephron, were Hollywood screenwriters. Her sisters are director/screenwriter Nora Ephron and novelist/screenwriters Delia and Amy Ephron. Hallie lives near Boston.

Books by Hallie Ephron writing as G.H. Ephron:

Amnesia
Addiction
Delusion
Obsessed
Guilt

The Table of
CONTENTS

FOREWORD

INTRODUCTION...1

HOW THIS BOOK WORKS..10

PART 1: PLANNING 12
Part 1: Introduction 13
Chapter 1: The Premise..14
Chapter 2: The Mystery Sleuth 18
Chapter 3: The Crime, Victim's Secrets..36
Chapter 4: The Villain 40
Chapter 5: Innocent Suspects 45
Chapter 6: The Supporting Cast 50
Chapter 7: Setting..57
Chapter 8: Staking Out the Plot..69
Chapter 9: Picking a Title 82
A Blueprint for Planning a Mystery Novel..86

PART 2: WRITING 92
Part 2: Introduction 93
Chapter 10: Writing a Dramatic Opening..96
Chapter 11: Introducing the Protagonist..103
Chapter 12: Introducing Major and Minor Characters..................108
Chapter 13: Dramatizing Scenes, Making Chapters 119
Chapter 14: Point of View..126
Chapter 15: Writing Dialogue 139

Chapter 16: Creating a Sense of Place 145
Chapter 17: Writing Investigation:
            Clues, Red Herrings, and Misdirection 152
Chapter 18: Writing Suspense... 163
Chapter 19: Writing Action... 171
Chapter 20: Puzzling it Out: Writing Reflection 179
Chapter 21: Layering in Backstory 186
Chapter 22: Writing the Coda... 194

PART 3: REVISING 198
Part 3: Introduction 199
Chapter 23: Flying High: Fixing Plot and Character 201
Chapter 24: Flying Low: Polishing Scenes and Sentences........... 206
Chapter 25: Hearing Criticism, Finding Your Own Fix................ 215

PART 4: SELLING YOUR MYSTERY NOVEL 224
Part 4: Introduction 225
Chapter 26: Targeting Agents... 226
Chapter 27: Targeting Small or Independent Presses 230
Chapter 28: Putting Together a Query Packet 234

APPENDIX OF RESOURCES FOR MYSTERY WRITERS 242

INDEX 246

foreword

Remember, in *The Wizard of Oz*, the sign Dorothy and her friends found as they approached the castle of the Wicked Witch of the West? It read, "I'd Turn Back If I Were You."

Well, I would.

If you're reading this book, or thinking of reading this book, you must want to write a mystery.

Big mistake.

In fact, writing any kind of fiction is a big mistake.

Really, take a look at it. What do you get?

1. Hours and hours of hard, lonely work. While other people go to the movies, play with their kids, walk their dogs, and do the laundry, you'll be up there locked away alone, putting the same comma in and out of the same line of dialogue for hours.

2. Self-doubt, embarrassment, and worry. You'll fear your characters are cardboard, you'll be afraid your setting's trite, you'll be sure your story's been told three hundred times already, every one of them better.

3. Rejection. If you do manage to finish the thing, at least one agent (and probably more) and at least one editor (and definitely more) will turn it down before someone agrees to take it.

4. More hours of hard work. When someone finally buys your book, you'll be editing and revising until you're sick of it. Then you'll go out on the road. You'll rush from one hotel to another, take off your shoes and empty your pockets in countless airports, and read in the evenings from this book you

can no longer stand. And, before rushing to the next airport, you'll fend off stern e-mails from your editor demanding to know why you're not making progress on your next book.

Turned back yet?

I didn't think so.

I never did either.

If you can't be discouraged by the almost certain scarcity of fame, fortune, and even convenience that attends the writing of a piece of mystery fiction, then chances are you really, *really* want to write one.

Welcome to the Land of Oz.

Things are crazy here. You'll meet all manner of beast and person. Many are engaged on the same journey you're on; the rest are here to comment, in their various ways, on your progress. It can be confounding, confusing, and downright scary here, but it's never boring.

In fact, it's the most thrilling place I've ever been. Everything is exciting. All the people are intriguing; each event is fascinating; nothing is wasted. It's all material. And you knew that. You've got a huge pile of this material; you've been collecting it for years, right? And now you're ready to write your book. You're ready to set off into the enchanted forest, but you're not sure which direction to go.

None of us were, when we started out. Some of us wandered in circles for awhile, tripping over roots, bopping our foreheads on branches. As often as not it was through sheer luck, or cussedness, that in the end we found our way.

But some people found guides.

And you're lucky enough to have found Hallie Ephron.

In this book, Hallie's giving you a map. The longest journey, as I know you know, begins with a single step. This book will help you take that step. And the step after that, and the next. It will show you the long view when you're feeling trapped in the thicket, and it will cut the towering peaks into manageable switchbacks. And when you find your writer's road blocked by a huge, unmovable boulder, it will show you how to push it aside, or find a route around or even over it.

The map in this book will make the process of writing your novel controllable, understandable, and as close to fun as it gets. You'll still have to do the work; this book won't write *your* book. But it will show you what work to do, so you can plan, structure, and write. And revise, rework, and rewrite. It will show you how to start, what to do when you're mired in the middle, and how to come to a triumphant finish. And, if you're still standing, it will help you market it to an agent and an editor so that your book can end up, finally, in the hands of those most elusive, legendary, and desirable inhabitants of this loony Land: readers.

And I can tell you this: It's too late for you. For anyone who's come this far, it's too late. You've reached the haunted wood and you can't turn back now.

So come on in.

—S.J. Rozan

S.J. Rozan is the author of eight novels in the Lydia Chin/Bill Smith series, as well as the standalone *Absent Friends* and many short stories. Her work has won the Edgar, Shamus, Anthony, Macavity and Nero for Best Novel and the Edgar for Best Short Story. She's a former Mystery Writers of America national board member, a current Sisters in Crime national board member, and President of the Private Eye Writers of America.

Introduction

> "The first person you should think of pleasing, in writing a book, is yourself. If you can amuse yourself for the length of time it takes to write a book, the publisher and the readers can and will come later."
>
> —PATRICIA HIGHSMITH
> *Plotting and Writing Suspense Fiction*

You know you're reading a great mystery novel when you're up at three in the morning, unable to put it down. When you finally fall asleep, the characters go romping around in your dreams. When you get to the final page, you smack yourself in the head because the solution seems obvious in retrospect yet came as a complete surprise.

Page-turning suspense. Rich characterization. A credible surprise ending. Sounds pretty simple, but writing a mystery novel is not for the faint of heart. Juggler, conjurer, and herder of cats—those are all in the job description. Be prepared to keep three or four intertwined plots spinning. Get ready to master the art of misdirection so readers will ogle those red herrings you've sprinkled while ignoring the real clues in plain sight. Don't be surprised when you find yourself riding herd on a load of characters who won't go where you want them to.

On top of that, you'll need dogged determination and intestinal fortitude to stick with it, through first draft and endless revisions, until your words are polished to lapidary perfection. It wouldn't hurt, either, to have the hide of a rhinoceros to withstand the inevitable rejections. Talent being equal, what separates many a published mystery writer from an unpublished one is sheer stamina and blind luck. Only gluttons for punishment need apply.

More complications: There is no formula for writing a popular mystery novel. Ask ten writers who've done it and you'll hear ten different approaches. That's because, just like you, every one of them has a unique assortment of strengths and weaknesses. Maybe your dialogue sings but your descriptions are pallid. Maybe you have a grand time coming up with plot twists and writing slam-bang action scenes, but your characters tend to be flat, without emotional insight. Maybe you write complex, interesting female characters but your men are cardboard cutouts. Your first draft will reflect whatever mixed bag you bring to the table.

This book presents a writing process that capitalizes on your strengths and shores up your weaknesses. Throughout, you'll find a range of strategies that have worked for successful mystery writers, along with invitations to try them and see what works for you. The baseline is to knock 'em dead with a great story, compelling characters, and plot twists that pull readers along and keep them guessing.

WHAT IS MYSTERY FICTION?

Simply put, at the heart of any mystery novel is a puzzle for the reader and a fictional sleuth to solve. There are one or more crimes, usually murders. Early on, the nefarious goings-on seem to be about one thing. In the end, however, they turn out to be about something else entirely, with twists and turns along the way. A teenage girl's accidental overdose turns out to be the murderer's carefully choreographed effort to eliminate her as an eyewitness to a crime. A botched mugging turns out to be a rape victim's revenge. A husband-wife mob hit turns out to be a mutual suicide pact.

To make the mystery work, the writer comes up with a string of events and reflects them in a series of funhouse mirrors. The main story gets intertwined with subplots and complicated by characters who may or may not have something to hide. In the end, the reader should be surprised when the truth is revealed.

From firsthand experience, I know that the author can be surprised, too. I write the Dr. Peter Zak mysteries with Donald Davidoff. Our protagonist is based loosely on Don, who in real life is a forensic neuropsychologist who consults as an expert witness in murder trials. We collaborate on story, but I do the writing. Together, we carefully outlined the plot of our first Peter Zak series novel, *Amnesia*. Before I started drafting the first chapter, we knew who did it and why—only we turned out to be wrong. I wrote a line of dialogue in a pivotal scene, based on what Don and I had discussed. I read what I'd written once, then again. In context, the dialogue took on an entirely new meaning: The character had just confessed to the murder. The solution made perfect sense and had the great virtue of being totally unexpected. If *we* were surprised, surely readers would be as well. When I went back to tweak earlier scenes to make the ending work, I found very little tweaking was needed. The killer's true identity was hiding in the novel all along, waiting for us to find it.

St. Martin's gave us a contract for *Amnesia* and a second series book. The editor said it was that surprise ending that sold her.

GENRE CONVENTIONS

People refer to mystery fiction as *genre fiction*, meaning there are certain conventions that readers know and expect. Here's a short list of them:

- The story is told from the point of view of the sleuth.
- The reader knows everything that the point-of-view character knows.
- Bad things happen; there's at least one murder.
- By the end of the novel, the reader knows who did it and why; all is explained, and loose ends are tied up.
- The reader feels satisfied that justice has triumphed in the end.

Does that mean that a mystery author has to write within the confines of these conventions? Not at all. Multiple points of view are common these days, especially in suspense. The occasional book marketed as a murder mystery has no murder in it. Plenty of authors leave plot strands dangling. Here's the governing rule: Write a good enough book, then you can break any rule and get away with it.

THE SUBGENRES

The label "mystery" covers a lot of turf, across a spectrum from soft- to hard-boiled. There is no standard list of subgenres, and many books straddle subgenres, but here's a sampling of the categories:

- **Cozy:** A mystery with a light tone and an element of fun; the setting is usually a small community and the protagonist is an amateur sleuth who's a member of the community. Sex and violence occur, for the most part, off-stage. Agatha Christie's Miss Jane Marple remains the quintessential cozy protagonist. Other exemplars include television's Jessica Fletcher and Lillian Jackson Braun's Jim Qwilleran with cats Koko and Yum Yum.

- **Caper:** An elaborate crime is planned and carried out; the characters are trying to break in somewhere impregnable and steal something heavily guarded. Donald Westlake is a master of both the comic and dramatic versions of this genre. *The Hot Rock*, the debut appearance of Westlake's bungling burglar Dortmunder (named after a German beer), is a classic example.

- **Police Procedural:** The protagonist is in law enforcement; the solution involves police procedure. Mystery authors who excel in this subgenre include Evan Hunter (aka Ed McBain), Loren D. Estleman, J.A. Jance, and Linda Fairstein.

- **PI:** The main character is a private investigator. This subgenre was perfected by the classic greats Dashiell Hammett (Sam Spade) and Raymond Chandler (Philip Marlowe); modern examples are Linda Barnes (Carlotta Carlyle), Sue Grafton (Kinsey Millhone), and Robert B. Parker (Spenser).

• **Historical:** The story is set in an earlier historical era. A classic is Josephine Tey's *The Daughter of Time*, in which a present-day police inspector unravels the murder of Richard III's young nephews. Other examples are Anne Perry's *A Breach of Promise*, Laurie R. King's *The Beekeeper's Apprentice*, and Sarah Smith's trilogy beginning with *The Vanished Child.*

• **Legal:** The playing field is the legal system, and the main player is an attorney. Believable courtroom drama is the centerpiece. Masters of the form include Scott Turow and Lisa Scottoline; British author John Mortimer's Rumpole series does a comedic turn on the genre.

• **Psychological Suspense:** The protagonist is usually a psychologist or psychiatrist, often working as an expert witness as well as solving a crime. The novel explores psychological issues. Of course there is G.H. Ephron, with protagonist neuropsychologist Peter Zak; Jonathan Kellerman, who writes child psychiatrist Alex Delaware; and Anna Salter, who writes forensic psychologist Michael Stone.

• **Forensic:** Examination of physical evidence takes center stage as the protagonist looks at fingerprints, bones, DNA, and other clues. Patricia Cornwell defined this popular subgenre with her series featuring medical examiner Kay Scarpetta. Kathy Reichs aces it with her forensic anthropologist/ sleuth Temperance Brennan.

• **Fem-jep:** "Female in jeopardy" puts a gorgeous woman in peril; she's stalked, kidnapped, or otherwise besieged by bad guys and has to be rescued by a knight in shining armor. Sometimes the chick saves herself. Mary Roberts Rinehart invented it; Mary Higgins Clark perfected it.

• **Genre Busters:** In recent years, books that defy categorization have captured readers' attentions. For example, Jasper Fforde's *The Eyre Affair* combines time travel and characters kidnapped from literature.

SERIES AND STANDALONES

A *series* mystery novel has repeating characters whose stories continue book to book and a puzzle that gets solved within the context of each book. A *standalone* is written as a one-off, without a plan for a prequel or sequel.

At the outset, it's a good idea to decide whether the book you're about to write is the first of a series or a standalone. This will affect many of the decisions you make—not the least of which is whether you can bump off your main character.

When my co-author and I started to collaborate, we envisioned our first novel as the beginning of a series. We thought our idea, a forensic neuropsychologist who solves crimes by studying psychological clues, not DNA or blood spatters, lent itself perfectly to a series format. Each book would explore a different psychological theme, starting with memory in *Amnesia*. Dr. Peter Zak, investigator Annie Squires, and a supporting cast would continue in subsequent books exploring topics such as paranoia, guilt, addiction, and obsession. Just for fun, we brainstormed a list of one-word titles and came up with about fifty of them.

In any established series, the plots have to continue to be good—but it's the repeating character that readers come back to. Time spent up front developing your protagonist for a series debut pays off big time in the long run.

There are a host of reasons to go the series route. You don't have to keep starting over. Create a rich set of repeating characters in book one, each with a backstory and issues, and continue to develop them book to book. From a business standpoint, there's somewhat less pressure to go supernova on the first book. With a supportive publisher, you have time to build an audience. Early books are more likely to stay in print as each new series entry pumps the sales of the previous ones.

By the third or fourth book, the downside of a series becomes clear. You have to find a fresh way to reintroduce the ensemble characters in each book without boring those who've read the previous books, while at the same time giving new readers a taste of each character's past without spoiling the earlier stories. You have to keep coming up with new catastrophes and life-changing crises to throw at the main characters.

In the happy event that you have a successful series, you may find after five or six series novels that writing a standalone and working on a broader canvas seems very appealing. Dennis Lehane published five moderately successful Patrick Kenzie/Angela Gennaro novels before hitting it big with *Mystic River*. Harlan Coben had seven Myron Bolitar sports agent series novels under his belt before writing standalone best-seller *Tell No One*. On the other hand, Sue Grafton looks like she really will get to *Z*.

WHAT MAKES A MYSTERY NOVEL POPULAR?

First let's take the high road: Whether it's hard-boiled or soft, cozy or caper, and regardless of whether there's a murder in the book at all, popular mysteries give readers something more than an edge-of-the-seat ride. Often they examine serious themes and social issues. Truth, culpability, love, racism, corruption, power, redemption—weighty matters such as these are at the core of the best mystery fiction. On top of that, the mystery has to be a fun read and a page-turner with a satisfying ending that leaves the reader wide-eyed in amazement, thinking: *I should have seen that coming.*

Now the low road: From a commercial marketing standpoint, it doesn't hurt to have a gimmick. This is particularly true when you're at the stage of getting a publisher interested in your work. Editors like books they can figure out how to market. So it's advantageous if your book has a hook, some unique feature you can communicate in fifteen seconds. A hook can be anything from your protagonist's unique occupation, to a particularly intriguing setting or backdrop, to an extra-added bonus beyond the mystery in the mystery.

Here are some examples:

Author	Hook
Rita Mae Brown and Sneaky Pie	The cat solves the crimes.
Margaret Coel	Stories are set among the Arapaho on the Wind River Reservation in Wyoming.
Susan Conant	The sleuth trains dogs.
Phillip R. Craig	The mysteries take place on Martha's Vineyard.
Diane Mott Davidson	Her culinary mysteries include recipes.
Dick Francis	Stories are about horseracing; author was a former jockey.
Kinky Friedman	The sleuth is a Jewish country-and-western singer.
Parnell Hall	The puzzle lady uses crossword puzzles and cryptograms to solve the crimes; puzzles are included.
Tamar Myers	The sleuth is an Amish innkeeper.
Margaret Truman	The mysteries take place at D.C. landmarks, and the author is the daughter of former President Harry Truman.

Having said that, there are plenty of star performers who deliver, year in and year out, best-sellers that are nothing more than good, old-fashioned crime fiction with a professional or semiprofessional sleuth. These include Michael Connelly, Janet Evanovich, Sue Grafton, Carl Hiaasen, Walter Mosley, Carol O'Connell, Robert B. Parker, and James Patterson. These authors tell great stories with great style, and any gimmicks are incidental to their success.

TUNING YOUR EAR: A READING LIST

Some authors find it difficult to read mystery fiction while they're writing their own. I understand the danger. I read my first Robert B. Parker novel while I was writing *Addiction*, and before I knew it, Dr. Peter Zak and Dr. Kwan Liu were trading banter that sounded suspiciously like Spenser and Hawk. *Delete. Delete. Delete.*

On the other hand, you can learn from the masters. Reading good mystery fiction tunes your ear. Books by Elmore Leonard are lessons in dialogue. Books by Jeffery Deaver are lessons in suspense. Read the titans of mystery fiction to see what makes readers respond. Read the Edgar-award winners to see what "quality" means. Read first mystery novels that turned into bestsellers. And don't forget the classics.

Here's a short reading list to get you started.

SOME NOVELS THAT SET THE STANDARDS

PLOT:
And Then There Were None: Ten Little Indians, Agatha Christie
An Unsuitable Job for a Woman, P.D. James
The Chill, Ross Macdonald

CHARACTER:
The Magician's Tale, David Hunt
The No. 1 Ladies' Detective Agency, Alexander McCall Smith
Blanche on the Lam, Barbara Neely
Winter and Night, S.J. Rozan

DIALOGUE:
LaBrava, Elmore Leonard
Looking for Rachel Wallace, Robert B. Parker

SETTING/DESCRIPTION:
Coyote Waits, Tony Hillerman
Devil in a Blue Dress, Walter Mosley
Winter House, Carol O'Connell

ACTION/SUSPENSE:
Bones, Jan Burke
The Bone Collector, Jeffery Deaver
Final Jeopardy, Linda Fairstein

HUMOR:
High Five, Janet Evanovich
Open and Shut, David Rosenfelt
The Hot Rock, Donald Westlake

A FEW BLOCKBUSTER DEBUT MYSTERY NOVELS:

- *The Black Echo*, Michael Connelly
- *When the Bough Breaks*, Jonathan Kellerman
- *Presumed Innocent*, Scott Turow

SOME CLASSICS THAT DEFINE THE GENRE:

- *The Moonstone* (1868), Wilkie Collins (the father of the English detective novel)
- *The Hound of the Baskervilles* (1901), Sir Arthur Conan Doyle
- *The Roman Hat Mystery* (1929), Ellery Queen
- *The Maltese Falcon* (1930), Dashiell Hammett
- *The Nine Tailors* (1934), Dorothy L. Sayers
- *Fer de Lance* (1934), Rex Stout
- *Death in Ecstasy* (1936), Ngaio Marsh
- *The Big Sleep* (1939), Raymond Chandler
- *The Murder at the Vicarage* (1930), Agatha Christie
- *I, the Jury* (1947), Mickey Spillane
- *Brat Farrar* (1949), Josephine Tey
- *The Talented Mr. Ripley* (1955), Patricia Highsmith
- *The Laughing Policeman* (1968), Maj Sjöwall and Per Wahlöö
- *Twice Shy* (1982), Dick Francis

NESTING INSTRUCTIONS

Virginia Woolf said it most eloquently: "A woman must have money and a room of her own if she is going to write." In today's equal opportunity environment, the adage applies to men as well.

If you're going to write, I have two pieces of advice:
- Set up a space for writing.
- Don't quit your day job unless you have an independent source of income.

When I started writing, I held on to my job but cut back to part-time so I'd have time to write. I set up my computer at the end of my bedroom and worked there with spotty results. I'd start writing and end up straightening my underwear drawer.

When my daughters outgrew the small, enclosed sunporch that had been their playroom, I turned that space into my office. I found that once I had a place dedicated to writing, I'd go in there and write. If I was in my office, everyone in the house knew I was working and to leave me alone.

If you don't have a spare room, then at least set up a separate space that no one else uses. Get a folding screen to close yourself off and to communicate to friends and family: Do Not Disturb. Then set a schedule.

Every writer has a different capacity for churning out pages. Robert B. Parker, who has been known to publish three books in a year and still manage to take six months off from writing, says he doesn't quit until he's written ten pages each day. He writes five days a week. At that clip, and because he does very little revision, he can complete a novel in six weeks.

Parker leaves the rest of us in the dust. I work everyday, seven days a week, except when I'm on vacation or on a break between books. On a good day, I can write 2,000 words. My self-imposed, daily minimum is 500 words—that's barely a page and a half. Not a whole lot. But write 500 words a day, everyday, and in six months you've got yourself a completed first draft.

Set a minimum goal for each day, placing the bar slightly above what you know you can do without breaking a sweat. Then stick to it. Set up a writing schedule that suits your biorhythms. Are you a lark or an owl? I get up at 7 A.M., make myself a cup of tea, and start writing. By two in the afternoon, my spark and creativity for the day are sapped, and I'm pretty much useless as far as writing first draft goes—though I can still revise and research.

Be sure you have everything you need right there in your office. A computer connected to the Internet has pretty much eliminated the need for those reference books that were once indispensable, not to mention trips to the library. The encyclopedia, dictionary, Bible, thesaurus, *Bartlett's Familiar Quotations*, and Strunk and White's *The Elements of Style* are all available in searchable format on www.bartleby.com/usage. My office has copies of each anyway, because I prefer real books. In addition, I have several handbooks on English usage, guides to forensics and crime-scene investigations, a *DSM-IV* (*Diagnostic and Statistical Manual of Mental Disorders*), a *Physician's Desk Reference*, *The Joys of Yiddish* plus a collection of books by my favorite writers (including my own).

Here are a few other essentials for a writing space:
• a comfortable desk chair with good back support
• a generous, well-lit work surface
• an electric pencil sharpener (I love this contraption, and though I rarely write in pencil, there's something very comforting about having a container full of sharpened pencils.)
• a computer with an Internet connection
• a reliable printer
• a phone (Yes, it's a source of interruption, but you won't have to leave the room to answer it.)

Finally, my office wouldn't be complete without fortunes stuck to my wall, saved from years of eating Chinese takeout because I was writing all day instead of shopping for food. I read them whenever I get discouraged. My favorite is at least a decade old and completely faded:

You will succeed in a far out profession.

How This Book Works

"Do you promise that your detectives shall
well and truly detect the crimes presented to
them, using those wits which it may please you
to bestow upon them and not placing reliance
on Divine Revelation, Feminine Intuition,
Mumbo-Jumbo, Jiggery-Pokery, Coincidence or
the Act of God?"

—MEMBERSHIP OATH OF THE DETECTION CLUB
founded in 1928; past presidents include
Dorothy L. Sayers and Agatha Christie

This book is designed to be interactive. It's loaded with *examples* for you to read and analyze, *Now You Try* exercises to do on the spot, and *On Your Own* end-of-chapter activities for follow-up. The more you do, the more you'll get out of it.

The book divides the writing process into five parts:

1. Part I: Planning. Beginning with a premise, this section provides a step-by-step guide to the process of planning a mystery novel. As you complete each chapter, you'll be instructed to go to the *blueprint* at the end of that section. Completing the blueprint is integral to the planning process. By the time you finish the planning section, you'll have a completed blueprint and be ready to write.

2. Part II: Writing. From compelling opening scene to climax to final coda, this section guides you through the writing process. It discusses writing scenes, introducing characters, writing the investigation, creating suspense and action, and suggests techniques to keep the reader turning the pages.

3. Part III: Revising. This section provides a range of techniques for polishing your novel within an inch of its life, as it must be in order to get out of an editor's slush pile. The chapters guide you through the revision process, first flying at high altitude and examining big issues such as pacing and characterization, then flying low examining scenes, sentences, and phrases.

4. Part IV: Selling. This section provides tips on finding an agent and a publisher, and how to prepare a query packet and send it out into the world. It includes tips for formatting a professional-looking manuscript and advice on handling rejection.

5. Appendix of Resources for Mystery Writers. Here you'll find information about organizations, mystery conferences, contests, and guidebooks to all things mysterious.

PaRt 1
planning

Introduction

> "Having a set of rules to follow as guidelines for writing a mystery makes sense for beginners, just as beginning artists learn the rules for color and perspective. Rules are fine until you get a feel for your own style and are skilled enough to stretch the limits of your writing. Certain rules, like playing fair with the reader, will always make sense."
>
> —RHYS BOWEN

Getting started writing a mystery novel can feel overwhelming. Where to begin? You may need to think about your story for weeks until it's sufficiently gelled to write an outline. Or you may need to jump in and write a chunk, and then do the planning. Or perhaps you are among the rare and fortunate few who write straight through from start to finish, barely pausing to take a breath.

As for me, I quickly hit a wall if I try to plunge ahead without a plan. A mystery novel is complex and must be well crafted, so I recommend standing back, early on, and thinking it through.

Turn to the end of this section (page 86) and look over the "Blueprint for Planning a Mystery Novel." It's a series of forms where you can record your planning ideas. At the end of each chapter, there will be an invitation to go to the blueprint and complete another section.

When you've finished the chapters in Part I, your blueprint will be complete and you'll be ready to write.

No one follows a plan to the letter. Major changes may be needed when a character you thought was going to be minor starts doing pirouettes, or when a plot point critical to your solution stretches credibility to the breaking point. But by getting down the basics early on and really thinking through your story and your characters, you give yourself a solid starting point.

CHaPtEr 1:
the premise

> "Anyone who ever waited for the great inspiration to strike is still waiting to write her first book or short story. I start with an idea, of course; something that intrigues me. Then I start asking myself three questions: Suppose, what if, and why?"
>
> —MARY HIGGINS CLARK

Start with *an idea*, something that intrigues you. Sounds easy enough. But where do ideas come from?

I used to think that I couldn't write fiction because I wasn't good at making things up. Turns out you don't have to be, because intriguing ideas are all around you. Learn to tune in, and pay attention when your brain says: *Oh, that's interesting.*

WHERE TO FIND IDEAS

Here are just a few places to find ideas:
- books (No, you can't steal the main idea of a book—that's plagiarism— but you can build on an image, a situation, or a line of dialogue, for example.)
- your own conversations
- overheard conversations
- television
- news and magazine stories
- something that happened to someone you know
- your own experience
- your dreams

Whenever I trip over a story idea, I jot it down and stash it in a folder labeled "compost." By now, the folder is bulging with clippings and handwritten notes.

Many of the story ideas I've saved have a psychological slant, because that's what interests me. Here are some of the news stories in my compost heap:

- A serial rapist brazenly shows his face during his attacks, defying the conventional pattern of such criminals and confounding profilers.
- Eight robbers who invaded a home are found living there a week later.
- A man tries to stage his own disappearance by murdering a look-alike he found on the Internet.
- A young man who writes his fantasies into his personal journal is sentenced to seven years in prison for making child pornography.

Start your own compost file, and save ideas that intrigue you.

MAKING THE LEAP FROM IDEA TO PREMISE

A *premise* is the basic proposition behind the book. Transforming an idea into a well-articulated premise is step one of writing a mystery novel.

Here's an example of a premise developed from one of the ideas in my compost heap.

Story idea from the news . . .	turned into a mystery novel premise using *suppose* and *what if*
A young man who writes his fantasies in a personal journal is sentenced to seven years in prison for making child pornography.	Suppose a troubled young man writes violent, explicit sexual fantasies into his personal journal and shares his journal with his therapist. And what if a series of violent crimes then occur that closely mirror the details of his fantasies . . .

The words **suppose** and **what if** anchor a well-articulated premise. Once you put it in that format, a premise shows you where you're going. It keeps you on track throughout the writing process, and it can be useful again when you're pitching your book to agents, editors, and ultimately to booksellers and readers.

Once the premise is articulated, it suggests all kinds of plot possibilities. Did the young man commit the crimes? Did his therapist? Did the therapist share that journal with someone, or did it get stolen, or maybe the young man copied those fantasies from somewhere or someone? The story could explore issues of culpability and privacy. And, and, and. . . .

With a good idea and a premise in hand, you're off and running.

Practice turning an idea into a premise. Go through the newspaper and clip articles that appeal to you and contain the germ of an idea for a mystery novel. Jot down each idea in the left column below. In the right column, transform it into a premise using suppose and what if.

Idea from the news	Mystery novel premise: *suppose* and *what if*

USING REAL EVENTS AND PEOPLE

A real person or an actual event can make an excellent jumping-off point for a mystery novel. But some real events are too bizarre for fiction. For instance, there's a news story in my compost heap about a highway toll collector who gets a call from a friend, warning her to be on the lookout for a 2003 white Chevy Silverado pickup being driven by a shooting suspect on the lam. Minutes later, that truck drives through her toll lane! Put that in a book and readers will cry foul because it seems so unbelievable. *But it really happened!*

you say. So what? Plenty of things happen in real life that you'd never get away with putting in a work of fiction.

A well-constructed fictional world isn't necessarily realistic, but it must be believable.

MARKET-DRIVEN IDEAS

Does your idea have to be marketable? Sure, what you're writing about has to be interesting to more than you and a few geeky professional colleagues. On the other hand, it's hard to predict what readers will find interesting. Can you imagine a book about the physics of icebergs appealing to lots of readers? No? Guess again. That's what best-selling suspense novel *Smilla's Sense of Snow* was about. Blockbuster *The Da Vinci Code* combined an international murder mystery with a minute analysis of esoterica culled from two thousand years of Western history. These authors make arcane content interesting by writing about it in a compelling way, and they tap into the mystery reader's appetite for learning new things.

Should you try to follow the trends and write what's hot? I don't recommend it. Readers are notoriously fickle, and what appeals to the crowd this year may be box-office poison three years from now when, if you're lucky, your book hits the shelves. Besides, readers are looking for something *new*.

Because it's all so unpredictable, the best advice is: *Write your passion.* Write what you care about, what interests and intrigues you. One thing's for sure, you'll be more likely to finish a novel if you care about it, and only finished books stand a chance of being published.

ON YOUR OWN: Finding ideas

1. Become an observer. The world around you is full of inspiration. Watch what goes on while you're riding a bus, drinking at a bar, waiting at an airport—wherever. Listen to conversations. Notice what people wear, their mannerisms. Take notes.

2. Be prepared when ideas strike. Carry a pad and pen in your pocket, keep them by your bed. You think you'll remember, but you won't.

3. Make a folder of ideas. Clip and save stories that intrigue you from newspapers and magazines. Throw in other ideas you jot down.

4. Carry a tape recorder. Do you get your best ideas while driving your car? I do. Keep a little tape recorder handy so you'll be able to capture those ideas without causing an accident.

Complete the Premise section of the blueprint. (Go to page 86 at the end of Part I to find these forms.)

CHaPtEr 2:
the mystery sleuth

> "A really good detective never gets married."
>
> —RAYMOND CHANDLER
> *Raymond Chandler Speaking*

An editor once told me that when she reads a manuscript, especially the first of a new series, first and foremost she's looking for a compelling mystery sleuth. In order to keep readers coming back, she said, the novel has to make the reader care about what happened to that character before the book opens and what's going to happen to that character after the book ends.

So what kind of character makes readers care? It goes without saying that the character must be fully realized and complex, not a cipher or a cliché. Does the character have to be likable? Sympathetic, at the very least. Perfect? No way. Perfectly moral, intellectually infallible, physically flawless characters are boring. Readers are far more taken with a character who is flawed in interesting ways. Michael Connelly's detective, Harry Bosch, is a haunted, emotionally bruised former cop who makes mistakes and steps on toes on the way to achieving justice. Sue Grafton's private investigator, Kinsey Millhone, sometimes lies "just to keep up [her] skills" and cuts her hair with nail scissors.

Harry Bosch and Kinsey Millhone are typical hard-boiled mystery protagonists: unattached and childless. Unencumbered sleuths live relatively uncomplicated lives. They can have romantic liaisons. They can go anywhere, any time, without having to call babysitters or dog walkers. Every time they rush headlong into danger, the reader isn't worrying about orphaned children or widowed spouses.

On the other hand, some of the most popular mystery series have main characters with plenty of personal baggage. Precious Ramotswe of Alexander McCall Smith's *The No. 1 Ladies' Detective Agency* gets married and adopts a child. Linda Barnes's Carlotta Carlyle series has become more compelling since Carlotta adopted "little sister" Paolina.

Start creating your mystery sleuth by getting to know him thoroughly, more intimately than you know your best friend. You don't need to tell the reader whether or not your character sleeps naked, but you should know.

Know how your character approaches an investigation. Is it going to be with bumbling and brute force, intellectual finesse and cunning, or cool professionalism and emotional detachment? Does he charge into an interrogation hurling threats and accusations, or lurk in a corner waiting for the suspect to make a gaffe?

Know what motivates your sleuth to solve crimes. Even if investigation is part of her everyday job, there needs to be some inner driving force that makes your character willing to take the risks necessary in order to ferret out a killer.

Though you'll never tell readers even half of what you decide, knowing your sleuth inside and out enables you to pick the telling details that make your character jump off the page.

A DARK PAST

Mystery fiction is riddled with sleuths who have been variously tortured by their authors: suffered physical or emotional abuse, addicted to drugs or alcohol, falsely convicted of a crime, suffered the loss of a loved one—the litany of woe goes on.

It's that dark past that motivates the character in the present. A character who investigates sex crimes may have survived a brutal rape. A police officer investigating police corruption may be haunted by his father's removal from the force under suspicion of misconduct. Our character, psychologist Dr. Peter Zak, lives with the knowledge that his actions evaluating an accused killer led to his own wife's murder.

When your sleuth has a dark past, it raises the stakes. Each time out, the sleuth not only solves a crime but also takes a personal journey and gets a chance to get it right this time.

HOW'D A NICE GUY LIKE YOU END UP . . . ?

Most of us trip over a dead body, we call the cops. End of story. A three-hundred-page mystery novel requires that the main character get mixed up in the investigation. You have to create a setup that makes it believable. That's easy if investigating crimes is a part of your main character's job but not so easy if you're writing an amateur sleuth.

How likely are these mystery sleuths to get involved in a murder investigation? Here is a short list of sleuths' professions that have found their way into mystery novels.

Not very	Well, maybe	Absolutely
Actor	Archaeologist	Bail bondsman
Art collector	Attorney	Expert witness
Cabbie	Clairvoyant	Federal agent
Caterer	Forensic psychologist	Fish and Wildlife Ser-
Banker	Forest ranger	vices special agent
Bookstore owner	Handwriting analyst	Medical examiner
Bum	Judge	Military police officer
College professor	Physician	Police officer or
Golfer	Nurse	detective
Horse trainer	Reporter	Private investigator
Housewife	Scientist	
Librarian	Thief	
Minister		
Museum curator		
Teacher		
Party planner		

Mystery readers are willing to go along with all kinds of amateur sleuths, as long as the character has a credible, compelling reason for investigating the crime. For example:

- The amateur sleuth possesses special expertise or inside knowledge that the police need.
- The amateur sleuth is married to (or otherwise related to) the homicide detective.
- A relative or friend is accused of the crime.
- The amateur sleuth is accused of the crime.
- The police investigators are corrupt or incompetent.
- The police are investigating the wrong person.
- The sleuth's reputation is at stake.
- The police don't believe there has been a murder.

When you pick a profession for your protagonist, keep in mind that the less likely your sleuth is to trip over a dead body, the more you'll have to work to establish a believable reason for him to investigate the murder.

RESEARCH YOUR CHARACTER

A credible main character gets you to that "look-ma-no-hands" moment in a mystery when the reader thinks: *Wow, this really could happen.*

The more you know the world your sleuth inhabits, the easier it will be to write a convincing character. Dashiell Hammett worked as a detective for the Pinkerton Agency in the years before he created his fictional PI, Sam Spade. Aaron Elkins was an anthropologist before he created fictional forensic anthropologist Gideon Oliver. Pam O'Shaughnessy worked for sixteen years as a trial attorney before she and her twin sister, Mary, became the pseudonymous Perry O'Shaughnessy and created lawyer/sleuth Nina Reilly. It's easier to write neuropsychologist Dr. Peter Zak because my co-author is a neuropsychologist.

Tear the illusion of authenticity and you stop the reader in his tracks. For instance, suppose you're reading a mystery novel about a judge who is presiding over a murder case. The judge runs into the jury foreman at a cocktail party, and they chat about the case. If you're like me, you'd stop reading. Judges don't chat with jury members during a trial.

If you give your sleuth a profession you haven't experienced firsthand, be prepared to do the research necessary to make your character ring true. Here are some ways to find out what you need to know:

- **Interviews:** Talk to someone who's in your sleuth's profession. Bring along a tape recorder, and be prepared with questions.
- **Tag-alongs:** Convince someone who does what your sleuth does to let you hang around for a few hours or days. Ride along with a cop. Get a criminal attorney to let you spend a day observing. Take notes.
- **Citizen's police academy:** Many communities have programs designed to acquaint citizens with the inner workings of their local police department. The training often includes the use of firearms and ride-alongs. Check if any are offered in your area. If you go, make friends with the officers you meet so you can follow up with questions that arise as you write.

FINDING EXPERTS

You will find that people are surprisingly willing to share their specialized knowledge. The trick is finding them.

- **Check out who you know:** You may already know someone who has the knowledge you seek. If you're writing a police procedural, you might be as lucky as I am and have a State Trooper living next door—he answered all my questions, put me in touch with a homicide detective, and even let me sit in his cruiser so I'd know what it looked, sounded, and smelled like to be in the driver's seat.
- **Ask your friends:** Maybe you know someone who knows someone who . . . You'll be surprised how few "degrees of separation" there are between you and the lawyer, archaeologist, or tennis pro you seek.
- **Go where your character would hang out:** Visit places where your character would inhabit and make friends. Roberta Isleib hung out at golf tournaments and met professional women golfers who helped her with the background she needed to write PGA golfer/mystery sleuth Cassie Burdette.
- **There's always the Internet:** Many Web sites are hosted by experts in

various fields and include both the person's credentials and their contact information. Identify the right person, and then get in touch. Or join an online group where you can pose queries. (For a list of Internet resources, see the Appendix.)

APPEARANCE: CONVEYING AND HIDING

Physical appearance translates into how other characters respond to your sleuth. So, even if you never give the reader a detailed description, you need to know what your character looks like. Does he look like a Marine, an over-the-hill prizefighter, or a used car salesman? Is she a hotshot lawyer in an Armani suit, a beauty queen who's all glam and gams, or a bag lady?

Personally, I prefer a main character who resembles a real person. But a little larger than life isn't a bad thing in a main character. As Janet Evanovich says of Stephanie Plum: "I wanted a heroine with big hair." Our main character, Dr. Peter Zak, is a somewhat idealized version of my co-author—a little taller, a decade younger, and a bit more conventionally handsome.

Characters who aren't what they seem at first blush intrigue readers. For example, a character who looks like a "dumb blond" might turn out to have a Ph.D. in chemistry. Or a character who blusters like a tough, hard-boiled cop might turn out to be an old softie. The pleasure for the reader comes in layers. First, there's the surprise in discovering hidden aspects of the character. Second, there's delight in watching suspects and other investigators fooled by the character's outward appearance.

Take Miss Marple, for example. Here's how Agatha Christie described her in the "The Tuesday Night Club," the 1927 short story in which she was first introduced:

> Miss Marple wore a black brocade dress, very much
> pinched in around the waist. Mechlin lace was arranged
> in a cascade down the front of the bodice. She had on
> black lace mittens, and a black lace cap surmounted
> the piled-up masses of her snowy hair. She was knit-
> ting, something white and fleecy. Her pale blue eyes,
> benignant and kindly, surveyed her nephew and her
> nephew's guests with gentle pleasure.

Outwardly, Miss Marple seems the quintessential ditzy old lady. But the white hair, old-fashioned getup, and knitting are pure camouflage for a sharp, logical mind and tenacious spirit. The pleasure for the reader comes when a police detective dismisses her as a dithery spinster and then gets his comeuppance when she discerns clues that he missed. Christie creates a gap between who Miss Marple is and who she appears to be, and then mines the gap.

Miss Jane Marple

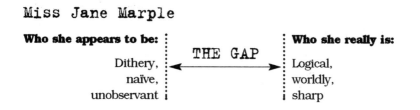

Who she appears to be: **Who she really is:**

Dithery,   ◀— THE GAP —▶   Logical,
naïve,   worldly,
unobservant   sharp

Think about which aspects of your main character's appearance are genuine reflections of character and which make up a misleading façade. Create a disconnect between your character's physical presence and true capabilities. Then mine the gap. Through plot and action, reveal who your character really is.

NOW YOU TRY: Appearance—what to convey, what to hide

List the qualities you want others to readily infer from your character's appearance; list other qualities you want to be hidden from others.

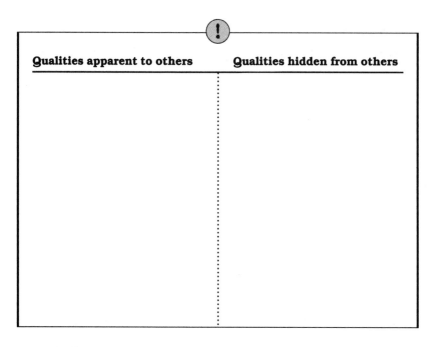

Qualities apparent to others	Qualities hidden from others

NOW YOU TRY: Appearance—get down the basics

Crystallize your character's features. Take all those ideas that are floating around in your head and get them in writing. Here's a list to get you started:

Gender:

Age:

Build:

Most striking feature:

Hair color, and if it's natural:

Hairstyle:

Wears what to work:

Wears what to a formal affair:

Wears what to bed:

Facial hair, tattoos, body piercings, scars:

Ethnicity, and from what physical features could others guess it:

Mannerisms, gestures:

Health problems:

What actor or actress you would cast in the role:

DISEQUILIBRIUM: PRESENT STATUS AND AMBITION

Disequilibrium makes for interesting characters and exciting plots. For instance, in Jan Brogan's *A Confidential Source*, reporter Hallie Ahern hates her job. It's her yearning to move from community reporting to an elite investigative team that drives her to write the account of a murder she witnessed, and soon she's plunged up to her neck in danger.

The right misfit between who your character is and who he aspires to be in the future can provide a compelling source of motivation in your plot. A character who is pursuing a promotion from desk sergeant to homicide detective might be willing to take risks to prove herself. A character who wants to dump her boyfriend and never get involved with another man as long as she lives might be easily deceived by another woman's claims that her husband abused her.

Think about who your character is when your story opens and what your character aspires to be in the future; use that disequilibrium to drive your plot.

NOW YOU TRY: Status and ambition

List your character's present status and aspirations for the future. Identify the misfits that you can take advantage of in building your plot.

	Present status	Aspirations for the future
Profession/job		
Income level		
Current residence		
Marital status		
Reputation		
Romantic attachments		
Children		
Pets		
Lifetime achievement		

BACKGROUND

Your character's background influences the way she responds to events and other characters. For example, S.J. Rozan's PI Lydia Chin is an American-born Chinese woman whose overprotective mother worked in a sweatshop while Lydia was growing up. So of course Lydia wants to help a young, up-and-coming Chinese fashion designer whose sketches are being held for ransom in *Mandarin Plaid*. Michael Connelly's detective Harry Bosch is a former foster child. So, in *City of Bones*, when buried bones turn out to be those of a foster child, of course he ignores orders from higher-ups to stop wasting his time trying to find the killer.

You can make your character an only child who is used to being the center of attention, or the third of nine siblings who learned early on how to get that coveted turkey wing. You can make her the only child of a concert violinist who has traveled the world, or the oldest daughter of an unemployed alcoholic who has never been out of Schenectady.

Knowing where your character comes from can help you create a complex, consistent human being. There are no right and wrong choices, but the background you invent should mesh with the direction you want your story to take. Whatever you pick, I recommend you give your character a background that is personally meaningful to you. That way, you'll be able to reach into yourself to guide your character's actions.

NOW YOU TRY: Make background decisions

Decide these aspects of your character's background.

Birth order:

Parents (occupations, education, and income):

Siblings:

Hometown:

Grew up in an apartment, ranch house, mansion, etc.:

Education:

Always wanted to be what:

Lost virginity when/how:

Past trauma, formative event:

Keepsake from the past and what it represents:

TALENTS AND SKILLS

Talents and skills give your character texture. Take Robert B. Parker's PI Spenser, for example. He's a large, powerfully built man who enjoys weight lifting and jogging. He also loves to cook. Linda Barnes's tough, taxi-driving protagonist, Carlotta Carlyle, spends her spare time playing volleyball. Unexpected contrasts make a character interesting.

It helps if you're familiar with the talents and skills with which you endow your sleuth, but not essential. Parker never boxed but he did lift weights for years, and he's modest about his cooking prowess. Linda Barnes did play volleyball, but not well. "What I do remember from volleyball," she told me, "is that spiking the ball is a wonderful form of anger management. The jargon of volleyball also seems apropos for a murder mystery: An unanswered spike is called a kill."

Are there things your character has to do that he hates? A reporter who dreads making cold calls? A police officer who hates target practice? Contradictions make for interesting characters.

Think about what your character is good at. Is he physical or cerebral? Artist or engineer? Are all her strengths right out there, or are some hidden? You'll be able to use your character's strengths in shaping your plot. Use hidden strengths to surprise the reader.

NOW YOU TRY: Talents and skills

What are your protagonist's talents and skills? Here's a list to get you started.

Most obvious skill:

Hidden skill:

Most obvious weakness:

Hidden weakness:

Talent:

Hates doing what:

PERSONALITY

Humor, anger, fear, love—what triggers these reactions in your character's emotional core? Is he fearless when climbing mountains but terrified by cockroaches? Does he have a lot of buddies but no close friends? Does he like puns but hate practical jokes?

The more you define your character's personality, the more you'll know how she'll react in the routine and extreme situations you're going to throw her into. You'll know what will make her persevere in the face of grave danger and apparently insurmountable obstacles, what kinds of pressure would make her buckle, and what would cause her to crack.

NOW YOU TRY: Personality traits

Answer each of these questions for your character:

Frightened by what?

Angered by what?

Finds what kinds of things funny?

Hates to be kidded about what?

Finds what attractive in others?

Finds what annoying in others?

Has what capacity for physical violence?

Has what capacity for intimacy?

Looks up to which heroes and role models?

Has what nervous tics and obsessive behaviors?

Uses what swear words when annoyed?

Angry?

Outraged?

UNDER DURESS

The nature of a mystery novel is such that your character will be tested. He'll be insulted, lied to, bullied, humiliated, cheated, threatened, and injured. He'll see other people duped, scapegoated, and hurt. Characters, like real people, show their mettle in do-or-die situations.

A news story a while back reported an armed confrontation among a group of young men on the subway, witnessed by many terrified passengers. Only one passenger got up and made his way through the train warning others. What would your character have done?

Think about how your character reacts under duress. Does she trade insult for insult or turn the other cheek? Does she go off half-cocked or simmer until she explodes? Does she rush into the middle of a confrontation or call 911?

NOW YOU TRY: Under duress

Jot down what your sleuth would do in each of these situations:

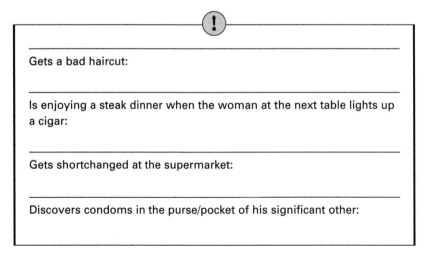

Gets a bad haircut:

Is enjoying a steak dinner when the woman at the next table lights up a cigar:

Gets shortchanged at the supermarket:

Discovers condoms in the purse/pocket of his significant other:

Hits a dog while driving, hurrying to the airport to catch a plane:

Gets propositioned by a beautiful woman/handsome man:

Breaks down at two in the morning on a deserted road:

Finds a diamond ring on a park bench:

Discovers that a best friend has been embezzling funds from a charity:

Discovers that her brother is a child molester:

TASTES AND PREFERENCES

This is the fun stuff. Tastes and preferences provide you with the grace note you need to express your character's personality. They give your character texture and flesh out his daily life.

Our character, Dr. Peter Zak, listens to folk music and jazz, has a passion for great ice cream, and gets his suits at bargain prices from Filene's Basement. These kinds of personality quirks can give your novel texture. We set scenes in a jazz bar and an ice cream parlor, and someday we may even plant a body in the ice cream freezer. Peter's bargain suits give his colleague a subject for frequent ribbing.

Think about your character's tastes and preferences. Is she likely to sit in a bar nursing a Bud or a glass of vintage Merlot? At home alone at night, is she likely to turn on the tube, read a book, or talk on the phone? Is she likely to wear vintage clothing snagged from a thrift store or hang around in sweats and sneakers? Does he frequent a local diner or gourmet French bistro? Does he have a passion for great pizza or great cigars? Details like these make your character come alive.

NOW YOU TRY: Tastes and preferences

Use this list to flesh out your character's tastes and preferences.

Favorite place to eat out:

Eats what for dinner, alone on a weeknight:

Usually orders what at a bar:

What book or magazine is on the bedside table:

Listens to what music in the car:

Favorite thing to do on a quiet Saturday afternoon:

Favorite thing to do on a Saturday night:

Ideal vacation:

Favorite place to hang out:

Has a weakness for what:

Collects what:

Political affiliation:

Activist for what cause:

NOW YOU TRY: Personality traits

Personality traits exist across a spectrum. Draw an *X* to show where your character belongs on each continuum:

Cautious	<1 — 2 — 3 — 4 — 5 — 6 — 7 — 8 — 9 — 10>	Impulsive
Aloof	<1 — 2 — 3 — 4 — 5 — 6 — 7 — 8 — 9 — 10>	Gregarious
Analytical	<1 — 2 — 3 — 4 — 5 — 6 — 7 — 8 — 9 — 10>	Emotional
Anxious	<1 — 2 — 3 — 4 — 5 — 6 — 7 — 8 — 9 — 10>	Easygoing
Charming	<1 — 2 — 3 — 4 — 5 — 6 — 7 — 8 — 9 — 10>	Abrasive
Cocky	<1 — 2 — 3 — 4 — 5 — 6 — 7 — 8 — 9 — 10>	Self-effacing
Fastidious	<1 — 2 — 3 — 4 — 5 — 6 — 7 — 8 — 9 — 10>	Sloppy
Honest	<1 — 2 — 3 — 4 — 5 — 6 — 7 — 8 — 9 — 10>	Deceitful
Optimistic	<1 — 2 — 3 — 4 — 5 — 6 — 7 — 8 — 9 — 10>	Pessimistic
Lethargic	<1 — 2 — 3 — 4 — 5 — 6 — 7 — 8 — 9 — 10>	Energetic
Practical	<1 — 2 — 3 — 4 — 5 — 6 — 7 — 8 — 9 — 10>	Dreamy
Sensitive	<1 — 2 — 3 — 4 — 5 — 6 — 7 — 8 — 9 — 10>	Thick-skinned
Stubborn	<1 — 2 — 3 — 4 — 5 — 6 — 7 — 8 — 9 — 10>	Accommodating
Vain	<1 — 2 — 3 — 4 — 5 — 6 — 7 — 8 — 9 — 10>	Modest

NAMING NAMES

Now that you know your sleuth inside and out, pick a name that fits. Mystery authors usually pick catchy, easy-to-remember names for their protagonists that suggest, by sound or meaning, something about their characters.

Janet Evanovich says she picked the name Stephanie Plum for her bounty hunter protagonist because of the way *Stephanie* rolls off the tongue, and because she likes the juicy ripeness of *Plum*. And besides, Evanovich says, there were a lot of Stephanies when she was growing up in blue-collar New Jersey, and Stephanie Plum is the quintessential "Jersey girl."

Think about the names Dashiell Hammett picked for two of his best-known sleuths: *Sam Spade* and *Nick Charles*. Even if you didn't know, you'd probably be able to guess which one is a hard-boiled, edgy, steely nerved San Francisco detective and which one is the dapper Manhattan man-about-town.

Sam Spade, with single syllables and repeated sibilance, sounds like a tough guy who *calls a spade a spade*. Sam is a working-class, no-nonsense first name. (Trivia fact: Sam was Hammett's real first name.) *Nick Charles* has a softer, more casual sound. We can easily imagine some hoity-toity Manhattan society matron pronouncing the last name *Chawles*. Still, *Nick* echoes the character's Greek-American background—he changed his unpronounceable last name to Charles when he retired from his job as a PI to manage his wife's sizable fortune.

So what's a good name for your protagonist? You've fleshed him out, decided what he looks like, his likes and dislikes, profession, locale, and so on. Now you're ready to choose a name that fits.

NOW YOU TRY: Match the sleuth to the description

Look at this list of popular mystery sleuths and try to match the characters to their locales and professions. Some you'll know, but for the ones you don't, think about why you made the match you did. What's in a name that says New York instead of New England or Louisiana? What says hard-boiled vs. cozy? Intellectual vs. working class?

Match these male mystery sleuths	To these locales/professions
Elvis Cole	New England, detective turned professor
Richard Jury	New York, aging unlicensed PI, alcoholic ex-cop
Homer Kelly	London, barrister, Old Bailey hack
Travis McGee	Louisiana, ex-cop, runs a bait shop
Gideon Oliver	Hollywood, wisecracking PI
Easy Rawlings	Scotland Yard, superintendent
Dave Robicheaux	Florida, houseboat-dwelling recoverer of stolen goods
Horace Rumpole	Seattle, physical anthropologist, "Skeleton Detective"
Matthew Scudder	Watts, African-American, recovered alcoholic, amateur detective

Match these female mystery sleuths	To these locales/professions
Carlotta Carlyle	Martha's Vineyard, feisty ninety-two-year-old poet
Lydia Chin	Botswana, lady detective
Faith Fairchild	Charlotte, North Carolina, antiques store owner
Victoria Trumbull	National Park Ranger
Anna Pigeon	New England, mother/caterer, minister's wife
Precious Ramotswe	Steel-town Pennsylvania, beautician
Abigail Timberlake	New York, Chinese-American PI
Bubbles Yablonsky	Victorian gentlewoman/Egyptologist
Amelia Peabody	Boston, redheaded cabbie turned PI

Solution: Match the sleuth to the description

Elvis Cole: Southern Hollywood, wisecracking PI (Robert Crais)

Richard Jury: Scotland Yard, superintendent (Martha Grimes)

Homer Kelly: New England, detective turned professor (Jane Langton)

Travis McGee: Florida, houseboat-dwelling recoverer of stolen goods (John D. MacDonald)

Gideon Oliver: Seattle, physical anthropologist, "Skeleton Detective" (Aaron Elkins)

Easy Rawlings: Watts, African-American, recovered alcoholic, amateur detective (Walter Mosley)

Dave Robicheaux: Louisiana, ex-cop, runs a bait shop (James Lee Burke)

Horace Rumpole: London, barrister, Old Bailey hack (John Mortimer)

Matthew Scudder: New York, aging unlicensed PI, alcoholic ex-cop (Lawrence Block)

**

Carlotta Carlyle: Boston, redheaded cabbie turned PI (Linda Barnes)

Lydia Chin: New York, Chinese-American PI (S.J. Rozan)

Faith Fairchild: New England, mother/caterer, minister's wife (Katherine Hall Page)

Amelia Peabody: Victorian gentlewoman/Egyptologist (Elizabeth Peters)

Anna Pigeon: National Park Ranger (Nevada Barr)

Precious Ramotswe: Botswana, lady detective (Alexander McCall Smith)

Victoria Trumbull: Martha's Vineyard, feisty ninety-two-year-old poet (Cynthia Riggs)

Abigail Timberlake: Charlotte, North Carolina, antiques store owner (Tamar Myers)

Bubbles Yablonsky: Steel-town Pennsylvania, beautician (Sarah Strohmeyer)

NOW YOU TRY: Name your sleuth

1. Think about what you want your character's name to convey. Strength? Vulnerability? Age? Region of origin? Ethnicity? Social class? Occupation? List at least eight characteristics you want the name to suggest.

1. _____

2. _____

3. _____

4. _____

```
5. _____

_____

6. _____

_____

7. _____

_____

8. _____
```

2. Now make a list of first and last names that meet your criteria.

```
_____

First Names:

_____

Last names:
```

3. Pick the first and last you like best.

4. Go to the Internet and search for the combination of names you picked (using quotes) to see how common it is. If there are too many hits, pick a different combination of names and search again.

ON YOUR OWN: Planning your sleuth

1. Write a five-minute, one-paragraph biography of your protagonist, something that could actually appear in the novel.

2. List four to six of the most significant, formative events in your main character's life. Briefly describe the impact each event has had on your sleuth.

3. Write a one-page, first-person monologue in your character's voice, talking about one of the events you listed in step two.

 Complete the Protagonist section of the blueprint. (Go to page 86 at the end of Part I to find these forms.)

CHaPtEr 3:
the crime,
victim's secrets

> "Everybody counts or nobody counts. That's it.
> It means I bust my ass to make the case whether
> it's a prostitute or the mayor's wife."
>
> —DETECTIVE HARRY BOSCH
> in Michael Connelly's *The Last Coyote*

At the center of every mystery is a crime. Someone does something bad, and someone else gets hurt or killed. The search for the culprit forms the backbone of the novel. Even if you don't yet know who did it, a good place to start planning your story is with the *crime scenario*: who gets hurt, how, and where.

The murder might take place when the novel opens or later when the story is well underway. It might have happened in the past and get told as a flashback. There are no rules about who gets killed or how, but readers who are expecting a more soft-boiled tale want their violence offstage and will be unhappy if you bump off cats, dogs, or children. Readers expecting a more hard-boiled tale have stronger stomachs.

THE VICTIM

How much you need to know about the victim depends on the story you're telling. You may need to know very little—only what put that character in harm's way. For instance, a novel about a museum heist in which a guard is killed may linger for only a few sentences on the victim: wrong place, wrong time, just doing his job, and the story moves on. But what if it turns out that this museum guard knew the robbers? Maybe he was an accessory or an unwilling pawn. Suddenly, understanding the victim becomes important to the plot, and the writer needs to flesh him out.

More often than not, the victim *is* essential to the story. For instance, in Scott Turow's *Presumed Innocent*, deputy chief prosecutor Rusty Sabich is asked to investigate the rape and murder of one of his colleagues, Carolyn Polhemus. Through dialogue and flashbacks, the reader learns that the victim was a strong, sensuous, and magnetic woman who made her share of friends and enemies. We also learn a secret: She was Sabich's former lover. When his relationship to the victim is discovered, Sabich finds himself the prime suspect.

VICTIM'S SECRETS

Hidden secrets are what propel a mystery novel forward. Everyone has them—the victim, innocent suspects, and the villain. The revelation of a secret sends the murder investigation in a new direction.

Here's an example of a crime scenario with a list of possible victim's secrets. As you read the list, think about how each victim's secret suggests a different path for investigators.

Crime scenario	Victim's secrets
Lorinda Lewis, a thirty-year-old bank teller, is kidnapped from in front of her home by carjackers who take her and her car. A short time later, she's killed when she's thrown onto the Hollywood Freeway.	Suppose she was about to expose a scheme to embezzle money from the bank. Suppose she was having an affair with her boss. Suppose she was a drug addict. Suppose she had a sister who looked just like her. Suppose she was a compulsive gambler. Suppose her boyfriend was a drug dealer. Suppose she was an adopted child who had just made contact with her birth mother.

How many secrets can a victim have in one novel? Two or three, maybe even four. Some secrets will turn out to be red herrings that make innocent suspects appear guilty; at least one secret will turn out to reveal the villain's identity.

Put your own crime scenario below, and brainstorm six possible victim's secrets. Think about which ones will work best in your novel.

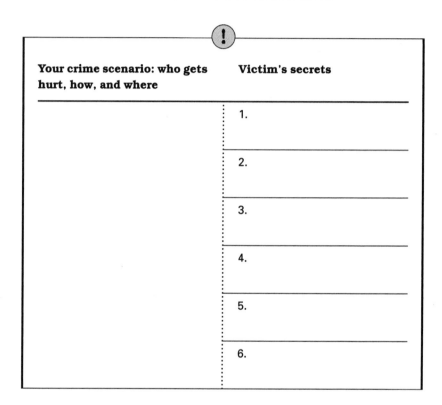

Your crime scenario: who gets hurt, how, and where	Victim's secrets
	1.
	2.
	3.
	4.
	5.
	6.

MAKING THE CRIME MATTER TO THE SLEUTH

Whether the crime is big and threatens the future of humanity or small and threatens a good person's reputation, it has to *matter to the sleuth*. There should be something about this crime or these victims that touches this particular protagonist in a profound and personal way. Here's where your sleuth's dark past comes into play.

For example, in our first book, *Amnesia*, Dr. Peter Zak is asked to evaluate a man accused of murdering his wife. Peter's wife was murdered by a man who tried to frame Peter for her death. Furthermore, he feels responsible—the killer targeted her to get back at Peter. Given an opportunity to help defend a man who may have been framed for his own wife's murder, Peter sees an opportunity to defend *himself*, and it's that parallel that draws him reluctantly into the investigation.

When the crime matters in a profound and personal way to the sleuth, the stakes get ratcheted up. By finding out whodunit and bringing the culprit to justice, the protagonist rights prior wrongs and restores honor. Failure and redemption become underlying themes.

Here are some of the plot devices authors use to make the crime matter to the sleuth:

- The victim is the sleuth's friend, colleague, lover, or relative.
- The next likely victim is the sleuth's friend, colleague, lover, or relative.
- The sleuth may be the next victim.
- The sleuth is accused of the crime.
- The sleuth identifies with the innocent person accused of the crime.
- The sleuth identifies with the victim.
- The sleuth or a loved one suffered a similar crime.

Come up with a crime and a reason that the crime matters to your sleuth. Create the connection that links victim to sleuth, and use that motivation to propel your story forward.

ON YOUR OWN: The crime, the victims

1. Create a simple scenario for each crime in your novel: Who gets hurt? How? Where?

2. Plan your victim(s). Create a thumbnail sketch, including:
   a. name
   b. age
   c. gender
   d. occupation
   e. appearance (a few physically distinguishing characteristics)
   f. significant personality traits (smart or stupid, generous or selfish, well liked or despised, etc.)
   g. a few telling details (something he owns, does, favorite expression, etc.) that define the victim
   h. what it is about the character that puts her in harm's way
   i. what secret(s) the victim is hiding

3. Figure out why your sleuth *needs* to solve this crime.

Complete the Crime section of the blueprint. (Go to pages 87 and 88 at the end of Part I to find these forms.)

CHaPtEr 4:
the villain

"If the bad guy in a book is a superficial
caricature, then the hero's victory against
him means little."

—JEFFERY DEAVER

As any mystery reader knows, today's villain is no Snidely Whiplash standing there twirling his moustache and sneering, a neon arrow blinking "bad guy" over his head. Any character who looks that nefarious is going to turn out to be innocent.

Readers are delighted when the bad guy turns out to have been hiding in plain sight, an innocuous-looking character who cleverly conceals his true self, luring trusting victims and then snaring them in a death trap. "The butler did it" won't wash in a modern mystery. Minor characters who are part of the wallpaper for the first twenty-eight chapters can't be promoted to villain status at the end just to surprise the reader. And you can't give a character a personality transplant in the final chapter. Disbelief will trump surprise unless you've left subtle clues along the way.

A LITTLE PLANNING SAVES TREES

Some writers know, from the get-go, which character is guilty. They start with the completed puzzle and work backwards, shaping the story pieces and fitting them together. Others happily write without knowing whodunit until the scene when the villain is unmasked. Then they rewrite, cleaning up the trail of red herrings and establishing the clues that make the solution work.

Which way is better? I need a plan. I have a friend, a many-times-published mystery writer, who boasts that she never plans. The identity of the villain comes as a complete surprise to her and the reader. In the next breath, she says she ended up having to dump the first two hundred pages from the draft of her latest novel. Having a plan up front can save a whole lot of rewriting in what should be the home stretch.

A VILLAIN WORTH PURSUING

You can't just throw all your suspects' names into a bowl and pick one to be your villain. For your novel to work, the villain must be special. Your sleuth deserves a worthy adversary—a smart, wily, dangerous creature who tests your protagonist's courage and detective prowess. Stupid, bumbling characters are good for comic relief, but they make lousy villains. The smarter, more invincible the villain, the harder your protagonist must work to find his vulnerability and the greater the achievement in bringing him to justice.

Must the villain be loathsome? Not at all. He can be chilling but charming, like Hannibal Lechter. Thoroughly evil? It's better when the reader can muster a little sympathy for a complex, realistic character who feels the crimes are justified.

So, in planning, try to wrap your arms around why your villain does what he does. What motivates him to kill? Consider the standard motives like greed, jealousy, or hatred. Then go a step further. Get inside your villain's head and see the crime from his perspective. What looks to law enforcement like a murder motivated by greed may, to the perpetrator, be an act in the service of a noble, even heroic cause.

Here's how a villain might justify a crime:
• righting a prior wrong
• revenge (the victim deserved to die)
• vigilante justice (the criminal justice system didn't work)
• protecting a loved one
• restoring order to the world

Finally, think about what happened to make that character the way she is. Was she born bad, or turned sour as a result of some early experience? If your villain has a grudge against society, why? If she can't tolerate being jilted, why? You may never share your villain's life story with your reader, but to make a complex, interesting villain, you need to know.

By understanding how the villain justifies the crime to himself, and what events in his life triggered these crimes, you give yourself the material you need to get past a black-hatted caricature and paint your villain in shades of gray.

Following is an example of the kind of information you need to decide about your villain, in advance.

Crime scenario	Who gets hurt, how, where	Lorinda Lewis, a thirty-year-old bank teller, is carjacked, thrown from the car, and killed.
Thumbnail sketch of villain	Basic information— name, age, job, physical description, family, background	Drew MacNee, bank manager, boyishly handsome; fiftyish; father of two teenage girls; married to the mousy but wealthy Marissa for twenty-five years; he lifts weights and runs thirty miles a week; he grew up the youngest and only son with five older sisters in an affluent household and always got what he wanted.
Motive	Ostensible reason for committing the murder	To keep Lorinda from revealing his many affairs with young, attractive bank tellers.
Motive 2	How the villain sees the crime	"Lorinda, that vengeful bitch, couldn't stand it when I dumped her; now she's going to destroy everything I've worked so hard for; I've got to stop her and protect my family."
Life trigger(s)	What, in the past, might explain why the villain commits this crime	Drew grew up the youngest in a family with five older sisters (his parents kept trying for a boy). He was catered to and assumed women were there to meet his needs. When he was captain of his high school football team, he and his buddies raped a girl and were protected from prosecution by the coach and town officials.

NOW YOU TRY: Noodling around in your villain's head

Think about the villain in your mystery novel. Jot down your ideas.

> **!**
>
> Crime scenario:
> _____
>
> Thumbnail sketch of villain:
> _____
>
> Motive—ostensible reason for committing the crime:
> _____
>
> Motive—how the villain sees the crime:
> _____
>
> Life trigger(s):

MAKE THE CRIME FIT THE VILLAIN

There are many ways to kill off a character. You can have him shot, stabbed, strangled, poisoned, or pushed off a cliff. You can have her run over by a car or bashed in the head with a fireplace poker. You get the picture.

The first issue to consider is: _Would your villain have the expertise and capability to commit this particular crime?_

Here's an example: Suppose there was a novel about a surgeon who, up to page 302, has been the soul of buttoned-down respectability. Suddenly, on page 303, he leaps from a hospital laundry bin and mows down his rival for hospital director with machine-gun fire. Never mind that up to that point in the novel this guy has done nothing more than attend board meetings, get drunk and obnoxious at a cocktail party, and perform heart surgery. Now suddenly he's The Terminator? The behavior doesn't fit the character. If he stabbed, poisoned, or pushed his rival off the hospital roof, the reader might swallow it. The author might get away (barely) with the shooting if hints were dropped earlier that this surgeon once served in military Special Forces.

Choose a modus operandi that your villain (and all your suspects) might plausibly adopt, and establish that your villain has the capability and expertise required. A murder by strangling, stabbing, or beating is more plausible if your villain is strong and has a history of physical violence. If your villain plants an electronically activated, plastic explosive device, be prepared to show how he learned to make a sophisticated bomb and how he got access to the components. If a woman shoots her husband with a .45 automatic, be prepared to show how she learned to use firearms and that she's strong enough to handle the recoil of a .45.

The second issue to consider: *Is the rage factor appropriate?*

The more extreme the violence, the more the crime is likely to be motivated by hatred and rage. A robber shoots a victim once; an enraged husband pumps bullets into the man who raped his wife until ammunition runs out. A villain may administer a quick-working deadly poison to a victim he wants out of the way, but a villain who hates his victim might pick a poison that's slow and painful and hang around to watch the victim die.

Adjust the violence quotient to match the amount of rage your villain has toward her victim.

NOW YOU TRY: Make the crime fit the villain

How would your villain kill his victim? Consider your villain's motive, strength, and expertise; consider the rage factor. Check the ones that could fit.

__ Asphyxiate by smoke inhalation   __ Push in front of a train
__ Beat to death   __ Run down with a car
__ Bury alive   __ Run over with heavy equipment
__ Bludgeon   __ Shoot with a pistol
__ Drown   __ Smother
__ Hang   __ Stab once
__ Mow down with machine-gun fire   __ Stab multiple times
__ Poison: mushrooms   __ Strangle
__ Poison: drug overdose   __ Slit throat

ON YOUR OWN: The villain

1. Reread a favorite mystery novel or read Scott Turow's *Presumed Innocent* or Linda Barnes's *Deep Pockets*. Pay special attention to the villain. Think about how the author creates a bad guy who is somewhat sympathetic and three-dimensional, and how the villain rationalizes the crime.

2. Brainstorm your villain and jot down your ideas: family background, physical appearance, education, formative events, and so on.

3. Pick a modus operandi that matches your villain, considering your villain's capabilities, expertise, and the rage factor.

 Complete the Villain section of the blueprint. (Go to page 87 at the end of Part I to find these forms.)

CHaPtEr 5:

innocent suspects

"Everybody has something to conceal."

—SAM SPADE

in *The Maltese Falcon* by Dashiell Hammett

"I've called you all together . . ." announces the great Hercule Poirot as he rearranges Staffordshire figurines on a marble mantle before turning his beady-eyed attention to the suspects gathered in the drawing room. With great drama, he lays out the case against suspect number one, only to reveal his innocence. He does the same with suspect number two, and so on around the room until, somewhere around suspect number five, Poirot spins around and confronts anew one of the earlier suspects—the killer.

Modern mysteries are rarely so heavy-handed, but the basic bait-and-switch principle still applies. There's a passel of suspects, each with a motive for murder, each with a secret or two. Attention moves from suspect to suspect until the villain is revealed. For the solution to surprise the reader—and credible surprise is what readers crave—either the most obvious suspect is not the killer or the crime is not what it appears to be.

How many suspects do you need? At least two (plus the true villain) will keep the reader guessing. More than five and it feels like a parlor game.

SUSPECTS' SECRETS

Create a cast of innocent suspects who have secrets—secrets can make characters look guilty or reveal them to be innocent.

A secret can be something the suspect doesn't know. For instance, a suspect doesn't know that her husband was once married to the victim. Or a suspect doesn't know that she's the prime beneficiary of her murdered aunt's estate.

A secret can be something the suspect knows and lies to cover up.

Or the secret can even be that the suspect doesn't exist. A clever villain plants evidence implicating someone who's dead or never existed at all.

Here are some examples:

Secret	Lie
A suspect is on the run from an abusive ex-boyfriend.	She lies about her true identity in order to keep her ex-boyfriend from finding her.
A suspect was robbing a bank across town when the murder happened.	He says he was with his girlfriend at the time of the murder; he's lying to avoid being arrested for the heist.
A suspect thinks her brother is guilty.	She says her brother was with her at the time of the murder in order to protect him.

MAKING INNOCENT SUSPECTS LOOK GUILTY

Virtually any character in your novel can be made to look suspicious. A rule of thumb that's familiar to any mystery reader: The guiltier a character looks at the beginning of the story, the more likely he will turn out to be innocent.

Here are some devices you can use to cast the shadow of guilt on innocent characters:

- **Obvious motive:** The character inherits the estate, or was having an affair with the victim's husband, or was being blackmailed by the victim, or had been jilted by the victim.
- **Vanishing act:** The character is nowhere to be found when investigators come to question him after the murder.
- **Stonewalling:** The character can't remember or refuses to tell the police where she was at the time of the murder.
- **Contradictory behavior:** A character who claims to be clueless about guns has an NRA membership card in his wallet; a character who claims to have been in love with the victim was having an affair with someone else.
- **Eavesdropper:** The character is overheard telling the victim, "Drop dead."
- **Enmity between the character and the victim:** The two are cutthroat business rivals or were engaged in a nasty lawsuit.
- **Overeagerness to answer questions:** The character goes to investiga-

tors and provides bushels of information that implicate others . . . only not all of it turns out to be true.

- **Rotten rep:** The character is known to be a swindler or compulsive liar.
- **Guilt by association:** The character hangs out with other unsavory characters or is married to someone who hated the victim.
- **Previously suspected:** The character was questioned in a similar homicide investigation—someone else was convicted, but now investigators wonder.
- **Previously convicted:** The character was convicted of a similar crime, though he's always claimed he was innocent.
- **Skeletons in the closet:** No one knows it, but the character was once (or still is) a compulsive gambler, alcoholic, drug addict, or pedophile.
- **Cracks in the veneer:** A flawlessly beautiful, kind, or generous character is seen kicking a dog, slapping a child, or grinding a delicate trinket under his heel.

PLANNING A SUSPECT: CREATING A THUMBNAIL SKETCH

A good way to prepare for bringing a suspect to life on the page is to create a thumbnail sketch. Think about the secrets you'll reveal about this character. Use unexpected contrasts to keep your suspects from turning into clichés. A jealous, bleached blonde, Armani-wearing wife might once have been a Peace Corps volunteer who still sponsors Bolivian orphans. A rigid, controlling bank manager might love to share knock-knock jokes with his five-year-old daughter. Contrasts give characters humanity.

A thumbnail sketch of the suspect should include:

- **Basic information:** Includes the suspect's name, relationship to the victim, age, gender, any distinguishing physical characteristics, anything significant about his personality or past; a few telling details (something he owns, does, favorite expression, etc.) that define him; include any quirky contrasts to make this character unique.
- **Motive:** Why this character might have committed the murder.
- **Lie(s):** The lie(s) this character tells.
- **Secret(s):** The hidden secret that makes this character look guilty; the hidden secret that demonstrates this character's innocence.

Here's an example of a thumbnail sketch of a suspect:

> **Crime scenario:** Martha Collicott, a wealthy, elderly widow, is strangled in her bed.
> **Suspect:** Terry Blaine

THUMBNAIL SKETCH:

BASIC INFORMATION

He's Martha's nephew, twenty years old, unemployed, handsome, fair-haired college dropout; bright but an underachiever; was always Martha's favorite nephew; drives a vintage Corvette and wears $200 sneakers; no regular address (says he's "staying with friends.") He's the only one who cried at Martha's funeral.

MOTIVE

He inherits Aunt Martha's money.

LIE

He says he was at a friend's home alone watching television at the time of the murder.

SECRETS

Secret that makes him look guilty: Terry is a compulsive gambler, deeply in debt, and being threatened by loan sharks; he needs Aunt Martha's money to save himself.

Secret that demonstrates innocence: Terry was dealing drugs at the time of the murder; that's why he lied about where he was.

NOW YOU TRY: Suspect's secrets

For one innocent suspect in your novel, come up with the following:

Suspect's name:

Basic information:

Motive:

Lie(s):

Secrets:

ON YOUR OWN: Innocent suspects

1. Watch a television crime show such as *Law & Order* or *CSI: Crime Scene Investigation*. List the characters who become suspects, and note the secrets that are revealed about each one. Notice that sometimes the secret makes a suspect appear to be guilty; other times the secret demonstrates a suspect's innocence.

2. Write a five-minute, one-paragraph description of each innocent suspect in your novel.

3. Pick one innocent suspect in your novel. Brainstorm and come up with a list of possible secrets that the suspect might be hiding.

4. Write a one-paragraph, first-person monologue in the voice of the suspect you picked in step three, talking about the secret that suspect is hiding.

Complete the Innocent Suspects section of the blueprint. (Go to page 89 at the end of Part I to find these forms.)

CHaPtEr 6:
the supporting cast

"Without Goodwin's badgering, Wolfe would surely starve, collapse under the weight of his own sloth . . ."

—LOREN D. ESTLEMAN
from the introduction to the 1992 Bantam
paperback edition of *Fer-de-Lance* by Rex Stout

Sir Arthur Conan Doyle gave Sherlock Holmes a full panoply of supporting characters. There was Dr. Watson, the quintessential sidekick, to act as a sounding board; Scottish landlady Mrs. Hudson to cook and clean and fuss over Holmes; Scotland Yard detective Inspector Lestrade, to provide a foil for Holmes's intuitive brilliance, as well as access to official investigations; the Baker Street Irregulars to ferret out information; and Mycroft Holmes, his politically powerful older brother to provide financial and strategic support.

Likewise, your cast of supporting characters should reflect what your protagonist *needs*. For instance, an amateur sleuth needs a friend or relative with access to inside information—a police officer, a private investigator, or crime reporter fit the bill. A character who is arrogant and full of himself needs a character to keep him from taking himself too seriously, maybe an acerbic co-worker or mother. You might want to show a hard-boiled police detective's softer side by giving him kids or a pregnant wife.

SECOND BANANAS

The most important supporting character is the sidekick. Virtually every mystery protagonist has one. Rex Stout's obese, lazy, brilliant Nero Wolfe has Archie Goodwin—a slim, wisecracking ladies' man. Carol O'Connell's slim, icy, statuesque blond detective Kathy Mallory has garrulous, over-weight, aging, alcoholic partner Riker. Robert B. Parker's literate, poetry-quoting Spenser has black, street-smart, tough-talking Hawk. Harlan Coben's former basketball star turned sports agent, Myron Bolitar, has a rich, blond, preppy friend, Windsor Horne Lockwood III.

See a pattern? It's the old opposites attract. Mystery protagonists and their sidekicks are a study in contrasts. Sidekicks are the yin to the protagonists' yang. The contrast puts the protagonist's characteristics into relief. For instance, the thickheaded Watson makes Holmes look smarter.

In our books, Peter Zak's sidekick is Annie Squires. She's also the love interest. Here's how she stacks up against Peter.

Peter Zak	Annie Squires (sidekick)
1. Male	1. Female
2. Neuropsychologist	2. Investigator
3. Cerebral	3. Physical
4. Analytic	4. Emotional
5. Would never carry a weapon	5. Carries mace and a gun when she needs to
6. Trained in therapy, psychological testing	6. Trained in judo, self-defense
7. Drives a Miata	7. Drives a Jeep
8. Loves Chinese dim sum, fine wine	8. Loves meatball subs, beer
9. Likes to row on the Charles	9. Likes to go rollerblading
10. His friends are mental health professionals	10. Her friends are cops
11. Jewish	11. Catholic

So, the place to start in creating a sidekick is the profile you developed of your sleuth. Think about what kind of opposites will work in a sidekick.

NOW YOU TRY: Traits for a sidekick

Make a list of your sleuth's characteristics; list the opposites you could invest in a sidekick. Circle the ones you like best.

Protagonist	Sidekick
1.	1.
2.	2.
3.	3.
4.	4.
5.	5.
6.	6.
7.	7.
8.	8.
9.	9.
10.	10.

THE ADVERSARY

Every protagonist/mystery sleuth needs an adversary, too. This is not the villain but a good-guy character who drives your sleuth nuts, pushes his buttons, torments him, puts obstacles in his path, and is generally a pain in the patoot. It might be an overprotective relative or a know-it-all co-worker. It might be a police officer or detective who "ain't got no re-spect" for the protagonist. It might be a boss who's a micromanager or a flirt.

For Sherlock Holmes, it's Inspector Lestrade and his disdain for Holmes's investigative techniques. In the same vein, Kathy Reichs's forensic anthropologist Temperance Brennan has a tormentor in the person of Mon-treal police detective Sergeant Luc Claudel. Their sparring is an ongoing element in her books. In *Monday Mourning*, Brennan finds out Claudel is going to be working with her on the case. She describes him:

> Though a good cop, Luc Claudel has the patience of a firecracker, the sensitivity of Vlad the Impaler, and a persistent skepticism as to the value of forensic anthropology.

Then she adds:

> Snappy dresser, though.

Conflict is the spice that makes characters come alive, and an adversary can cause the protagonist all kinds of interesting problems and complicate your story by throwing up roadblocks to the investigation.

An adversary may simply be thickheaded—for example, a superior officer who remains stubbornly unconvinced and takes the protagonist off the case. Or an adversary may be deliberately obstructive. For example, a bureau-crat's elected boss might quash an investigation that threatens political cro-nies, or a senior reporter may fail to pass along information because he doesn't want a junior reporter to get the scoop.

In developing an adversary, remember it should be a character who is positioned to thwart, annoy, and generally get in your sleuth's way. With an adversary in the story, the sleuth gets lots of opportunities to argue, strug-gle, and in general show her mettle and ingenuity.

NOW YOU TRY: Finding an adversary

Think about the characters you have planned for your novel. Which ones can act as adversaries? List the possibilities below, and brainstorm how each character can complicate your character's life or obstruct the investigation.

Potential adversary	Complications, obstructions

THE SUPPORTING CAST

A supporting character can be anyone in your sleuth's life—a relative, a friend, a neighbor, a co-worker, or a professional colleague; the local librarian, waitress, or town mayor; even a pet pooch. A supporting character may get ensnared in the plot and land in moral peril or even take a turn as a suspect. In a series, supporting characters return from book to book and can have ongoing stories of their own.

Supporting characters come with baggage, so pick yours carefully. If you give your protagonist young kids, you'll have to deal with arranging for child care. A significant other? Be prepared to handle the inevitable attraction to that sexy suspect. A pet St. Bernard? Beware—he'll have to be walked.

Supporting characters give your character a life, but each one should also play a special role in the story. Here are some of the roles the supporting characters can play:

- sounding board
- possessor of special expertise
- provider of access to inside information
- bodyguard/tough guy
- caretaker, worrywart
- drudge
- mentor
- mole
- moneybags
- influential cutter of red tape
- love interest

Supporting characters might start out as stereotypes: a devoted wife, a nagging mother-in-law, a bumbling assistant, a macho cop, or a slimy lawyer. It's okay to typecast supporting characters during the planning phase. When you get into the writing, you'll want to push past the stereotypes and flesh out supporting characters, turning them into complex characters who do things that surprise you and the reader. You don't want supporting characters to hog the spotlight, but bland and uninteresting characters shouldn't be clogging up your story either.

NAMING SUPPORTING CHARACTERS

Give each supporting character a name to match the persona, and be careful to pick names that help the reader remember who's who.

Nicknames are easy to remember, especially when they provide a snapshot reminder of the character's personality (Spike, Godiva, Flash) or appearance (Red, Curly, Smokey). Throwing in some ethnicity makes a character's name easy to remember, too (Zito, Sasha, Kwan). Avoid the dull and boring (Bob Miller) as well as the weirdly exotic (Dacron).

It's not easy for readers to keep all your characters straight, so help them out. Don't give a character two first names like William Thomas, or Susan Frances. Vary the number of syllables in character names—it's harder to confuse a Jane with a Stephanie than it is to confuse a Bob with a Hank. Pick names that don't sound alike or start with the same letter. If your protagonist's sister is Leanna, don't name her best friend Lillian or Dana.

Names are hard to come up with when you need them. An obvious source for inspiration is your local telephone directory. There are books of baby names. Another resource is the Internet. You'll find Web sites with lists of surnames and first names from Aaron to Zinnia, in every ethnicity and culture. Search for "dictionary names" and you'll find a lot of information sources waiting to be exploited.

Create a list of names that you consider "keepers," and add to it whenever you find a new one you like.

ON YOUR OWN: The supporting cast

1. Name and profile your sidekick(s):
   a. name
   b. occupation
   c. major roles vis-à-vis your protagonist (sounding board, love interest, etc.)
   d. personality
   e. background
   f. strengths/weaknesses

2. Name and profile your adversary:
   a. name
   b. position that enables this character to obstruct your sleuth
   c. relationship between your protagonist and this adversary

3. Make a list of the other supporting characters your story needs. For each one, create a brief profile, including:
   a. name
   b. role in the story
   c. brief description (including age, gender, appearance, personality, and anything else you feel is important about this character)

Complete the Supporting Cast section of the blueprint. (Go to page 90 at the end of Part I to find these forms.)

CHaPtEr 7:
setting

"My books begin with a place, the feeling I
want to set a book there, whether it's an empty
stretch of beach or a community of people."

—P.D. JAMES
interview with Salon.com

It's been said that a vivid setting is like another main character in the novel, and sometimes it is. At the very least, your setting has to be credible and fit your story's plot, characters, theme, and general emotional tone.

Setting includes these dimensions:

- **When:** Year and season
- **Where:** Geographic locale, exteriors, and interiors
- **Context:** Activities and institutions that provide the primary backdrop

Pick your settings carefully because whatever you choose both constrains and enriches your story's possibilities.

Before you start writing, make a list of possible times and places where you're going to set scenes. Then research them and explore their dramatic possibilities. If you can, pay a visit to each place. Take pictures and take notes. If you can't visit, then find photographs and written descriptions, and talk to people who've been there. When it comes time to write, you'll be able to use real details and add plausible fictional touches.

WHEN: THE YEAR

When your novel takes place—in the present, the past, the future, or even a made-up time—has a major impact on all aspects of the book. It affects what characters wear, what they worry about, what their homes are like, how they get around, and so on. It also constrains the kind of crime investigation that can take place. Laurie R. King's sleuth, Mary Russell, apprentice to Sherlock Holmes, relies on old-fashioned observation and deduction. Kinsey Millhone is stuck in a 1980s time warp, so Sue Grafton never has to work her plots around cell phones or DNA evidence. Kathy Reichs sets her Temperance Brennan series in the present, so she has all the trappings of modern forensic science at her disposal. Give the investigators in your novel the tools appropriate to the time period.

Setting your story in a particular historical time frame allows you to intertwine your story with concurrent events. The Great Depression, the Roaring Twenties, World War II—virtually any time period can provide a rich historical context with real individuals and events you can use as part of your story. Sarah Smith set her historical mystery *The Knowledge of Water* in Paris 1910, and the rains of the Great Flood that year are integral to her plot and provide a backdrop for her most dramatic scenes. You can even have historical figures take part in your drama.

Set your story in the present and you can include current events. The downside is that current events can make your story seem dated. Remember, even for published writers cranking out a book a year, it usually takes two years between when a book is started and when it's published. In addition, most of us lack perspective on current events. What seems like a major news story when you're writing your novel may be a big yawn a year later. So only include current events that matter to your story.

Some events feel too big to be left out of any story set in the fictional present. The 9/11 terrorist attacks are a case in point. Many authors were in the middle of writing set-in-the-present novels when the terrorists struck. Some rewrote their novels to include the attacks.

For example, Jim Fusilli had sent his second Terry Orr novel to Putnam when the World Trade Center was attacked. This is how he explains his difficult decision to recall the book and rewrite it completely, incorporating the terrorist attacks into the book:

> I insisted on rewriting *A Well-Known Secret*, and did so after spending some time in the neighborhood, talking to residents, business owners, policemen, and National Guardsmen, and getting the silt in my throat and dust in my hair.
>
> My purpose was twofold: to anchor the series in an accurate depiction of New York City; and to allow readers who lived outside of the downtown Manhattan area to experience September 11 as if they had lived through it. *A Well-Known Secret* was the first novel to address September 11, and I'm glad I wrote it the way I did.

At the same time Fusilli was deciding to rewrite his novel, my co-author and I were putting the finishing touches on our mystery about paranoia, *Delu-*

sion. Like his novel, ours was set in the fictional present. News stories of the attacks would have pushed the paranoid husband in our story over the edge. Did that mean we had to incorporate 9/11 into our novel? After a long talk with our editor, we decided not to mention it. We could get away with it in part because our book was set in Boston, not New York, and the terrorist attacks weren't germane to the story we were telling.

Make a conscious, reasoned decision on whether to include concurrent events in your novel. Weigh the pros and cons, the advantages and limitations.

NOW YOU TRY: Including concurrent events, weighing the pros and cons

Make a list of the events that are concurrent with your novel's time frame. List reasons in favor of including or excluding those events.

(!)

When: The year:

Concurrent Events:

Reasons to Include:

Reasons to Exclude:

WHEN: THE SEASON

You can exploit the season in which your story takes place in several ways. Extreme weather—hurricanes, monsoons, blizzards—can create a dramatic backdrop. In this example from Raymond Chandler's short story "Red Wind," a description of Southern California Santa Ana winds provides a powerful way to open the first scene:

> There was a desert wind blowing that night. It was one of those hot, dry, Santa Anas that come down through the mountain passes and curl your hair and make your nerves jump and your skin itch. On nights like that, every booze party ends in a fight. Meek, little wives feel the edge of the carving knife and study their husbands' necks. Anything can happen.

The season—or seasons, if your novel's time frame is long enough—you pick creates story possibilities. In winter, an ice storm in Vermont can shut down roads and delay a medical examiner trying to reach a crime scene; a summer heat wave in Kansas City can leave elderly shut-ins dead, one of whom turns out to have been murdered; soaking spring rains can turn roads to mud, send hillsides sliding into houses, and leave your protagonist stranded by the side of the road and chilled to the bone.

Be aware of the nuisance factor in the season you pick. Set your story in a New England winter and your characters are going to have to bundle up and de-ice their car windshields whenever they go out. If you want your character to take a pleasant stroll and come across a body washed up at the edge of a creek, make sure it would be warm enough at that time of year for strolling and creeks wouldn't be dried to a trickle. You can't have a character skulking about in pools of darkness between the street lights at eight o'clock on a July evening—the sun wouldn't have set.

Whatever time period and season you choose to set your story, spend some time planning how you'll put those choices to work in your story.

NOW YOU TRY: Making the most of "when"

Write down the year(s) and season(s) you've chosen to set your novel. Brainstorm and make a list of how your choices can affect your story in terms of investigational techniques, concurrent events, weather, and so on.

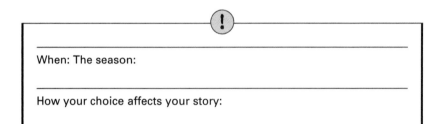

When: The season:

How your choice affects your story:

WHERE: GEOGRAPHIC LOCALE

The geographic locale where you set your novel provides you with a range of possible dramatic landscapes in which to bring your story to life. A small town presents as many possibilities as a big city. The quiet Kentish village of St. Mary Mead provides a perfect backdrop for Agatha Christie's Miss Marple. Venice, with its mist-shrouded canals and palazzos, makes a rich backdrop for Donna Leon's Commissario Guido Brunetti novels.

Readers love local color, and the audience for most mystery series grows out from its geographic location. On the other hand, exotic locations entice readers who yearn for the unknown. What matters is that you know your setting, bring it alive on the page, and take advantage of the opportunities your setting presents.

Let the geographic locale shape your characters' behavior. New Yorkers avoid eye contact with strangers while Texans say "howdy" to everyone. A Milwaukee police officer might have a passion for bratwurst; one of Chicago's finest might be an aficionado of Red Hots.

Here are some ways your novel might reflect the geographic locale you pick:

- how characters talk—word choice, speech patterns, and dialect
- what characters wear
- what characters eat and drink
- how characters get places
- how people treat strangers
- what sports teams characters root for

Here's an example from Laura Lippman's *The Sugar House*. Through the details Lippman chooses, she makes Baltimore come alive.

> Sour Beef day dawned clear and mild in Baltimore
> Other cities have their spaghetti dinners and potluck at
> the local parish, bull roasts and barbecues, bake sales
> and fish fries. Baltimore had all those things, too, and
> more. But in the waning, decadent days of autumn,
> there came a time when sour beef was the only thing to
> eat, and Locust Point was the only place to eat it.

Like so many mystery writers, Lippman writes about her series setting so vividly because she lives there. If you set your novel where you've lived, you can use your insider's knowledge. If you set your story somewhere you've never lived, leave yourself time during the planning stages to visit and research the locale thoroughly.

WHERE: EXTERIORS

Once you've picked your geographic locale, think about the exterior settings you can use. If you're using real exteriors, make them as accurate as possible. Readers don't like it when your sleuth drives the wrong way up a one-way street or when a well-known restaurant has suddenly been relocated to a different neighborhood.

Jan Brogan painstakingly researched the Providence street exteriors she used in *A Confidential Source*, a mystery about lottery corruption and talk radio. Here's a brief excerpt:

> I scanned the streets, looking for help, and saw a police
> cruiser in front of Union Station, waiting for the light.
> Tucking my knapsack under my arm, I ran down Foun-
> tain Street and across Dorrance. On the other side of

Dorrance, I came to a stop. The sidewalk was filled with
pedestrians headed toward WaterFire, a clog of slow-
moving tourists taking in the sights.

Jan told me that she knew those streets because she used to work nearby.
But after she wrote the scene, she went back, map in hand, and walked the
area by foot to be sure she'd written it correctly. Likewise, she made multiple
trips to WaterFire, the summer event when crowds fill Waterplace Park in
downtown Providence, to make sure that the staircases and ramps that her
heroine traverses in the novel's climactic chase scene were accurate.

Not every exterior setting you use has to be real. Made-up exteriors work
fine, as long as the details are plausible for the area. An adobe hacienda in
the middle of Boston won't wash, nor will cobblestone streets in San Diego.
A good way to conjure a made-up exterior is to combine elements of real
ones and mix them together with elements from your own imagination. Some
writers draw maps of the exteriors they invent in order to keep themselves
oriented and keep their story consistent.

WHERE: INTERIORS

Your novel may have as many as a dozen interior settings. A recurring interior will probably be your protagonist's home or office.

Our protagonist lives in a turn-of-the-century, two-family house he
shares with his mother. The kitchen hasn't been updated (Peter doesn't
cook), but in the basement there's a state-of-the-art wine cellar (Peter's a
wine snob). Since his wife's murder, he's kept her ceramics studio on the
top floor intact, and when he hits a rough patch he goes there to think.

Review the profile of your protagonist and think about what you want
your character's home or office to express. If your character is anal and
methodical, you might go for steel-and-glass furniture and a Mondrian print
on the wall. If your character is absentminded and careless, his desk might
be adrift in paperwork and the rug frayed at the edges. If your character is
cheerful and optimistic, her home would be freshly painted and filled with
bright colors. If he's morose and brooding, maybe the windows are shrouded
with dusty, green velvet drapes.

In your mind, transport yourself there. Is it a mansion, apartment,
mountaintop cabin, or homeless shelter? Is it filled with fine antiques, battered items picked from yard sales and thrift stores, minimalist designer
furniture, or unopened storage boxes? Is there a large-screen television or
a vintage radio? Does the kitchen have all the latest gadgets or just a micro-
wave for reheating takeout? Each choice should be a reflection of your character's personality and where he is at this juncture in life.

Other interiors relate to your protagonist's job. If your protagonist is an
attorney, you'll probably write scenes that take place in a jail and a court-

room. If your protagonist is a medical examiner, you'll need an autopsy room and a morgue. Most novels featuring a homicide detective have scenes that take place in squad cars and police station interiors.

Have at the ready some interiors where your protagonist goes to relax. A recurring interior for us is Toscanini's Ice Cream, a real place in Cambridge with world-class ice cream. It's the place where Peter and his girlfriend Annie go to talk. In Sue Grafton's novels, Kinsey Millhone finds safe refuge at a dingy local tavern serving Hungarian food cooked up by Rosie, a colorful recurring character.

It's fun to use real interiors to set scenes. Local readers enjoy finding places they recognize. A good rule of thumb is: It's okay to use a real place if nothing terrible happens there. Use a real restaurant if your characters go there and have a wonderful meal; use a made-up restaurant if your character is going to get food poisoning after eating there. You don't want to make enemies out of restaurant owners, and you certainly don't want to get sued.

NOW YOU TRY: Making the most of "where"

Pick a geographic location and list all the interior and exterior settings where you've chosen to set your novel. List the aspects of setting that you'll be able to use to advantage in your story.

	!	
Geographic locale		Aspects you can use in your story
Interior settings		Aspects you can use in your story
Exterior settings		Aspects you can use in your story

CONTEXT: ACTIVITIES AND INSTITUTIONS

The activities and institutions that provide the backdrop for your story are another dimension of setting. In most mysteries, there's the context in which the sleuth operates, plus the context in which the crime occurred. For example, the most common context for a mystery is law enforcement—the main characters are police detectives; the activities are basic interrogation and investigation; and the institutions are those that make up the criminal justice system, from police departments to jails to courtrooms. Still, each police procedural has an added context—the backdrop for the crime. For example, if the police are investigating art theft, their investigations might take them into artists' studios, art museums, galleries, or auction houses. If you're writing an amateur sleuth, the backdrop becomes your sleuth's day job and the world your sleuth inhabits.

The backdrop you pick for your book is an important factor in marketing your novel. A mystery set in a medical examiner's office featuring graphic autopsies is going to repel the more squeamish reader. A mystery set at a bird sanctuary featuring a birder who witnesses a crime while tracking down a red-footed falcon probably won't appeal to readers who like their mysteries fast paced and hard-boiled.

Here are some examples of backdrops that have been used in mystery novels:

Activities	Institutions
Art collecting	Museums, auction houses, art galleries
Medical research	Hospitals, universities, private labs
Gambling	Racetracks, casinos
Smuggling endangered species	U.S. Fish and Wildlife Services, U.S. Customs
Drug dealing	Organized crime, street gangs
Golfing	The PGA tour, country clubs, golf courses

Pick a backdrop that you know intimately or one that interests you enough that you won't mind doing the research necessary to make it come alive.

Here are some of the aspects of backdrop to research in advance:
- **Uniforms:** The formal or informal dress codes that determine what people wear; how clothing indicates status.
- **Jargon:** The special terms and expressions that are widely used.
- **Equipment:** Special equipment and tools, how it operates, safety precautions.
- **Pecking order:** The high- and low-status jobs, and how people at various levels recognize and treat one another.
- **Schedule:** The events that happen in a typical day or night, week, or month.
- **Behavior:** The written and unwritten codes that influence how people behave in typical and extreme situations; what boundaries they're not supposed to cross.

NOW YOU TRY: Making the most of the backdrop

Write down the institutions and activities that provide a backdrop for your mystery novel. Make a list of the questions you need to answer in order to write the backdrop convincingly.

!

Backdrop—institutions and activities:

Questions to be researched:

MAKING A SETTING FEEL REAL

As a writer, your goal is not to re-create a place and time—leave that to history books and travel guides. The last thing you want to do is bog down your story with pages of descriptive detail, no matter how evocative.

Whether a setting is real or imaginary, you need to know it inside and out before you start writing so you can create a credible sense of place. Put pink flamingos on suburban lawns in Chicago and you'll blow your cover as a Floridian. Plausibility is what you're after. The telling detail is what counts. With a few strokes of physical and sensory descriptions, a few telling details, you want to bring a particular setting to life.

That's where research comes in. How much research you have to do depends on how familiar you are with the setting you've chosen to write about and what resources you can access. I rely on my collaborator for details about routines on a psychiatric ward. But to write a chase scene through the tunnels that connect the buildings of our fictional Pearce Psychiatric Institute, I paid a visit to the tunnels at Harvard's McLean psychiatric hospital and captured the kinds of details I'd have been hard pressed to make up.

Painstaking research informs the setting in this passage from Sarah Smith's *The Knowledge of Water*, set in Paris in 1910 when record rainfall caused a devastating flood:

> By the glass peristyle and the doors to the Orsay station, the crowd was elbow to elbow, craning forward. The main entrance to the Gare d'Orsay was on the second level, above the tracks. The water was almost up to the level of the doors. The vast green-glass-and-studded-iron arches of the station, the café, the benches, the mahogany stands for postcards, books, and newspapers stood ready for crowds of travelers hurrying to catch their trains; the green-and-gilt railroad clock loomed over everything, though it had stopped; but the lower level of the station, where the tracks had been, was an enormous swimming pool, a dimly reflecting darkness whose surface was lit by the gray snowlight.

Sarah told me that she visited Paris and did research in order to write that kind of vivid description of the flood. With research in hand, she bent the facts to suit her fiction.

> I started with a picture of the flood. Then I read the Paris newspapers from the period, found an album of pictures at Harvard, and had the great good fortune to find some old issues of a Paris civil engineering journal at the New York Public Library. These had a detailed description of what flooded when, tram line by tram line, subway station by subway station, day by day.
>
> With that material, I could construct a timeline of the flood. I got very detailed about this step and constructed maps day by day, with the flooded areas indicated, lists of events, copies of newspaper stories sorted by date.
>
> . . .
>
> Of course, once I had all this excess of information, I was free to ignore it for the story. For instance, in real life the Gare d'Orsay disaster happened at 1 A.M. What a waste, because the electricity had failed in that part of the city by then and no one could have seen it. I moved it by twelve hours so everyone could see the windows exploding and millions of gallons of water erupting down the streets.

Even if your story takes place in a made-up time or place, the details have to feel dead-on. Draw maps of your locations, jot down the distances, and note the prominent geographic features. Refer to your notes as you write, adding to the map as you embellish the fictional place with realistic detail.

GETTING THE INFORMATION YOU NEED

Here are some suggestions for getting the information you need:

• **Go there:** Pay a visit to the places where your mystery is set. Go as an *active observer*, not as a tourist or resident.
  • Look at the people: Who's there, how do they look, what are they doing?
  • Look around and identify the props that define the place.
  • Use all your senses: Are there distinctive sounds and smells?
  • Check out the local newspaper.
  • Collect maps, tourist guides, and postcards.
  • Bring a tape recorder, a notebook, a camera; capture the details.

• **Talk to people who've been there:** If you're writing a police procedural set in a big city, talk to big-city cops; if you're writing a cozy set in a New England inn, interview a New England innkeeper. Don't know any innkeepers? Call or e-mail a couple of inns and plead your case. Many people are delighted to share their knowledge and expertise.

• **Read diaries and letters:** First-person accounts and memoirs are a rich source of information for the writer, especially if the setting is historical. There's no better source for domestic detail, for example. Find them in libraries, historical society archives, and on the Internet.

• **Find newspaper accounts:** Your library can give you access to newspaper archives where you may find photographs to give you visual detail.

• **Search the Internet:** The Internet is full of pictures and descriptions of real places, as well as links to people with special interests and special expertise. My favorite search engine is Google. Enter a place name to find links to pages of information; click the Images tab to see if there are any pictures.

• **Find books in bookstores and libraries:** With so much information now accessible via the Internet, it's easy to forget about books. For rich descriptions and photographs, check out travel guides and coffee-table books that contain photo essays about a particular place. Buy them at bookstores or borrow them from the library where you'll find the writer's best friend: the librarian. With libraries online and networked together, I find that within a week I can get my hands on virtually any book in print. At online bookstore Amazon.com, you may find what you need using the "search inside the book" feature; just enter search words and you'll get access to the three or four pages of text and pictures surrounding each instance of those words in the book.

• **Be methodical:** Impose a method on your information gathering. Some people copy facts onto index cards, others use spreadsheets or text files. Be sure to capture the information *and also its source.*

ON YOUR OWN: Setting

1. Draw up a list of questions you need to research in order to create a convincing setting.

2. Visit as many of your novel's settings as you can; take along a notebook, a camera, and a tape recorder. Spend at least an hour observing and taking notes or recording.

3. Research the settings you can't visit. Use books, magazines, newspapers, the Internet, or interview people who've been there. Be methodical; record facts and their sources.

4. Write a five-minute, one-paragraph description of your sleuth's home or office, something that could actually appear in the novel.

 Complete the Setting section of the blueprint. (Go to page 90 at the end of Part I to find these forms.)

CHaPtEr 8:
staking out the plot

> "I'm a ferocious outliner. I can't begin a book
> unless I know where it's going and how it gets
> there."
>
> —Val McDermid

> "I never outline. I try to feel the same ex-
> citement that I hope the reader will: never
> knowing what comes on the next page."
>
> —Lee Child

A seasoned mystery writer with an established audience can get away with a ho-hum plot. For the new mystery writer, the plot has to be great—surprising, believable, and compelling. Imagine a roller coaster ride with a climb and a steep plunge at the start. There's a brief respite before the ride starts going fast and then faster, rising steadily. Then, there's a hairpin turn and an even steeper drop. You barely catch your breath and the ride gains speed again, rising to yet another twist and plunge. There's a final twist and heart-stopping plunge, then you coast back to the platform, exhilarated and wanting to take the ride again.

In more mundane terms, a mystery novel is comprised of groupings of scenes that can be thought of as acts, sandwiched between a dramatic opening that sets up the novel at the beginning, and a coda that explains all at the end. During each act, tension rises to a dramatic climax and plot twist, resulting in a major reversal for the protagonist in his quest to find the killer. At or near the end of the last act, there's a slam-bang dramatic finale in which the sleuth is in jeopardy and the truth revealed. At the end, loose ends are tied up and the world is safe from evil once again.

THE SHAPE OF A MYSTERY PLOT

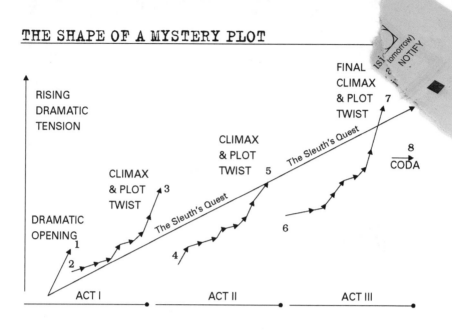

THE SLEUTH'S QUEST

What unifies a mystery novel is the sleuth's quest to find the killer. What keeps the reader hooked are all the roadblocks and setbacks the sleuth has to overcome. Drama works in direct proportion to how miserable you make your protagonist.

Here are some ways to plague your protagonist:

• **Plague your character with discomfort.** The hungrier, thirstier, colder (or hotter), achier, and generally more pissed off he becomes, the more heroic the quest. Give him a scraped knee, sprained ankle, dislocated finger, bloody nose, broken arm, or gunshot wound, and show how he pushes past pain and disability in order to continue his pursuit. Make sure the reader knows he feels the pain, but be careful about letting him bitch and moan too much about it—no one likes a whiny hero.

• **Plague your character with inner demons.** If you throw your character into a snake-filled pit, be sure to establish beforehand that he's terrified of snakes. If your character is an alcoholic trying to stop drinking, make his quest for the killer take him into bars.

• **Plague your character with mishaps.** Throw obstacles at your character to slow him down. His car can break down, or he can be set upon by thugs who turn out to be protecting the villain, or his car can roll over and end up in a ditch after being nudged off the highway by a semi. Maybe your character learns something damaging about one of the suspects, but she can't get anyone to listen to her. After each setback, the sleuth comes back stronger and more determined.

• **Modulate the misery.** Begin with minor woes and build as the story progresses to its final climax. From time to time, things should improve. Then, just when it looks as if your protagonist is out of the woods, let the next disaster befall him.

• **Raise the stakes.** On top of all those plagues, keep raising the stakes so your protagonist's need to bring the killer to justice gets stronger. For example, an innocent character is about to be convicted of the crime. Or maybe the protagonist or a loved one is in jeopardy. Or a villain threatens to escalate his attacks, and your protagonist is the only one who can stop him.

Reaching the end goal should feel heroic, worth all the pain and misery your protagonist had to overcome along the way.

NOW YOU TRY: Your sleuth's quest

In a sentence or two, describe your sleuth's quest. What does he want or need to achieve before the novel ends? Where does the quest start, and where does it end? Then make a list of plagues—potential setbacks, roadblocks, and other forms of misery you might throw in the way. Finally, decide how you're going to raise the stakes.

(!)

Your Sleuth's Quest:

Plagues:

How the stakes are raised:

A DRAMATIC OPENING: THE SETUP

Open your mystery novel with a dramatic scene in which something out of the ordinary happens. It might be a murder, or just some out-of-whack event, to borrow a term from science-fiction writing, with an element of mystery to it.

Your novel might open with the murder itself. Or it might begin with your protagonist discovering that someone has been murdered. Or it might start with an event that happened years before the main story begins.

Your book has to get off to an exciting or intriguing start, posing an unanswered question that provides a narrative hook that pulls the reader forward. Avoid the clumsy device of having an opening prologue that flashes forward to the murder, then chapter one begins some time earlier. You don't have to have a body drop in the first chapter. There are plenty of successful novels where no one is murdered until after page sixty.

Here are some examples of award-winning best-sellers in which the opening scene sets up the book and pulls the reader forward without a murder:

- **Out-of-whack-event:** A baby is found abandoned on the steps of a church. (*In the Bleak Midwinter*, Julia Spencer-Fleming)
  Unanswered question: Who left the baby on the church steps, and what happened to the baby's mother?
- **Out-of-whack-event:** A criminal defense attorney meets her new client—a woman accused of killing her cop-boyfriend. The woman extends a hand and says, "Pleased to meet you, I'm your twin." (*Mistaken Identity*, Lisa Scottoline)
  Unanswered question: Is this woman the defense attorney's twin, and is she a murderer?
- **Out-of-whack-event:** PI Bill Smith receives a late-night telephone call from the NYPD, who are holding his fifteen-year-old nephew Gary. (*Winter and Night*, S.J. Rozan)
  Unanswered question: Why would Gary ask for Smith? Smith hasn't seen Gary for years and is estranged from Gary's parents.

A warning: Don't allow your opening scene to steal your book's thunder. My co-author and I learned that the hard way. We wrote a chilling opening for *Obsessed*, written from the point of view of the bad guy. In it, he vandalizes Emily Ryan's car in a deserted parking lot, leaves a clear threatening message, and then hides in the underbrush. He watches Emily return and react to his handiwork, then terrifies her some more. Peter Zak arrives, just in the nick of time, but never actually sees the stalker.

What was the hitch? That opening scene tipped our hand—because the scene was written from the stalker's point of view, the reader knew there really was a stalker. The book worked much better if the reader wasn't sure. We wanted doubt to grow, with Emily becoming an increasingly ambiguous character and the reader questioning everything she said. A few weeks before the manuscript was due, we dumped the opening and wrote a new one— this time from our protagonist's point of view. Peter finds Emily in the parking lot terrified, her car vandalized. The result is a slightly less riveting opening but a much more interesting and suspense-filled novel.

So, pick your opening gambit and examine it with a critical eye. Be sure it sets up your novel, propels the reader forward, and doesn't rob your story of potential suspense by revealing too much.

NOW YOU TRY: Find your opening scene

Review your crime scenario and your sleuth's quest. Think about where you want your story to start, and find a dramatic opening scene. Is it the crime itself? The start of the investigation? Or is it some other dramatic prelude to your story?

Write a one-paragraph description of your opening scene. Be sure your scene meets the criteria shown below.

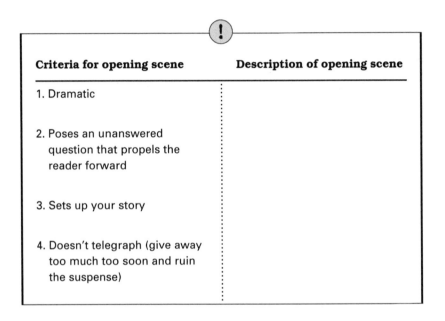

Criteria for opening scene	Description of opening scene
1. Dramatic	
2. Poses an unanswered question that propels the reader forward	
3. Sets up your story	
4. Doesn't telegraph (give away too much too soon and ruin the suspense)	

PLOT TWISTS AND DRAMATIC CLIMAXES

Plot twists are one of the most basic ingredients in a mystery. The unanswered question posed at the end of your opening scene is your novel's first plot twist. There should be a lot of them in your story, and each act should end with a *major* plot twist.

A plot twist might raise the stakes, making it more urgent that the sleuth find the villain; a plot twist might exonerate one suspect or implicate another; the twist might even completely change the reader's understanding of the crime.

Plot twists should be surprising and credible at the same time. If the reader sees it coming, it's not a twist. As you develop your plot, keep asking yourself: What does the reader expect to happen next? What could happen instead? Brainstorm the possibilities, and go in an unexpected but plausible direction.

Here are just a few of the many ways to twist your plot:
- A witness is discredited.
- A witness recants his story.
- A witness disappears.
- New evidence is discovered implicating a new suspect.
- The true implications of evidence that was previously misinterpreted are revealed.
- Evidence is discredited.
- Evidence disappears.
- A secret in a victim's past is revealed.
- A secret in a suspect's past is revealed.
- A threatening message is received.
- Another victim is murdered.
- A witness dies or is murdered.
- The prime suspect dies or is murdered.
- The sleuth is attacked.

At the end of each act, plan a dramatic climax that provides an ending to the story so far and a major plot twist that propels the reader forward to the next act.

THE FINAL CLIMAX

Most mystery novels have a final climactic action scene, fraught with mortal danger, during which the sleuth and the villain duke it out, if not physically then verbally. That scene contains the payoff for the entire novel. It's one of the most important scenes in your book—second only to the dramatic opening. After that comes a coda, a more contemplative scene in which all is explained. You can write three hundred pages of great book, but if the final twenty don't fulfill the promise, it's a washout.

In most mysteries, the protagonist triumphs, the villain is defeated, and justice is served. The ending should be plausible, surprising, and most importantly, satisfying. Don't feel rule-bound if some unusual ending suits your story, but be sure that in the end it is crystal clear whodunit, why, and how. Your reader should never be left scratching his head.

Plan a dramatic action scene (or several) near the end of the third act, culminating in a confrontation between the protagonist and the villain as the final shoe drops.

In planning the ending, here are some things to avoid:

- **Duh:** An ending that's obvious to everyone but the sleuth. This happens when you've telegraphed the ending to the reader (the shadowy figure with bad breath that the sleuth keeps ignoring).
- **Over-the-top:** An ending with an overdose of violence. The villain holds the sleuth at bay with a machine gun while systematically cutting off the hands and ears of his victims and blowing up houses in a nearby suburb.
- **You've got to be kidding:** The villain seems incapable of such a crime (the anorexic teeny-bopper strangler).
- **Spill all:** The villain, for no apparent reason, begins to talk-talk-talk, spilling every detail about the crime.
- **And then I woke up:** An ending that suggests that the rest of the book was a dream or didn't really happen.
- **If only I'd known:** Yeah, you could have solved it, too, if the sleuth hadn't withheld key information.
- **Out of sight:** The all-important confrontation takes place off stage.
- **But, but, but:** The ending fails to tie up all the loose ends and explain how and why everything happened.
- **Yeah, right:** The ending leaves the reader having to assume that some key part of what happened was due to coincidence.

PAGES, SCENES, CHAPTERS, AND ACTS

Scenes are the building blocks of a mystery novel. A scene contains the dramatic telling of an event that occurs at a single time in a single place. When the time or place changes, there's a new scene. Every scene in a mystery novel should have a *payoff*: Something happens or changes that propels the story forward. Several scenes may be grouped into a *chapter*, or a chapter may be comprised of one long scene.

The *acts* in your novel are dramatic structures. There's no message in the text that says "End of Act I." The end of an act looks like the end of any chapter, but it should feel to the reader as if a major part of your story has ended—tension has risen to a crescendo and there's been a major plot twist. The beginning of the next chapter is the beginning of the next act, and it feels as if the momentum is starting to build all over again, with tension ratcheted down at the start and the characters take time out to digest the implications of the latest plot twist.

There are about ten to thirty scenes per act in a mystery novel, and a total of forty to ninety scenes in all. Here's an example of how a 280-page novel might break down:

	# Pages	# Scenes	# Chapters	Ending plot twist
Dramatic opening	10	1	1	Julia's car is vandalized and she realizes she's being stalked.
Act I	60	13	7	Sleuth investigates; identifies Lenny as the likely stalker and is closing in . . . **Plot twist:** Lenny is murdered.
Act II	100	24	10	Sleuth continues to investigate, suspicion shifts to Julia's boyfriend. **Plot twist:** Boyfriend is run down in a parking lot, Julia is arrested.
Act III	100	26	10	Sleuth continues to investigate, realizes stalking was a smokescreen to cover up true motive. **Final plot twist:** Sleuth confronts the villain, injures him; villain is arrested.
Coda	10	2	1	Julia is released from jail. Discussion, reflection of what happened; final secret revealed.
Total	270	65	28	

NOW YOU TRY: Analyze plot structure

To get the hang of how a mystery works, analyze the plot of a standard, one-hour television crime show. These tend to be structured like mystery novels. They begin with a dramatic opening, and the commercial breaks impose a four-act structure. Usually there's a plot twist before each commercial. Often they end after the final dramatic scene, dispensing with the mopping-up of a coda.

Watch a show and analyze the structure of the plot by filling out this scorecard:

	Description	Most likely suspect at the commercial break
Opening scene—short scene at the very beginning (before the first commercial)		
Plot twist before the next commercial break		
Plot twist before the next commercial break		
Plot twist before the next commercial break		
Final climactic scene; final plot twist and resolution		

SUBPLOTS

Mysteries have secondary plots interwoven with the main one. Subplots make the novel more complex and interesting and also provide the reader with a breather from the ongoing, increasing tension of the main plot.

Subplots can be heavy or lightweight, but they should always be integral to the novel, not slapped on. They should tie directly to the main plot, echo the themes explored in the main plot, complicate the crime investigation, or provide the main character an opportunity to address inner demons.

Here are some different kinds of subplots:

• **A romance.** The main character becomes romantically involved. Now we have a character the protagonist cares about, someone who can be put in jeopardy, ratcheting up the stakes. A romance provides an opportunity to make your main character more three-dimensional and gives you a chance to write a really juicy sex scene.

- **Trials and tribulations of the main character's friends/family.** Colorful relatives or friends can provide comic relief and can also complicate the protagonist's quest in interesting ways.
- **Health issues.** This could be a character attempting to lose weight, getting pregnant, or fighting a life-threatening disease.
- **Challenges of the protagonist's "day job."** Ongoing rivalry with a co-worker, dealing with a demanding boss, tangling with bureaucracy, getting fired—there are many ways to use the drama of the character's day job to complicate the story.
- **Investigation of another, apparently unrelated crime.** A major plot twist occurs when this second crime ties into the main one.
- **Unresolved event in a character's past.** The narrative flow seesaws back and forth between the present action and some unresolved past event. The ending of the book is doubly satisfying when the crime is solved *and* a past wrong is righted.

How many subplots does your story need? There should be at least one. In *Amnesia* we had three. The main plot about a woman who claimed to remember who shot her in the head was interwoven with a subplot about a woman with recovered memories of childhood abuse. A second subplot involved Peter's coming to terms with his own complicity in his wife's death. A third was developed about his burgeoning romance with investigator Annie Squires.

While you should resolve the main plot at the end of the novel, a subplot can be left hanging. This is especially useful if you're writing a series. For instance, you can bring a romantic subplot to the brink of intimacy, and then leave the reader panting to read the next book.

TO OUTLINE OR NOT TO OUTLINE

Is a detailed outline essential or a waste of time? Some writers can't start writing without one. Others say outlines are stifling and dry up their creative juices, preventing their characters from "taking over."

My characters never take over. How I wish they would. Without an outline, I'd end up wandering around aimlessly with them in the desert. I need an outline to remind me where we're all headed.

My outline tends to be spare. There's nothing dramatic about it. It's a working document, pure and simple. Here's an example of the outline of the first three scenes in *Guilt:*

Writing and Selling Your Mystery Novel

Outline for each scene includes:

- Scene 1, 2, . . . Number scenes sequentially
- Day 1, 2, . . . Number days sequentially to show elapsed time since the start of the novel
- Time of day
- Setting
- Characters in the scene
- What happens
- Which character is the narrator and has the point of view (POV)

Outline example from *Guilt* by G.H. Ephron

Scene 1: Day 1 (early September, present) Weekday, late morning. Storrow Hall at Harvard Law School. Mary Alice meets with Jackie to finish paperwork for restraining order against Jackie's husband. Mary Alice finds a backpack containing a bomb. It explodes, she's killed. Mary Alice's POV.
Scene 2: Same time/same day. Il Panino's café near Harvard Square. Annie Squires and Peter Zak meet for lunch. Traffic tie up, sirens. They see Jackie on sidewalk, "walking wounded." Jackie tells them about the explosion. Peter's POV.
Scene 3: Same day. In the car. Annie and Jackie go to elementary school to find Jackie's daughter Sophie. Annie convinces Jackie to talk to the police. They get Sophie. Annie's POV.

This kind of outline is a working document for the writer's eyes alone. It's not something you'd ever show to an agent or editor. It keeps your place, keeps track of time elapsed, and provides scaffolding on which to hang your story. It's also easy to revise—you can move whole clumps of scenes from one place to another with a quick cut-and-paste.

If you create an outline, and I recommend that you do, treat it as a working document and revise it as you go along.

WRITING A BEFORE-THE-FACT SYNOPSIS

In addition to an outline, you may want to write a "before-the-fact" synopsis of your book. This kind of synopsis tells the story dramatically, from start to finish, with sufficient detail so you can expand it into a book.

Author Jessica Speart writes a fifty-page synopsis for each of her wildlife agent Rachel Porter mysteries. She says: "It's during this process that characters spring to life, clues fall into place, and dialogue starts to flow. It gives me the freedom to concentrate on details once I sit down to write the actual novel, and I've found it to be an essential tool in building an airtight plot."

A fifteen-page synopsis for a three-hundred-page novel is more my speed. Here is an excerpt from the before-the-fact synopsis for the same first three scenes in *Guilt*. Notice this synopsis is written in present tense and tells the story dramatically. Compare this to the outline of these scenes.

Before-the-Fact Synopsis: *Guilt* by G.H. Ephron

When bombs start going off in his Cambridge neighborhood, Dr. Peter Zak allies himself with the police investigators to find the bomber. For the first time in Peter's career as a forensic neuropsychologist, he's not working for the defense.

It begins at Harvard Law School with an explosion that narrowly misses Jackie Klevinski, a recovered drug addict and mother of seven-year-old Sophie. Killed in the blast is law student Mary Alice Boudreaux, who'd been working with Jackie. Mary Alice had been meeting with Jackie to have her sign a request for a restraining order against her abusive husband, Joe Klevinski.

Peter and investigator Annie Squires find Jackie wandering the street, dazed and in shock, soon after the explosion. Jackie has been a student in Annie's self-defense class, and Annie has a special affinity for her because Jackie reminds Annie of a childhood friend, Julianne, whose father was abusive. Jackie tells them about the bombing and shares her fear that her husband may have been behind it. Perhaps he found out about the impending restraining order and planted the bomb to avoid losing his daughter Sophie. Maybe even now, he's gone to Sophie's school to take her away.

Annie drives Jackie to the elementary school where they find Sophie safe and sound. They bring Sophie back to Annie's office.

A synopsis like this can be shown to an editor or agent. In fact, some publishers require authors to submit a synopsis as the first deliverable of a book contract.

As a working document, a before-the-fact synopsis is not quite as useful as an outline. It's not broken down into scenes, doesn't show a time frame, and lacks the detail of an outline. It's not practical to revise it as you write. On the other hand, writing this kind of synopsis makes you think through all the plot twists and turns and articulate how one part of the story connects to the next. Once I've written a thorough synopsis, I find I'm less likely to write myself into a corner.

ON YOUR OWN: Staking out your plot

Outline your plot. You don't have to outline every single scene in your novel at the outset. You can seesaw back and forth between planning and writing—

do some detailed planning at the outset, write some, then return to planning, then writing, and so on. This approach can be less overwhelming than having to outline the entire plot before you start writing.

1. Create an outline that includes:
   a. the opening scene (the out-of-whack event)
   b. the rest of the scenes in Act I; remember, every scene should have a payoff that moves the story forward
   c. the final scene in Act I containing a dramatic climax and plot twist
   d. a brief summary of what happens in Act II, plus a description of the climax and major plot twist
   e. a brief summary of what happens in Act III, plus a description of the climax and major plot twist
   f. the solution: whodunit and why

2. After you've written the scenes in one act, outline the scenes in the next act; and while you're at it, revise the outline reflect what you actually wrote.

3. Repeat step two until you've finished the book.

Write a before-the-fact synopsis. Start small, then add on.

1. Write a one-paragraph synopsis that contains a dramatic summary of your novel. Include at least a summary of the dramatic opening, the crime, the investigation, and the solution.

2. Expand the synopsis to one page, adding a summary of each act and the major plot twists.

3. Expand it again, adding in subplots.

4. Keep expanding until everything in your head is down on paper.

Complete the Plot section of the blueprint. (Go to page 91 at the end of Part I to find these forms.)

CHaPtEr 9:
picking a title

The last step in planning is to pick a title for your novel. Of course you don't *need* a title to get started writing, but just like typing THE END when you're done, there's something therapeutic about typing a title at the beginning— if only to show yourself that you're officially off and running.

Most writers consider the title they pick at this stage to be a "working title," subject to change. Sometimes the book you start writing gets transformed by the time you get to the end, and you need a different title. Later, your publisher or agent may suggest a title change for what they perceive as marketing exigencies. Raymond Chandler wanted to call one of his novels *The Second Murder;* his publisher changed the title to *Farewell, My Lovely,* a change we can all agree was for the better.

WHAT'S IN A TITLE?

Like the graphic on the cover, the title should intrigue potential readers. You want a title that will pique the interest of readers who will love your book. The title should tease with a hint of what lies between the covers. So, don't call it *Sex and Bondage* unless it delivers both. False advertising won't build a following of devoted readers.

Mystery writers often give their series titles a common element. Sue Grafton captured the alphabet with her titles, beginning with *A Is for Alibi.* John D. MacDonald colors his Travis McGee novel titles, starting with *The Deep Blue Good-by.* My co-author and I give our Peter Zak series novels one-word titles from psychology. *Amnesia* is about memory. *Delusion* is about paranoia.

A useful rule: Think short. A short, snappy title is better than a longer one because it's easy to remember. Want proof? Here are the twenty mystery and crime fiction best-sellers listed on www.barnesandnoble.com for a week in May, 2004:

1. *Therapy* by Jonathan Kellerman
2. *Ten Big Ones* by Janet Evanovich
3. *3rd Degree* by James Patterson
4. *The Full Cupboard of Life* by Alexander McCall Smith
5. *Hidden Prey* by John Sandford
6. *Reckless Abandon* by Stuart Woods
7. *Doctored Evidence* by Donna Leon
8. *The Narrows* by Michael Connelly
9. *Guardian of the Horizon* by Elizabeth Peters
10. *Monday Mourning* by Kathy Reichs
11. *A Spectacle of Corruption* by Donald Liss
12. *The Bones in the Attic* by Robert Barnard
13. *1st to Die* by James Patterson
14. *2nd Chance* by James Patterson
15. *The Kalahari Typing School for Men* by Alexander McCall Smith
16. *Bad Business* by Robert B. Parker
17. *Dead to the World* by Charlaine Harris
18. *In the Bleak Midwinter* by Julia Spencer-Fleming
19. *Uniform Justice* by Donna Leon
20. *Lake House* by James Patterson

Here's how the list breaks down in terms of word count:

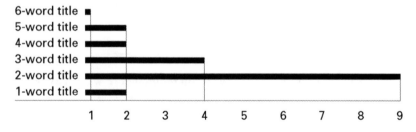

Two-word titles are by far the most common. The outlier on the list, *The Kalahari Typing School for Men*, was originally published in Scotland. That might explains how it escaped with its glorious, six-word title.

A number of books on this list have recognizable series titles. James Patterson's *3rd Degree* follows *2nd Chance* in his Women's Murder Club series. *Ten Big Ones* is the tenth book in Janet Evanovich's Stephanie Plum series that began with *One for the Money*. Charlaine Harris always uses the word "Dead" in her Southern Vampire series titles.

Other titles provide a glimpse of setting (*Lake House*; *The Narrows*; *In the*

Bleak Midwinter). Others mine the theme of the book with an image or a phrase with a double meaning (*Doctored Evidence*; *Uniform Justice*). Alliteration makes a title easier to remember (*Bad Business*; *Monday Mourning*).

Quotes from Shakespeare, the Bible, nursery rhymes, images from fairy tales, and historical references frequently show up as mystery titles. *Guardian of the Horizon* refers to the Egyptian Sphinx, hence a perfect title for a mystery novel featuring an archaeologist's return to Egypt.

It's also clear from a quick glance at the list: Far more important than a book's title is the author's name. Most of these guys, and they are mostly guys, have a long track record of best-sellers. Sad but true, names sell books, titles don't. If no one knows your name, that's even more reason to have a great title. *In the Bleak Midwinter* (#18 on the best-seller list) was Julia Spencer-Fleming's first novel.

Whatever title you pick, it should:
- accurately pitch your book
- intrigue potential readers
- be easy to remember

Titles can't be copyrighted, so there's no law against naming your book *Misery* or *The Da Vinci Code*. But I wouldn't pick a title that's so instantly recognizable. On the other hand, if your favorite title happens to have been used on a book no one remembers, feel free to use it.

NOW YOU TRY: Examining your favorite titles

Think about what you like in a book title. List five of your favorites—they don't have to be mysteries. What is it about each title that made you able to remember it, and what does that title evoke about the book itself?

Five Favorite Titles	Why you remember it; what it evokes
1.	
2.	
3.	
4.	
5.	

1. Brainstorm title ideas. Pay special attention to the premise, the backdrop and setting, the major plot points, and the main character. Free associate; make a list of the words and images that come to mind. Circle five or ten you like best, and turn them into titles.

2. Look up each of the five titles in an online bookstore (or in your library's copy of *Books in Print*) to see how often it's already been used.

3. Search your possible titles on the Internet and check each word in an online slang dictionary; that way, if you use a word like *shag* in your title, at least you'll know up front that it has more than one meaning.

4. Pick a title.

Write the title in the final field of the blueprint (on page 91), and then type it on the first page of your manuscript. You're ready to start writing.

A BLUEPRINT FOR PLANNING A MYSTERY NOVEL

PREMISE: Suppose... and what if....

PROTAGONIST: The mystery sleuth

Name:

_____

Reason for getting mixed up in investigating crimes:

_____

Physical appearance:

_____

Present status and ambitions:

_____

Background:

_____

Talents and skills:

_____

Personality:

_____

Tastes and preferences:

THE CRIME(S)

	Crime 1	Crime 2	Crime 3
Crime scenario: Victim, MO, scene of the crime			
What appears to have happened			
What really happened			
Why this crime matters to this sleuth			

THE VILLAIN
Name:

Thumbnail sketch:

Apparent motive:

How this character justifies the crime(s):

VICTIMS

Victim's name:

Thumbnail sketch:

What put this victim in harms way: | Secrets:

Victim's name:

Thumbnail sketch:

What put this victim in harms way: | Secrets:

Victim's name:

Thumbnail sketch:

What put this victim in harms way: | Secrets:

INNOCENT SUSPECTS

Suspect's name:	Relationship to victim:

Thumbnail sketch:

Apparent motive:	Secrets and lies:

Suspect's name:	Relationship to victim:

Thumbnail sketch:

Apparent motive:	Secrets and lies:

Suspect's name:	Relationship to victim:

Thumbnail sketch:

Apparent motive:	Secrets and lies:

Suspect's name:	Relationship to victim:

Thumbnail sketch:

Apparent motive:	Secrets and lies:

SUPPORTING CAST

Name	Relationship to sleuth (boss, brother, etc.)	Role in the story (adversary, sidekick, etc.)

SETTING

TIME year, season, concurrent events	
LOCATION geographic locale, exteriors, interiors	
CONTEXT institutions and activities that provide the backdrop	

THE PLOT: Main turning points

DRAMATIC OPENING (out-of-whack event)	Description:
END OF ACT I climax and plot twist	Description:
TWIST OF ACT II climax and plot twist	Description:
END OF ACT III climax and plot twist	Description:
SUBPLOTS	Description:

WORKING TITLE

PaRt 2:

writing

Introduction

> "For me and most of the other writers I know, writing is not rapturous. In fact, the only way I can get anything written at all is to write really, really shitty first drafts."
>
> —ANNE LAMOTT
> *Bird by Bird: Some Instructions on Writing and Life*

Okay, you've spent tons of energy and done a bang-up job with your plan. Now the real work begins: Writing the first draft.

At its most elementary, you'll be writing scenes that combine description, movement, dialogue, and internal dialogue to create these basic components of a mystery:

- **Investigation:** Questioning suspects, examining the crime scene, stakeouts, searches, and so on.
- **Suspense:** Rising tension, there's potential danger as the investigation continues; anticipation builds that something is *going* to happen.
- **Dramatic action:** Physical drama such as a car chase, a gunfight, or an assault.
- **Reflection:** Pondering over what just happened and sifting through clues and red herrings; then a moment of realization as a light bulb goes off in the character's (and the reader's) head, and the story is propelled forward.

To see how these elements work together, read the three-scene synopsis that follows.

Investigation	Concerned when lawyer Bill Fellon fails to show up in court, private investigator Jason Armitage goes to Fellon's apartment to look for him.
	Jason finds Fellon's Porsche in the parking lot outside his apartment; the engine is cool.

Suspense	Jason goes to Fellon's apartment. The door is ajar. Cautiously he enters. He checks out the kitchen, the living room. Everything seems normal.
	He notices an acrid smell. He enters the bedroom and finds Fellon lying on the bed, holding a pistol, a bullet wound to the head. Jason picks up the phone to call the police when he hears a toilet flush.
Dramatic action	The bathroom door opens and a man wearing a ski mask emerges.
	They struggle. Jason grabs for the gun, but before he can shoot the man, he's bashed in the head with the base of the telephone and it's lights out.
Reflection	Jason wakes up in an ambulance. At first he can't recall what happened. Then it comes back to him. He remembers going to his friend's apartment and finding him dead in what was meant to look like a suicide. Jason is angry, upset; he knows his friend was depressed, but he'd never shoot himself. Jason tries to visualize the intruder he saw coming out of the bathroom and wonders why the man only hit him in the head and didn't kill him. Then he realizes that his own clothes are covered in blood, his fingerprints are all over the gun that killed his friend, and the police officer leaning over him is reading him his Miranda rights.

Generally speaking, a mystery novel unfolds in waves of investigation, suspense, action, and reflection. Early on in the novel, there's more investigation; toward the end there's more suspense and action. A well-paced novel takes time to develop characters, to create a sense of place up front, all the while moving the story forward.

GETTING IT DOWN

Writing a first draft is like knitting a very long scarf. Your blueprint, outline, and synopsis provide a pattern to follow. Start at the beginning, write scene one and then scene two. Keep at it, carrying along and interweaving the threads of subplots while you build the main story, varying the pattern and improvising as inspiration strikes. Sooner or later, you've inched your way to the end.

For me, the first draft is excruciating. I can plan to beat the band, research for hours on end, revise 'til the cows come home, but writing that first draft—every sentence, every page feels like pushing wood through a meat grinder. I read e-mail or play solitaire to avoid writing. I'll even do laundry or balance my checkbook rather than write. Mystery author Kate Flora suggests hanging a sign *inside* your office door that says KEEP OUT. I tried it, but it didn't work.

I have no magic bullet. But it helps if I give myself permission to drop stitches. Writing badly on a first draft is absolutely acceptable. So silence your inner critic and get the first draft nailed. If your first attempt is rife with highfalutin metaphors, arcane vocabulary, and long descriptive passages, you'll cut and simplify later. If your writing is skeletal, more movie script than novel, don't worry about that, either. You'll layer on nuance, character, and description when you revise.

Some writers start writing the first scene and steam ahead, writing scene after scene through to the end. But for the rest of us, writing is three steps forward, two steps back. Every morning when I sit down to work, the first thing I do is reread and revise the scene I wrote the day before. Sometimes I revise an even larger chunk before writing new material. This is good, but only up to a point. You've heard that old saying, "Great is the enemy of good?" Well, "great" is also the enemy of "finished." And you've got to finish the first draft so you can get on to the revisions that will make it shine.

This section provides you with instruction and practice exercises for writing the first draft.

MANUSCRIPT LENGTH

There are no hard and fast rules, but generally speaking a publisher expects a manuscript for a mystery novel to be somewhere between 70,000 to 90,000 words. Using 12-point Times New Roman font, double spacing, and inch-wide margins, that's about 250 to 400 pages. If your manuscript is more than 450 pages, it'll be hard to get an editor to consider it. A 150-page manuscript, even one that deals with lightweight content, probably won't make it out of the slush pile either.

CHaPtEr 10:
writing a
dramatic opening

No pressure, but the opening of your book is the gatekeeper in determining whether your novel will sell. If your opening is weak, it won't matter if chapter two is a masterpiece. Editors and agents will stop reading before they get to it.

If you completed your blueprint, you've already scoped out a dramatic scene to open your novel. You know who's in the scene and what's going to happen to propel the novel forward.

Your opening scene can be long or short. It can be action packed or moody, rich in description, or skeletal and spare. It may contain a vivid sense of setting or a strong shot of character. Regardless of what's in that scene, the reader should have some idea what the story is going to be about after reading it, or at least have a good sense of the theme and be eager to turn the page.

ANALYZING A DRAMATIC OPENING

So what makes a good dramatic opening? In the absence of any useful rules, the best I can offer is an example. Consider this abridged excerpt from the opening scene of Julia Spencer-Fleming's award-winning first novel, *In the Bleak Midwinter*, and think about how it's done.

• How does the opening sentence set up the scene?
• What's the out-of-whack event, and how does it pull the reader forward?
• In what tense is this told, and from which character's point of view?
• What do we know about the setting?
• What's the weather and time of day?
• What do we learn about Russ Van Alstyne?
• Why does this event matter to this protagonist?
• What does this opening scene suggest that the book is going to be about?
• Does this opening develop plot or character?

Opening Scene From *In the Bleak Midwinter* by Julia Spencer Fleming

It was one hell of a night to throw away a baby. The cold pinched at Russ Van Alstyne's nose and made him jam his hands deep into his coat pockets, grateful that the Washington County Hospital had a police parking spot just a few yards from the ER doors. A flare of red startled him, and he watched as an ambulance backed out of its bay silently, lights flashing.

"Kurt! Hey! Anything for me?"

The driver waved at Russ. "You heard about the baby?"

"That's why I'm here."

Russ waved, then pushed open the antiquated double doors to the emergency department.

[. . .]

"Hey! Chief!" A blurry form in brown approached him. Russ tucked his glasses over his ears and Mark Durkee, one of his three night shift officers, snapped into focus. As usual, the younger man was spit-and-polished within an inch of his life, making Russ acutely aware of his own non-standard-issue appearance: wrinkled wool pants shoved into salt-stained hunting boots, his oversized tartan muffler clashing with his regulation brown parka.

"Hey, Mark," Russ answered. "Talk to me."

The officer waved his chief down the drab green hallway toward the emergency room. The place smelled of disinfectant and bodies, with a whiff of cow manure left over by the last farmer who had come in straight from the barn.

[. . .]

"How's the baby look?"

"Fine, as far as they can tell. He was wrapped up real well, and the doc says he probably wasn't out in the cold more'n a half hour or so." Russ' sore stomach eased up. He'd seen a lot over the years, but nothing shook him as much as an abused child. He'd had one baby-stuffed-in-a-garbage-bag case when he'd been an MP in Germany, and he didn't care to ever see one again.

Discussion

Plot and character take equal weight in this excerpt. It's as much about introducing a main character as it is about setting a story about an abandoned baby spinning. Every sentence, every detail is a deliberate choice, and by the end, the reader knows that the novel is going answer two questions: Who abandoned that baby and why?

It was one hell of a night to throw away a baby. This grabber opening is internal dialogue that puts the reader firmly in the head of Russ Van Alstyne. The point of view is the third-person limited, and we experience this scene as if the camera is looking through Van Alstyne's eyes. His thoughts filter the images we see. It's written in the past tense but it feels immediate. Right away, there's the out-of-whack event—a baby has been abandoned.

The cold pinched at Russ Van Alstyne's nose and made him jam his hands deep into his coat pockets, grateful that the Washington County Hospital had a police parking spot just a few yards from the ER doors. You've heard that old author's adage "show don't tell"? In this brief passage, Spencer-Fleming shows what Van Alstyne is like. She shows that he is chief of police: The ambulance driver addresses him as "Chief," and he parks his car in a "police parking spot." She also shows how cold it is with *the cold pinched his nose,* and with the way Van Alstyne jams his hands into his pockets. The bitter cold isn't there just for ambience. It brings home to the reader how dangerous it was for that baby.

The place smelled of disinfectant and bodies, with a whiff of cow manure left over by the last farmer who had come in straight from the barn. In a few descriptive phrases, we get a visceral sense of place. We know this is a hospital, and we know it's somewhere rural.

We get a detailed description of what Van Alstyne's wearing (*wrinkled wool pants shoved into salt-stained hunting boots . . .*) as he mentally compares himself to the younger officer (*spit-and-polished within an inch of his life*). Van Alstyne is a guy with more than a few miles on him who doesn't fuss with his appearance.

How's the baby look? Van Alstyne asks, and already we're wondering: who left this baby on the church steps, and what happened to the baby's mother? *"He was wrapped up real well, and the doc says he probably wasn't out in the cold more'n a half hour or so."* Clues!, thinks the astute reader. Someone cared enough to make sure the baby was wrapped up well. Maybe that someone was even watching to be sure the baby was found in time.

Here's what Spencer-Fleming doesn't give us: a whole lot of backstory. Backstory is background information about how a character arrived at this particular place and time. It's a sure sign that the novel is written by a novice when a load of backstory is dumped into the opening chapter. Yes, we get a whiff of Van Alstyne's past, and a hint of why an abandoned baby matters to him: *He'd had one baby-stuffed-in-a-garbage-bag case when he'd been an MP in*

Germany, and he didn't care to ever see one again. That's all the reader needs to know at this point.

NOW YOU TRY: Analyze a dramatic opening

Reread the opening scenes of some of your favorite mystery novels. Pay careful attention to how the author handles these three elements:

1. The opening paragraph

2. The final paragraph

3. The out-of-whack event and how it sets up the novel

SKETCHING OUT A DRAMATIC OPENING

As an exercise in chapter eight, you wrote a description of your opening scene. If you have a clear picture in your mind of exactly what happens in the scene, you may feel you can jump right in and write the dramatic opening of your novel. If you find that blank page daunting, sketch out the scene before you try to write it.

Here's an example of what a "sketch" of a scene looks like, using the opening of *In the Bleak Midwinter*.

Scene sketch	Describes these elements
Miller's Kill, small town, Adirondacks, winter; hospital parking lot and ER	Where
Present, bitter cold winter night	When
Russ Van Alstyne (police chief, narrator); Kurt (ambulance driver); Officer Mark Durkee	Characters in the scene
Van Alstyne is in parking lot of Washington County Hospital; it's cold; an ambulance is leaving Van Alstyne chats with the ambulance driver; finds out about a baby left on St. Alban's doorstep Van Alstyne goes into ER; talks to Durkee; is relieved to find out baby is fine, was well wrapped up; remembers the discarded baby he found as MP in Germany	What happens
Who abandoned the baby and why?	Question that propels the reader forward

Review your description of your dramatic opening. Then visualize the scene in your mind. Sketch it out below.

!

Sketch out these elements

Where:

When:

Characters in the scene:

What happens:

Questions that propels the reader forward:

HOW TO BEGIN THE DRAMATIC OPENING

A good way to start the opening scene is by jumping right into the action. Here are some opening lines that catapult the reader into the story:

> When the first bullet hit my chest, I thought of my daughter. (*No Second Chance*, Harlan Coben)

> She'd been brutally stabbed and slashed more times than Carella chose to imagine. (*Widows*, Ed McBain)

> Gordon Michaels stood in the fountain with all his clothes on. (*Banker*, Dick Francis)

> The house in Silverlake was dark, its windows as empty as a dead man's eyes. (*The Concrete Blonde*, Michael Connelly)

> I was fifteen years old when I first met Sherlock Holmes, fifteen years old with my nose in a book as I walked the Sussex Downs, and nearly stepped on him. (*The Bee-keeper's Apprentice*, Laurie R. King)

> They were thirty-five nautical miles off the coast of Rhode Island. (*The Mayday*, Bill Eidson)

> Eight-thirty A.M., and I was running late. (*The Dead Stone*, Vicki Stiefel)

Your opening line is important, but don't obsess about it. Just write an opening line that puts the reader into the scene, get past it, and keep going. You can make it "perfect" later.

WRITING THE DRAMATIC OPENING

The first scene of your book presents some unique problems. Your primary job is to get your story moving while at the same time introduce your reader to the characters and setting.

Keep your eye on the story you're setting up—something intriguing has to happen. Lay in just enough character and setting description to orient the reader. You have the rest of the book to fill in the blanks.

Write the opening scene using the elements you sketched out. You can make revisions later as you learn more in the chapters of this book that cover topics such as setting the scene, introducing characters, writing dialogue and internal dialogue, and creating action.

ENDING WITH FORWARD MOMENTUM

End your dramatic opening scene with an unanswered question that is implied or stated. Your goal is to make it impossible for the reader to put down your novel.

Here's how Harlan Coben ends the opening scene of *No Second Chance*:

> So I like to think that as the two bullets pierced my body, as I collapsed onto the linoleum of my kitchen floor with a half-eaten granola bar clutched in my hand, as I lay immobile in a spreading puddle of my own blood, and yes, even as my heart stopped beating, that I still tried to do something to protect my daughter.

The reader wants to know: Does he die? And what's he trying to protect his daughter from?

Review the sketch of your opening scene. Decide how you should end it in order to achieve maximum forward momentum.

ON YOUR OWN: Write a dramatic opening

1. Write the opening scene for your novel.

2. Go back and review your scene, and examine your choices:
   a. Does the first sentence set up the scene?
   b. What's the out-of-whack event?
   c. Have you ended with an unanswered question?
   d. In what tense is this told, and from which character's point of view? Are you happy with these choices?
   e. Have you dumped a load of backstory that you don't need into the opening?

3. Revise and move on.

CHaPtEr 11:
introducing the protagonist

"Years ago I was in Botswana, staying with friends in a small town called Mochudi. A woman in the town wished to give my friends a chicken to celebrate Botswana National Day. I watched as this woman—traditionally built, like Mma Ramotswe—chased the chicken round the yard and eventually caught it. She made a clucking noise as she ran. The chicken looked miserable. She looked very cheerful. At that moment I thought that I might write a book about a cheerful woman of traditional build."

—ALEXANDER McCALL SMITH
from an interview on www.randomhouse.com

In mystery fiction as in life, first impressions matter. Make the most of your sleuth's first appearance on the page.

Raymond Chandler introduces his protagonist with *description* and sets the bar high in this introduction to Philip Marlowe in *The Big Sleep*, the first of the Philip Marlowe novels published in 1939:

> It was about eleven o'clock in the morning, mid October, with the sun not shining and a look of hard wet rain in the clearness of the foothills. I was wearing my powder-blue suit, with dark blue shirt, tie and display handker-chief, black brogues, black wool socks with dark blue clocks on them. I was neat, clean, shaved and sober, and I didn't care who knew it. I was everything the well-dressed private detective ought to be. I was calling on four million dollars.

Aside from being beautifully written, this introduction is packed with information about Marlowe. As a first-person narrator, Marlowe talks directly to the reader. He tells us he's a private dick and a clotheshorse in his powder-blue suit, fancy hankie, and socks with clocks—Bogie's portrayal of the character notwithstanding. You can almost smell the aftershave. We know he likes his liquor hard, otherwise why mention *sober*. Then he gives the in-your-face *and I didn't care who knew it*. Here's a guy with a chip on his shoulder, an outsider. *I was everything the well-dressed private detective ought to be*—we know he's also a self-deprecating smartass. Immediately we get a hint of what he's up to: *I was calling on four million dollars.*

Robert B. Parker uses dialogue to introduce his main character, Spenser, in this excerpt from *Bad Business*:

> "Do you do divorce work?" the woman said.
>
> "I do," I said.
>
> "Are you any good?"
>
> "I am," I said.
>
> "I don't want likelihood," she said. "Or guesswork. I need evidence that will stand up in court."
>
> "That's not up to me," I said. "That's up to the evidence."
>
> She sat quietly in my client chair and thought about that.
>
> "You're telling me you won't manufacture it," she said.
>
> "Yes," I said.
>
> "You won't have to," she said. "The sonovabitch can't keep his dick in his pants for a full day."
>
> "Must make dining out a little awkward," I said.
>
> She ignored me. I was used to it. Mostly I amused myself.

No description. No setting. With a deadpan stylishness, Parker jumps directly into a verbal sparring match between Spenser and a woman who wants to hire him to snoop on her soon-to-be ex. We get a strong taste of Spenser's wry sense of humor, we know he's a detective, and we easily infer that he can take or leave this particular assignment.

A third way to introduce a protagonist is to drop in on him in the middle of action. That's how Michael Connelly introduces police detective Harry Bosch a few pages into his award-winning debut novel, *The Black Echo*.

> Harry Bosch could hear the helicopter up there, somewhere, above the darkness, circling up in the light. Why didn't it land? Why didn't it bring help? Harry was moving through a smoky, dark tunnel and his batteries were dying. The beam of the flashlight grew weaker ev-

ery yard he covered. He needed help. He needed to move faster. He needed to reach the end of the tunnel before the light was gone and he was alone in the black. He heard the chopper make one more pass. Why didn't it land? Where was the help he needed? When the drone of the blades fluttered away again, he felt the terror build and he moved faster, crawling on scraped and bloody knees, one hand holding the dim light up, the other pawing the ground to keep his balance. He did not look back for the enemy he knew was behind him in the black mist. Unseen, but there. And closing in.

When the phone rang in the kitchen, Bosch immediately woke.

This is an action sequence that turns out to be a dream. Immediately we suspect that Bosch fought in the military, and we get hints of his darkest fears and of a tragedy in his past.

Description, dialogue, action—any of these can be used effectively to introduce your protagonist. Whatever method you choose, your goal is to create a sense of immediacy, to give the reader a sense of the character's physical presence as well as personality. The character should pop off the page. Then, while the reader is paying attention to the fireworks, you slip in basic information.

GIVING THE READER THE BASICS

There's much debate among writers concerning how much the reader needs to be told right away about a main character. Lawrence Block never describes Bernie Rhodenbarr, his series protagonist, and readers don't complain. Sarah Caudwell wrote a series of suspense novels featuring Professor Hilary Tamar of Oxford and never told the reader if Professor Tamar was a man or a woman. Nevertheless, within the first few pages or so of a character's first appearance, most mystery authors let the reader know this basic information: name, gender, approximate age, job, and physical appearance.

It's important to give the reader a hint, at least, of your character's physical presence right away. In the absence of a description, readers will quickly form their own competing images.

The challenge is to slip in the facts without giving a boring curriculum vitae. If you're writing a character who acts as a narrator, speaking directly to the reader, telling the basics is no problem at all. Sue Grafton writes this information dump and gets away with it handily in *G Is for Gumshoe*:

> For the record, my name is Kinsey Milhone. I'm a private
> investigator, licensed by the State of California, (now)
> thirty-three years old, 118 pounds of female in a five-

foot-six frame. My hair is dark, thick and straight. I'd been accustomed to wearing it short, but I'd been letting it grow out just to see what it would look like. My usual practice is to crop my own mop every six weeks or so with a pair of nail scissors. This I do because I'm too cheap to pay twenty-eight bucks in a beauty salon. I have hazel eyes, a nose that's been busted twice, but still manages to function pretty well I think. If I were asked to rate my looks on a scale of one to ten, I wouldn't. I have to say, however, that I seldom wear makeup, so whatever I look like first thing in the morning at least remains consistent as the day wears on.

Like a character in a movie who suddenly turns and addresses the audience, Kinsey speaks directly to the reader. In one dense paragraph, we get all the basics about her, plus a shot of her feisty, nonconformist personality.

Here's another example from *The Magician's Tale* by David Hunt (aka William Bayer). Though the passage is also written in the first person, this character (photographer Kay Farrow) describes herself as part of the storytelling rather than speaking directly to the reader.

The sun is about to set. I check myself in the mirror—glowing eyes, dark brows, small triangular face, medium-length hair parted on the side. I brush down some wisps so they fall across my forehead, then dress to go out—black T-shirt, jeans, black leather jacket, sneakers, Contax camera around my neck.

I wear black to blend in. My hope is that by dressing dark and with my face half concealed by my hair, I can slink along the streets, barely seen, covertly stealing images.

I pause at my living room window. Dusk is magic time, the sky still faintly lit. Streetlamps are on and lights glow from windows, making the city look mysterious and serene. The view's so spectacular it's hard to tear myself away: North Beach, Telegraph Hill, the Bay Bridge sharply defined, all still, silent, glowing behind the glass.

Hunt has his character look into a mirror and tell us about her own appearance. Plenty of books on writing tell you this is hackneyed, but it turns up all the time in very good novels, and here you see how well it can be done.

From the telling details Hunt reveals, the reader infers a great deal. This character is young (*black T-shirt, jeans* . . .), a resident of San Francisco (*North Beach* . . .), and a photographer (*Contax camera around my neck*). The character feels somewhat androgynous, but the *medium-length hair* suggests she's a woman. Beyond that, we know she's highly visual, curious, and secretive. A page later, she's prowling an unsavory neighborhood and a street kid calls out to her: "You blind, girl? What's with the shades, Bug?" Her response tells us that she suffers from complete color blindness. Soon she meets a man who addresses her as "Kay" and we know her name. Within the first four pages, Hunt covers all the basics, introducing his protagonist and blending the information seamlessly into an ongoing narrative.

Linda Barnes takes another approach to introduce Carlotta Carlyle in *The Big Dig*:

> He was studying my face like he'd never seen green eyes,
> a pointy chin, or flaming hair before. Made me wonder
> whether I looked drawn or pale. I widened my smile,
> hoping the extra wattage would substitute for a blusher.

Notice that Barnes has another character look at Carlotta Carlyle, and Carlotta tells us what she thinks he sees.

There will be a lot that you want to convey to your reader about your main character. Restrain yourself. There's no rush. Make the introduction memorable but not overwhelming. Carefully select details to show. Reveal your character's backstory as you go along and in support of ongoing drama.

NOW YOU TRY: Give the reader the basics

1. Refer to your blueprint. Make a list of twenty things about your protagonist's past, personality, or appearance that you want the reader to know right away.

2. Cross out the fifteen that can wait until later in the novel.

3. Write (or rewrite) the first scene your protagonist appears in, getting across those five basic things about your character without writing a character-information dump.

ON YOUR OWN: Introducing the protagonist

1. Look at a half-dozen of your favorite mysteries. Analyze how the author introduces the protagonist:
   a. Does the author use description? Dialogue? Action?
   b. How (and when) does the author convey the character's name, gender, job, age, and physical appearance?
   c. What character traits does the author initially reveal, and how?
   d. How much of the character's background does the reader learn at the beginning?

2. Try different approaches to introducing your protagonist. Try first-person narration. Try dialogue. Try action. See which one works best.

CHaPtEr 12:
introducing major and minor characters

> "Don't say the old lady screamed. Bring her on and let her scream."

— attributed to MARK TWAIN

Not all characters are created equal, but each one has that moment when he appears on the printed page and gets to make a first impression. How big an impression should be in direct proportion to the size of the role that character plays in the novel.

- **Major characters** get to have opinions and take action; they're necessary to the integrity of the story. Take one out and the plot collapses. Major characters in a mystery include the villain, all the suspects, the sidekick, and the supporting cast.
- **Minor characters** play small but necessary roles. They may appear only once or twice. For instance, the barmaid who serves up that double Scotch and listens to your sleuth complain about the case; or the victim's bereaved mother whom your protagonist questions to get the names of the victim's close friends.
- **Walk-ons** are usually nameless characters who deliver, at most, a few lines of dialogue; their presence lends a dash of realism to a scene, then they are seen no more.

MAKING INTRODUCTIONS: CONJURING THE DETAILS

When a character first appears in your novel, take a few paragraphs to create an impression. Here's the kind of impression you want to avoid making:

> An attractive young brunette sat at the desk. She had on glasses, and she wore a dark top. She looked up and saw me.

What's wrong with this introduction? It's pallid and generic. Words like *attractive* don't carry any specific meaning. *Dark top?* Was it a scruffy T-shirt? A ruffled blouse?

Is this any better?

> A skinny adolescent girl sat at the desk. She had dark
> eyes and pale skin, and her short dark hair was streaked
> with red. She had on wire-rimmed glasses and wore black
> jeans and a black T-shirt. A leather lace was tied around
> her wrist, and there were silver rings on all her fingers.

At least there are more details. Too many, in fact, and the details are pure surface—eye color, skin color, glasses, clothing, jewelry. We barely get a sense of who this character is. Verbs like *sat* and *had on* and *wore* are weak and fail to communicate anything about the character's presence. We know she's probably an edgy teenager, but she's more shop-window mannequin than real human being.

How about this description?

> Olivia was slumped at a desk facing me, staring intently
> at a computer screen. She looked nothing like the lively
> six-year-old or the mousy preadolescent I remembered.
> A long neck and bony elbows stuck out of her loose black
> T-shirt. But the hair was what you noticed—black spikes
> with poster-paint red streaks running through them.
>   She took off her round, wire-rimmed glasses, picked
> up a bottle of eye drops from alongside her keyboard,
> tipped her head back, and squeezed some drops into
> each eye. She had a leather lace tied around her wrist
> and silver rings on all her fingers, including the thumb.

Now the character makes more of an impression. It's in the details like that long neck and bony elbows sticking out of a loose black T-shirt, the *poster-paint red streaks* in her hair, and the thumb ring. These are more than a bunch of descriptions that communicate appearance; they are details that show who Olivia is. More information is conveyed by what she does—she puts drops in her eyes.

This description comes from *Addiction*, the second Dr. Peter Zak novel, and we were laying the groundwork for a character who, the reader will later discover, abuses Ritalin. She's more than edgy; she's the equivalent of high on speed and isn't getting enough sleep.

Where do you reach to find the details you need? How do you get past clichés? I know there are writers who conjure intriguing characters from dust. I can't. Sometimes it feels as if all I've got in my head are caricatures from Charles Dickens and *Love Boat*.

Fortunately, the world is full of real people who can provide the inspiration for fictional characters. For example, Olivia grew out of a girl who sat across from me on a subway.

All kinds of people make good jumping-off points for characters. Yourself, for example. The villain in one of our novels, I won't say which, feels intensely autobiographical to me. She's got my hair, stature, and inability to suffer fools.

I don't recommend creating a character who walks and talks like your best friend, but certainly you can create a character who is a composite of relatives, friends, or acquaintances. In our series, Peter's mother is a loose amalgam of my husband's mother and his aunt.

Public figures or actors make good starting points for fictional characters, as do strangers. Watch people. Take advantage of the time you spend waiting in a doctor's office or airport terminal, or riding a bus.

Can you create a nosy next-door neighbor based on your boss? A nefarious killer based on your ex? A two-bit crook based on the bully who tortured you in high school? Sure. But make sure that by the time you're finished, the real person is unrecognizable. You don't want to get sued.

INTRODUCING MAJOR CHARACTERS

When a major character appears, take the opportunity to make proper introductions. In these memorable paragraphs, Raymond Chandler introduces the villain of his short story, "Spanish Blood":

> Big John Masters was large, fat, oily. He had sleek blue jowls and very thick fingers on which the knuckles were dimples. His brown hair was combed straight back from his forehead and he wore a wine-colored suit with patch pockets, a wine-colored tie, a tan silk shirt. There was a lot of red and gold bands around the thick brown cigar between his lips.
>
> He wrinkled his nose, peeped at his hole card again, and tried not to grin. He said: "Hit me again, Dave—and don't hit me with the City Hall."

This is the essence of showing, not telling. Here are some of the basics to get across to the reader whenever you introduce a major character:

• **Full name and gender.** *Big John Masters was large, fat, oily.* Right away, the reader finds out the character's name and that he's a man. The name itself (*Big John Masters*) suggests a large, imposing figure. If your point-of-view character doesn't know the name right away, refer to the character some other way. For example, you might refer to a character by profession: "the lawyer"; relationship to another character: "Liam's boss"; physical feature: "Scar Face"; or item of clothing: "Pinstripes." Start using the character's name as soon as your point-of-view character learns it.

Q&A: Basing characters on real people: The legal risks

Q. *Suppose a character in your novel is based on a real person. Can that person sue for libel?*

A. Maybe. The law defines libel as the publication of a false statement of fact that harms the reputation of a living individual. (The dead cannot be defamed because, the law says, a person's reputation dies when a person dies.) So yes, living individuals can be libeled in works of fiction. They can sue you.

Q. *What does someone need to win the case?*

A. To win, the person must show (a) that the portrayal is recognizable, and (b) that her reputation has been damaged as a result. If the person is a public official or public figure, in addition she must prove that the portrayal is false and was published with "actual malice." The Supreme Court defines actual malice as knowledge of a statement's falsity or reckless disregard for a statement's truth.

Q. *So, what's the bottom line?*

A. Protect yourself and disguise the character. Change the name, gender, ethnicity, age, physical description, geographic location, job function or title, and alter the details of the events to make an individual unrecognizable.

Q. *Does disguising a character provide sufficient protection?*

A. Usually. But be careful that the features you use to disguise the character are not themselves defamatory. If you disguise your former teacher as a physically repulsive woman, the disguise itself may be defamatory.

• **Physical appearance.** *He had sleek blue jowls and very thick fingers on which the knuckles were dimples.* Hair, clothing, and finally the cigar—not a single piece of the description is throwaway. Sketch out your character's physical features and/or clothing with a few telling details. His cologne, a broken nose, and a bulge under the arm of his suit jacket that suggests the gun he's packing may be enough. Don't go on and on with paragraphs of description.

• **Personality.** *He wrinkled his nose, peeped at his hole card again, and tried not to grin. He said: "Hit me again, Dave—and don't hit me with the City Hall."* Convey the impression your character makes—his attitude, affect, and demeanor. In this example, Chandler uses a *one-two punch* character intro. After a description, the character does something—in this case, he looks at his cards, tries not to grin, and delivers a line of dialogue. This combination of description with action and dialogue effectively communicates attitude and personality. How your character stands, moves, talks, breathes, and chews his food can be used to convey a sense of someone who's flat and depressed, larger-than-life and menacing, all business and professional, or jovial and easygoing.

• **Relationship to the point-of-view character.** The reader should know immediately whether this character is a stranger, an acquaintance, a colleague, or a long-time friend of the character who's telling the story. In this case, this is a fellow poker player, and though Chandler never says it outright, the reader also gleans that he's a corrupt politician.

NOW YOU TRY: Analyze the introduction of a major character

Analyze this passage where Linda Barnes introduces detective Eddie Conklin, a former cop who offers Carlotta Carlyle a job investigating in *The Big Dig*. Use the questions on the left to guide you.

How does the author convey:

• physical appearance
• profession
• personality
• his relationship to Carlotta; their history
• Is this an impartial picture of Eddie?

Excerpt from *The Big Dig* by Linda Barnes

I used to work with Happy Eddie Conklin when I was a cop . . .

Eddie, now head of Foundation Security's Boston office, was early, wearing a gray suit that did its best to make him look ten pounds lighter, seated at a table barely big enough to handle two plates and a teapot. He rose, clasping my hand in both of his, yanking me into an embrace.

"Business, I tell ya, fantastic. Boomin' don't come close to it. Lack of trust in this town, geez, it's amazin'. Due diligence alone, bodyguardin' alone—I could run my own freakin' police department, ya know? Ya like this place? Ya want something to start?" He relayed my order of hot and sour soup to the hovering waiter and demanded "egg rolls, spring rolls, whatever ya call 'em," as well. "Bring that sweet sauce, ya know? The duck kind."

I poured steaming tea into small white cups.

Eddie looked preposterous from his silk tie to his tasseled slip-ons. His gray hair was short, his jaw freshly shaven. He glanced around to discourage eavesdroppers to neighboring tables, lowered his voice half a notch. "So how's your boy Mooney?

Discussion

Happy Eddie makes a strong first impression. Did you notice the use of contrast to show us how big he is? The guy is wearing a suit designed to make him look thinner, and he's sitting at an itty-bitty table with dainty teacups.

He's gruff and kind of goofy, the way he *yanks* Carlotta into his embrace and asks her if she likes the restaurant. The dialogue is written in dialect, suggesting a Boston accent: "*I tell ya . . .*" and "*. . . geez it's amazin'*" The grammar shows us Eddie hasn't gone to Harvard: "*Boomin' don't come close to it.*"

Eddie could have been a typical, hard-boiled private detective, but he's much more interesting. He's garrulous and anxious to please, more over-stuffed teddy bear than stuffed shirt. Whenever you bring on a character, think about what the stereotype would be; then surprise yourself by writing something different.

Is this an objective picture of Eddie? Of course it isn't. That's because we're seeing him through Carlotta's eyes. She's the narrator, and this description is all internal dialogue coming from Carlotta's head, so we get a strong sense of Carlotta's *attitude* toward Eddie. There's more affection than disdain in her description of him, though it's clear she thinks he's a bit of a buffoon. She comes right out and says, "He looked preposterous . . ." From the way he embraces her, we suspect they go way back.

When you write a description of a major character, keep the narrator's voice in your head, and describe the character showing your narrator's attitude to that character. Read the example below—here are two similar descriptions, but the narrator's attitude toward the character is quite different.

Example 1	Example 2
Lola stepped into the room and started for the corner. She was gorgeous, as always, with her flaming red hair and dress that fit her like quicksilver. She seemed oblivious to all the men in the room who were watching her, like a pack of hunting dogs who'd just caught the scent.	Lola slinked into the room and started for the corner table. That silver lame dress looked as if it had been painted on. She tossed her silky red hair back, like she didn't notice the men's eyes following her.

With subtle differences (*Lola stepped* versus *Lola slinked*, for example), the first description conveys sympathy; the second description conveys contempt. By carefully picking the words you use to describe a character, you can show the reader both the character's presence and the narrator's attitude.

NOW YOU TRY: Introduce a major character

1. Write the first appearance of a major character using the one-two punch method—first describe the character. Show with telling details. Then have him say and/or do something.

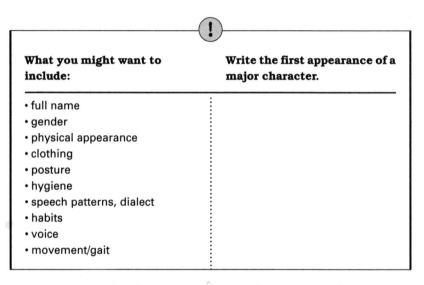

What you might want to include:

- full name
- gender
- physical appearance
- clothing
- posture
- hygiene
- speech patterns, dialect
- habits
- voice
- movement/gait

Write the first appearance of a major character.

2. Now revise that first appearance, tweaking your word choices to convey as much as you can about the *narrator's attitude* toward this character.

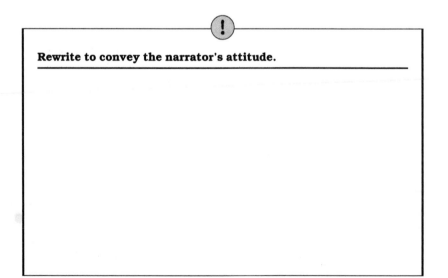

Rewrite to convey the narrator's attitude.

INTRODUCING MINOR CHARACTERS

Minor characters should make an impression when they come on the scene, just not a big splash. You don't want the reader to get too attached to them.

Here's how Jasper Fforde introduces Chief Boswell, the protagonist's boss in *The Eyre Affair*:

> I worked under Area Chief Boswell, a small, puffy man who looked like a bag of flour with arms and legs. He lived and breathed the job; words were his life and his love—he never seemed happier than when he was on the trail of a counterfeit Coleridge or a fake Fielding.

For all its brevity, this description shows the reader what Boswell looks like, what he does, and that he loves his job. And talk about terrific visual images—you can't beat *a bag of flour with arms and legs*.

Here's another example from *Devices and Desires* by P.D. James. With a flash of vivid description, action, and dialogue, Manny Cummings makes his debut:

> The door was already closing when he heard running footsteps and a cheerful shout and Manny Cummings leapt in, just avoiding the bite of the closing steel. As always he seemed to whirl in a vortex of almost oppressive energy, too powerful to be contained by the lift's four walls. He was brandishing a brown envelope. "Glad I caught you, Adam. It is Norfolk you're escaping to, isn't it? If the Norfolk CID do lay their hands on the Whistler, take a look at him for me, will you, check he isn't our chap in Battersea."

Is Manny tall or short? Fat or thin? Balding or sporting a crew cut? Who knows and who cares. It's what he does that counts: He leaps into the elevator, arriving like a whirlwind, delivers three lines of dialogue with a hint of an Irish brogue, and gives the protagonist an all-important brown envelope that pushes the plot along.

Despite the lack of particulars, Manny makes a vivid impression. Then the reader is content to let him fade into the background.

A minor role is no place for a complex character. Don't imbue one with a lot of mystery that your reader will expect you to explain. A name, a few quirky details, and a bit of action or dialogue are more effective than a long, drawn-out description.

NOW YOU TRY: Introduce a minor character

Write a one-paragraph first appearance of a minor character.

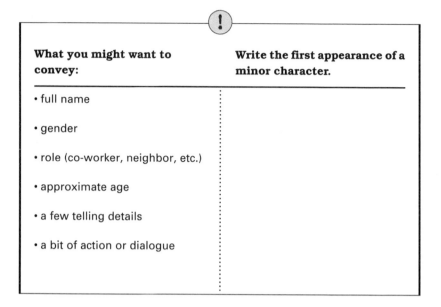

What you might want to convey:	Write the first appearance of a minor character.
• full name	
• gender	
• role (co-worker, neighbor, etc.)	
• approximate age	
• a few telling details	
• a bit of action or dialogue	

INTRODUCING WALK-ONS

The world of your novel will be full of walk-on characters who provide texture and realism. Each one may also have some small role in facilitating the plot, but for the most part, walk-on characters are there to make scenes feel authentic. Your protagonist takes a stroll, the street needs pedestrians; she goes to the bank, the bank needs bank tellers and security guards; and so on with hotel clerks, waitresses, salesmen, and all the rest.

Walk-ons should get no more than a sentence or two of introduction. They don't need names, and a touch of description is plenty. The details you choose can be a kind of shorthand commentary on the neighborhood or context. Maybe the playground skateboarder is dressed in baggies and a Rasta hat. Or a PTA mother has a four-carat rock on her finger. Used in this way, walk-ons are as much elements of *setting* as they are characters.

A walk-on can also provide side commentary on the action. For example, here's a stroller-pushing pedestrian and a pair of toddlers from the Peter Zak novel *Guilt*. They appear when Peter and Annie are getting a bit amorous in public:

> An older woman walked by pushing a double stroller holding a pair of identical, tow-headed toddlers. She cleared her throat and looked down her nose at Peter and Annie with distaste.
>
> Annie pulled away. "Oh dear. Mustn't set a bad example."

That's it. The stroller-pusher appears, makes Annie feel self-conscious, and in the next sentence she and her tow-headed charges are gone. In addition, these characters suggest the presence of other pedestrians on the city street.

Be careful not to mislead the reader. If you go on for sentences about what a walk-on looks like, you set the expectation that the character will have a prominent role in the book.

Occasionally you'll write a walk-on who refuses to simmer down. When a walk-on starts to "act out," keep writing and see who this character is, what he does, and what interesting detours he inserts into your story. If all he creates is an unnecessary diversion, you'll have to stifle him. But if he adds just the spice your story needs, then by all means, promote him to a bigger role and integrate him into the plot.

NOW YOU TRY: Introduce a walk-on

Write the first appearance of a walk-on character. All it takes is a sentence or two.

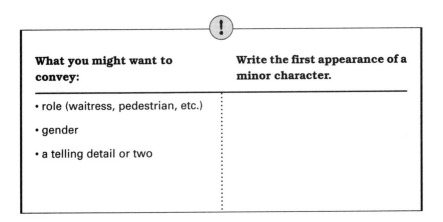

What you might want to convey:	Write the first appearance of a minor character.
• role (waitress, pedestrian, etc.) • gender • a telling detail or two	

WHAT DID YOU SAY YOUR NAME WAS?

Ever start reading a book and feel like your brain is about to explode because the author has introduced a dozen characters in the first ten pages and you can't keep them straight?

If you try to introduce too many characters too soon, you'll thoroughly confuse the reader. Spread out character introductions. I'd avoid party scenes, for example, until your protagonist and a few other main characters are well established.

Another way to confuse readers is to refer to the same character by a bunch of different names. Suppose you introduce Officer James Dazzle. A sentence later you write "James went to the door." A paragraph later, it's "Dazzle's jaw dropped." A page further on, "Jim scowled." Later, "The patrolman scratched his head." The hapless reader thinks these are five different characters. Do this with two characters in the same scene and what's supposed to be an intimate conversation reads like a crowd scene.

When a character is introduced for the first time, tell the reader the character's whole name. After that, call the character by one name and stick with it in the narrative. This is not a case where you have to worry about overusing the same word.

The only exception is in dialogue. For instance, we always refer to Peter Zak in the narrative as *Peter*. But in dialogue, much to his chagrin, his mother calls him *Petey*. Patients address him as *Dr. Zak*.

ON YOUR OWN: Introducing major and minor characters

1. Take along a little notebook or index cards when you're out, especially when you know you're going to be waiting. Observe people. Capture telling details that you might use in writing characters. Jot down snippets of conversation.

2. Create a file where you save your observations—manila or electronic.

3. Scan a favorite mystery novel for character introductions. Look at how the author does it:
   a. Is this an introduction of a walk-on, a minor, or a major character? How can you tell?
   b. What telling details does the author pick?
   c. How does the author convey the impression this character makes on others?
   d. How does the author convey this character's relationship to other characters?

4. Pause before you write each character's first appearance. Get a firm visual image of the character, then think about what you want to convey to the reader and how you can *show* rather than tell. For any major character, try writing a one-two punch intro—description then action and/or dialogue.

5. Give each character in your book a full name and decide how you will consistently refer to that character throughout the narrative. Decide how others in the book will address that character.

CHaPtEr 13:
dramatizing scenes, making chapters

> "Usually, when people get to the end of a chapter, they close the book and go to sleep. I deliberately write a book so when the reader gets to the end of the chapter, he or she must turn one more page. When people tell me I've kept them up all night, I feel like I've succeeded."
>
> —SIDNEY SHELDON

On the first day of a class I once took on writing fiction, the instructor said, "The most important single piece of advice I have for anyone trying to write fiction is this: Write scenes." I later wrote those words on a sticky note and stuck it to the wall by my computer.

Write scenes. In other words, don't *tell* the story, *show it*. Bring it to life. Make it unfold cinematically. This is excellent advice, given how the current generation of readers has been weaned on movies and television.

TURNING A SCENE DESCRIPTION INTO DRAMATIC FICTION

A scene is the dramatic telling of an event that takes place in one place at one time in the novel. The scene descriptions in your outline are a starting point for writing the drama. A few sentences of scene description in an outline can turn into pages of drama.

Here's an example of a short passage of dramatic fiction based on a scene description presented in the introduction to Part II: Writing. As you read, think about what makes it dramatic.

Scene description	Dramatic fiction
Day 1, 20 minutes later.	Jason stepped out of the elevator. Traffic had been light, and he'd gotten there in less than twenty minutes.
Jason Armitage goes to Drew Fellon's apartment. The door is ajar. Cautiously he enters. He checks out the kitchen, the living room. Everything seems normal.	He didn't remember the gold-flocked wallpaper or the brass wall sconces that lined the hall, but then it had been a year at least since he'd last been to Fellon's apartment. His old friend had been married back then to the woman he now referred to as Bonnie Simple.
He notices an acrid smell. He enters the bedroom and finds Fellon lying on the bed, holding a pistol, a bullet wound to the head.	The door had been recently painted too, a creamy white, now scuffed and gouged along the bottom, like someone had kicked at it with steel-toed boots. Jason reached up to knock when he noticed the door was ajar.
	He tried to ignore the queasy feeling in the pit of his stomach. Nothing to worry about. His friend probably overslept and left in such a rush that he forgot to lock up. Jason pushed the door open a crack. Maybe. But where was Drew's dog? Usually the damned Doberman started barking the minute the elevator doors opened. Yapping and snarling. Had the beast escaped?
	Jason cast an uneasy glance up and down the hallway, hoping that the sound he heard was the elevator descending and not Fang's teeth-bared snarl.
	A jolt went down Jason's spine when the phone in the apartment rang. He inhaled and pressed his shoulder against the wall. *Rrrring.* No claws scrabbling on the wood floor. *Rrrring.* No footsteps. *Rrrring.* A click, and there was Fellon's voice. "Sorry I can't come to the phone . . ."

Here are some tips for turning scene description into dramatic fiction:

• **Begin the scene as late as possible.** *Jason stepped out of the elevator.* Notice that I didn't bother to write Jason driving over, parking the car, or getting into the building. Begin a scene as late as possible, when the drama begins. Avoid any to'ing and fro'ing that doesn't serve your story.

• **Orient the reader.** *. . . he'd gotten there in less than twenty minutes.* Near the beginning of the scene, tell the reader where we are and how much time has elapsed since the previous scene ended. Make it brief. This isn't drama, but it keeps the reader from being confused and therefore distracted from the drama you're creating.

• **Put the reader in one character's head.** *He tried to ignore the queasy feeling in the pit of his stomach. Nothing to worry about.* Write the scene as if you are inside a character's head using internal dialogue (the character's thoughts). In a mystery, that character is often the sleuth. Here, the reader walks down the hall with Jason, sees what Jason sees, is privy to Jason's thoughts and, along with Jason, grows increasingly uneasy.

• **Show some telling details.** Pick ordinary details like the *gold-flocked wallpaper,* and extraordinary details like the bottom of the door that looked *like someone had kicked at it with steel-toed boots.* In a mystery, some of these details turn out to be clues.

• **Exploit the senses.** *Rrrrring.* Give the reader the sounds, smells, and other sensations that the point-of-view character would experience.

• **Keep it relevant.** In an earlier draft of this scene, there was a whole description of the exterior of the building, parking the car, a conversation with the doorman, a paragraph-long description of Fellon's ex-wife, and some sentences about fall weather in New England. It got cut because the story didn't need it. Avoid pointless dialogue, aimless introspection, unnecessary travel, weather, setting, food, or even sex if it doesn't *serve your story.*

• **Give yourself permission to write beyond the scene you planned.** Where did that ringing phone and the dog come from? Neither was in the scene description. Writing is an organic process. All I can tell you is that when I went to write the scene, I put myself in Jason's head and the missing dog showed up and the phone rang. Unexpected plot points like Fang appear uninvited as you write, and it's glorious when they do. It's up to you to deal with these unexpected guests. Maybe the dog will show up dead in the bedroom with the deceased lawyer . . . or maybe not. Readers of mystery fiction are not as partial to dead dogs as they are to dead lawyers.

• **End a scene as early as possible.** Don't allow a scene to trail off at the end. Instead, wind up with a punch, something that makes the reader want to turn the page.

NOW YOU TRY: Continue writing the scene

Continue the scene. You decide if the caller hangs up or says something. You furnish the apartment. Is it a jumble of legal briefs and law books covering coffee table and desk, or is it neat as a pin, all chrome and glass on white carpeting? Pick details that convey to the reader, in a few brushstrokes, something about the attorney who lives there. Put us inside Jason's head as he moves from room to room. What does he think when he notices the acrid smell? What does he see when he gets into the bedroom? Where's the Doberman? Convey how Jason feels by *showing the reader his reaction*, not by telling.

Continue the scene.

A jolt went down Jason's spine when the phone in the apartment rang. He inhaled and drew back, pressing his shoulder against the wall. Rrrring. A click, and there was Drew's voice. "Sorry I can't come to the phone . . ."

THE PAYOFF

In a mystery, every scene should contain a *payoff*—something that happens, some change that occurs that propels the main plot or one of the subplots forward. In the scene above, the payoff is Jason finding his friend dead.

The payoff might be immediate. Maybe the sleuth learns something that brings investigators a step closer to discovering the truth (a clue) or learns something that sends the investigators down a blind alley (a red herring). Maybe something dramatic happens that ratchets up the tension—the sleuth receives a message warning her to *back off, or else*. Or something happens that raises the stakes, like a character gets kidnapped. Or a roadblock is thrown at the sleuth—he might get pulled off the street and put on desk duty by the superintendent in charge of the investigation.

A scene might have a delayed payoff. For example, in an early scene, the protagonist might meet her old friend, Denise, for lunch. While they're looking at the menus, Denise talks about her recent divorce, how she's starting a new life, and how surprised she is that her ex has agreed so readily to the terms of the divorce. When her salad arrives, Denise sends it back because it has peanuts in it. The reader barely notices this detail. Chapters later, Denise dies from what turns out to be a severe allergic reaction to peanuts. Her ex-husband tells investigators that Denise didn't know she was allergic to peanuts. Now comes the payoff to that earlier scene, as the reader and the protagonist remember the salad Denise sent back because it contained peanuts. Conclusion 1: Denise knew she was allergic to peanuts. Conclusion 2: Her ex-husband is lying. The story is propelled forward by the realization that Denise's death couldn't be accidental.

The payoff of the book's opening scene is the narrative hook that propels the book forward. The payoff of the final scenes of Act I and Act II are the major plot twists in the novel.

If a scene has no payoff, it doesn't belong in your mystery novel.

SUBTLE ORIENTEERING

When you come to the end of a scene within a chapter, insert a double space (or put a place marker such as ** on a line) to indicate to the reader that a scene has ended and another one is about to begin. Chapters end with a page break.

The next scene could be five minutes or five days later, still in Clancy's Liquor, or on a mountaintop twenty miles away. The new scene may have the same characters or different ones from the preceding scene. Some writers think it builds suspense if the reader has to wait to discover this kind of basic information. It doesn't. All it builds is confusion. A reader who is confused about the who-where-when of a scene is likely to scan ahead and destroy the impact of the author's carefully wrought drama.

Whenever you start a new scene, one way or another you must quickly make the reader aware of the following:

- *when* it takes place and how much time has transpired since the last scene ended

- *where* it takes place
- *who* is in the scene and who is telling the story

Avoid orienting the reader with a clunky "Three hours later, Mrs. McGilli-cuddy and I were walking on the beach . . ." It can be done unobtrusively, as Laura Lippman does in the beginning of this scene from *The Sugar House*:

> Within a day, dental records obtained from a Silver Spring orthodontist made it official. The Dead Girl Formerly Known as Jane Doe was Gwen Schiller. Martin Tull was impressed, and generous enough not to hide it.
>
> "I can't believe how much you did with so little," he kept saying to Tess. They were sitting in a sub shop near police headquarters.

Without feeling at all like a news bulletin, Lippman lets the reader know where we are (the sub shop), when it is (a day later), and who is in the scene (Tess and Martin Tull).

CHAPTER TRANSITIONS

You can end a chapter at the end of a scene or in the middle of one, depending on the dramatic effect you want to create.

Ending the chapter at the end of a scene gives the reader a sense of completion as a series of events has come to its conclusion. A settled ending gives the reader time to take a breath before continuing.

You get the opposite effect when you end a chapter in the middle of a scene at a particularly suspenseful moment. The reader feels breathless as forward motion is suspended in midair. With a cliffhanger ending, you make it hard for a reader to put down the book.

Kathy Reichs is a master of the cliffhanger chapter ending. Here are a few chapter endings and next-chapter beginnings from her novel *Monday Mourning*:

> **Chapter end:** The line went dead.
> **Next chapter start:** I jiggled the button, trying to get the switchboard operator's attention.
>
> **Chapter end:** Black space gaped between the open door and jamb.
> **Next chapter start:** Through the gap, I could make out disordered shadows and an odd luminescence, like moonlight on water.
>
> **Chapter end:** My heart dropped like a rock.
> **Next chapter start:** LaManche's voice grew distant. The room receded around me.

Both settled and cliffhanger chapter endings belong in your novel. Settled endings are good early in an act. Cliffhanger endings are useful as your book barrels along toward an act-ending climax.

A WORD ABOUT PACING

As you write, keep an eye on pacing—controlling and modulating the speed and intensity of your story. Bunch up all your suspense and action sequences together and the reader will turn numb from over-stimulation; pile on too many paragraphs of plot exposition and lush, descriptive setting and the reader's thoughts are apt to drift to unfinished chores.

Generally speaking, the intensity of your story should build, with more leisurely storytelling at the beginning, more tense suspense and slam-bang action toward the end.

ON YOUR OWN: Writing scenes

1. Pick a favorite mystery by an author whose work feels like what you aspire to.
    a. Notice how the story is divided into scenes and the scenes grouped into chapters.
    b. Skim through, reading chapter endings and next-chapter beginnings. Notice chapters that have settled endings and chapters that end with cliffhangers.
    c. Pick several scenes at random and read them carefully, noticing how the author orients the reader at the beginning of each scene. Also notice how the author brings the drama to life. Think about why the author started and ended the scene where he did. Find the scene's payoff.

2. Continue writing scenes. Use this checklist to guide your work:

__ Orients the reader at the outset to who/where/when

__ Starts as late as possible, ends as early as possible

__ Dramatically conveys what the point-of-view character sees, hears, smells, touches, thinks, and feels

__ Has a reason for being in the novel: a payoff

__ Ends with a punch

CHaPtEr 14:
point of view

"I think point of view is a bugaboo for many beginning writers because so many terrifying things have been said about it. It is entirely a matter of feeling comfortable in the writing, the question of through whose eyes you should tell the story."

—Patricia Highsmith
Plotting and Writing Suspense Fiction

Writing is all about making choices, and one of the first choices you make when you sit down to write is point of view. There are two decisions to make:
• to write the story in the first person or in the third person
• to have one or more than one character tell the story

Sounds pretty simple, and sometimes it's clear to the writer what point of view will work best for a given novel. Other times the writer struggles, starting the novel in first person and partway through discovering it's too limiting; or starting the novel in the third person with multiple narrators and feeling dissatisfied because there's not a strong enough sense of the main character.

Of course you can begin writing in the first person, for example, and then decide the third person works better. But you'll have to rewrite everything you've written up to that point. I know because I've done it. To avoid a major rewrite halfway through, experiment early on with different point-of-view choices. See which feels right for the story you want to tell.

Here are the point-of-view choices:
• **First person:** One character holds the camera; the narrative is written in the first person.
• **Third person limited:** One character holds the camera; the narrative is written in the third person.

- **Multiple third person:** One character *at a time* holds the camera; the narrative is written in the third person.
- **Omniscient:** The camera can be anywhere; the narrative is written in the third person.

Let's take a closer look at each of these choices. It's all about trade-offs.

FIRST-PERSON POINT OF VIEW

Many traditional mysteries are written from the point of view of a sleuth who is a first-person narrator. Series authors often choose first person because it helps create a bond between the reader and the protagonist, which is essential in a successful series.

Robert B. Parker wrote *Hugger Mugger*, a Spenser series novel, in the first person. Read this example to see how well he makes it work:

> I was at my desk, in my office, with my feet up on the windowsill, and a yellow pad in my lap, thinking about baseball. It's what I always think about when I'm not thinking about sex. Susan says that supreme happiness for me would probably involve having sex while watching a ball game. Since she knows this, I've never understood why, when we're at Fenway Park, she remains so prudish.

With a first-person sleuth narrator, Parker gives the reader an intense and personal, inside view of his character. First-person narrative also reinforces the illusion that the sleuth and the reader are solving the puzzle together. The reader and the sleuth work together, finding clues, pursuing blind alleys, experiencing heart-pounding suspense, and finally discovering the truth.

Other series authors with first-person sleuth/narrators include some of the biggies: Sue Grafton, Jonathan Kellerman, Lawrence Block, Linda Barnes, Kathy Reichs, Linda Fairstein, and James Patterson.

A single, first-person narrator is the simplest to manage for new writers. It's easier to get a single point of view under control, and you only have to create one strong narrator's voice.

But here's the rub. When a first-person narrator gets locked in a dark, dank basement for days, your story gets held captive with him. If your first-person narrator isn't present when something dramatic (like the murder) happens, you can't dramatize it. Your character has to find out indirectly by visiting the scene of the crime, hearing it described by another character, reading the autopsy report or newspaper article, or interviewing surviving witnesses. Events perceived after the fact or secondhand don't pack nearly the wallop of a dramatic scene experienced firsthand.

THIRD-PERSON-LIMITED POINT OF VIEW

You can convey an equally strong sense of the main character by writing in the third person limited. The story is still narrated by one character, and the pronouns "he/she" and "him/her" are used instead of "I" and "me." Writing in the third person limited enables you to insert more distance between the character and the reader, providing a narrator's filter for the point-of-view character's experience.

Consider this example from P.D. James's *Devices and Desires*. This passage is written in the third person, from the point of view of Alice Mair.

> By four o'clock in the morning, when Alice Mair woke with a small despairing cry from her nightmare, the wind was rising. She stretched out her hand to click on the bedside light, checked her watch, then lay back, panic subsiding, her eyes staring at the ceiling, while the terrible immediacy of the dream began to fade, recognized for what it was, an old spectre returning after all these years, conjured up by the events of the night and by the reiteration of the word "Murder," which since the Whistler had begun his work seemed to murmur sonorously on the very air.

Did you notice how James inserts distance between the reader and the point-of-view character? It's written as if we're looking down on Alice, interpreting her actions, reading her thoughts.

If you want to insert this kind of distance between your point-of-view character and the narrative, you'll want to write in the third person instead of the first person. You'll be able to draw back the camera, from time to time, and show the reader a bigger picture that your point-of-view character may not be able to see. Keep in mind, though, that narrative written in the third person limited is more difficult to control than narrative written in the first person. It's easy to find yourself slipping out of one character's head and into another. And you're still limited in what you can show the reader, since a single character tells the story.

MULTIPLE-THIRD-PERSON POINT OF VIEW

More and more crime fiction writers are opting for multiple points of view. They write in the third person, with the camera close over the shoulder of one character at a time. Different scenes can be narrated by different characters.

With multiple points of view, you have more flexibility in telling your story. For example, suppose you have two main characters, partner sleuths. When one of them gets trapped in a damp cave, you can shift to the point of view of the other character who is trying to find her. Shift back to the trapped partner and feel him getting colder and wetter as the water rises. Shift back to the other partner, searching frantically, trying to find the cave entrance. Shifting the point of view enables you to create considerable dramatic tension and suspense.

The first four Peter Zak novels are written in the first person, from Peter Zak's point of view; in the fifth one, *Guilt*, we wanted investigator Annie Squires to tell some of the story. So, we shifted the narrative into the third person and alternated chapters between Peter and Annie.

This paragraph is written from Peter's point of view:

> Even from the street, Peter could see that Il Panino, the storefront café on a nondescript patch of Mass Ave. about a half-mile from Harvard Square, was packed with its usual lunch-time throng. He admired the way Annie Squires maneuvered into a parking spot out front, just barely bigger than her Jeep, perfect on the first try. It was one of many things he admired about her.

This paragraph is from Annie's point of view:

> Leaves swirled through the air as Annie stared down at the grave. Her arm was still in a cast, and she held it cradled in front of her. Her wrist ached in the cold. Peter put his arm around her shoulders and pulled her close.

Using multiple points of view can be liberating. You can dramatize virtually anything—just shift the point of view to a character who is there. You can even write scenes from the villain's point of view.

Big-name authors who excel at using multiple points of view include Lisa Scottoline, Val McDermid, Naomi Rand, Tony Hillerman, and Dennis Lehane. These authors are also big talents with a lot of writing experience under their belts.

Don't underestimate the skill it takes to create a single strong, distinct narrator's voice, never mind more than one. Too often, inexperienced writers attempt to write in multiple points of view and the book ends up feeling disjointed, without a coherent story line.

For your first mystery novel, I recommend you stick to a single character as narrator and write in the first or third person. Get a single point of view nailed before you move on to multiple viewpoints.

OMNISCIENT POINT OF VIEW

Some authors use the voice of a godlike narrator who sees all and knows all, who hovers above the action and is simultaneously inside each character's head. Jane Austen used omniscient third person in *Pride and Prejudice*. She took the reader inside the heads of Jane, Mr. Darcy, Mr. Bingley, and all the rest of her characters, while at the same giving a satiric running commentary on the mores of the time.

An advantage of the omniscient-third-person point of view is that the narrator can go anywhere and see anything. If the sleuth gets trapped in a cave, the narrator can describe the deserted scene outside, where birds are singing and the sun shining a few feet beyond the cave's wall.

A disadvantage is that an omniscient narrator who picks and chooses what to share with the reader can make the reader feel distanced and manipulated. The mystery can end up feeling like more of a tease than a puzzle. In addition, using the omniscient third person can make it harder to create a close bond between the reader and the sleuth.

Many authors shun the omniscient voice, concerned that it seems stilted and old-fashioned. Still, it has its place. Plenty of authors use it occasionally to pull the camera way back and show the reader a bird's-eye view of the goings on.

A good example of a modern master using the occasional omniscient point of view is S.J. Rozan in *Absent Friends*. Rozan moves nimbly from one character's head in one chapter to another character's head in the next. Every once in a while, as in the example below, the narrator is omniscient:

> The thunderbolt of Harry Randall's death hit Phil Con-
> stantine at Grainger's Tavern. It was thrown from the
> TV over the bar by a glossy-haired anchorwoman in an
> insistent blue suit. The news blasted him with a power-
> ful jolt, though no one watching would have seen that:
> just his eyes opening slightly, his jaw tightening as his
> focus narrowed and intensified.

We get both a description of Phil's feelings (*the news blasted him with a power-ful jolt*) and how he appears (*eyes opening slightly, his jaw tightening . . .*). Only an omniscient narrator can both be inside Phil, privy to his feelings, and at the same time outside Phil, aware of how he looks.

SLIDING POINT OF VIEW: A NO-NO

Reading a scene where the point of view slides from one character's head to another can feel like riding in a car with loose steering. It feels out of control and confusing.

Whether you tell your story in the first or third person, have a single point-of-view character or several, it's best to anchor the narration in each scene in a single character's head. You can have a different narrator tell the story in the next scene. But don't allow the point of view to slide within a single scene.

For instance, suppose you write a scene in which the police arrive and investigate a shooting. You begin writing the scene from the point of view of the detective in charge. You can show the detective's observations of blood spatter, gunshot residue, and the position of the corpse. You can show the detective questioning the victim's boyfriend and interpreting his reactions. But to reveal what the boyfriend really thinks and feels would require a shift in point of view. Stay in one character's head per scene.

In order to keep the point of view from sliding, keep asking yourself: Who is narrating this scene? Then, as you write, keep yourself anchored in that character's head. Write the scene as that character experiences it, revealing his thoughts and feelings, his *observations* of other characters, and his *interpretation* of what other characters might be thinking and feeling.

Point-of-view differences can be subtle. For example, if Bob's the narrator, you can show his thoughts and feelings:

• Bob *was afraid* he was going to throw up.

If Linda is the narrator, the same content becomes:

• Bob *looked like* he was going to throw up.

Linda can only tell the reader what she observes; she doesn't know for sure what Bob feels.

Here's another example. Cover up the discussion on the right and try to find the slips in point of view. Then read the discussion.

Passage with point-of-view slips	Discussion
Cecilia tiptoed to the door. She peered out and listened. All quiet. At last, she could share what she'd learned.	No problem here. We're in Cecilia's point of view. She's the narrator.
She closed the door and addressed William with a solemn face, her voice ominous.	Cecilia can't see her own face. The point of view has slipped to omniscient.
William tried not to show his disdain. She was so full of herself.	These are William's thoughts. The point of view has slipped; William is now the narrator.

NOW YOU TRY: Slipping and sliding point of view

1. Read the passage below and find the point-of-view shifts.

Read this passage.   **Note the point-of-view shifts.**

When Corrigan looked up, he saw Mary gazing at him like a lost puppy. He looked away, got up, and made for the door. As she watched him leave, her look hardened.

"So you think you don't owe me anything?" she said, her voice raspy and dull.

He whipped around, his eyes blazing. "I don't owe you a damned thing."

He had no business treating her like that. Mary stumbled to her feet, her fists clenched.

2. Revise the entire passage so Corrigan is the narrator.

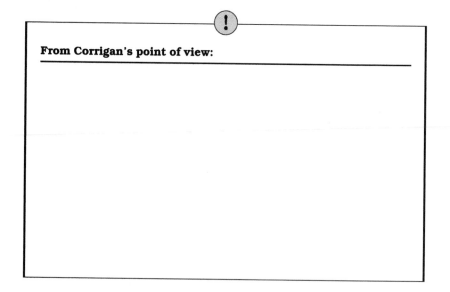

From Corrigan's point of view:

3. Revise the passage again so Mary is the narrator.

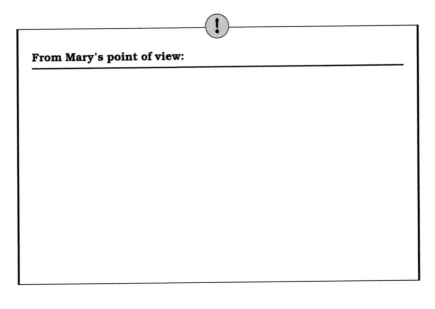

From Mary's point of view:

PICKING POINT-OF-VIEW CHARACTERS

If Conan Doyle were writing the Sherlock Holmes stories today, he surely would have made Holmes the point-of-view character rather than Watson. Why? Because Holmes is at the center of the action. He should be telling the stories.

Ask yourself *whose story it is* that you're telling—that character should be a point-of-view character. Usually in a mystery, the sleuth tells some or all of the story. Any other character who is at the center of some important action is another potential narrator, particularly if only that character experiences events you want to dramatize.

CHANGING POINT OF VIEW, CHANGING STORY

A story changes depending on who tells it. Imagine a scene in which Betty Blondell is stalked by Cal Carver, while Detective Dennis Detroit observes from a parked car. Write the scene from Betty's point of view and it's full of suspense. You can even keep the reader in the dark as to whether there really is a stalker; when Detective Detroit appears to save the day, it's a complete surprise. Write the scene from Cal's point of view and the reader knows there's a villain and knows exactly what this cad has in mind for Miss Blondell. But we get a big surprise when Detective Detroit spoils Cal's party. Write it from Detective Detroit's perspective and we can watch both Cal and

Betty. The drama comes from whether he's going to intervene in time to prevent Betty from getting hurt.

Here are two versions of the same action, written from the point of view of two different characters. Read the two versions and think about how the change in point of view affects the story. Notice that only the dialogue (bolded) remains the same.

Sharon's point of view	Bob's point of view
"Sharon?" The voice echoed in the courtyard.	When I got there, Sharon was walking across the courtyard. Looked as if she was heading for her car. A minute later and I'd have missed her.
I turned and immediately wished I'd just kept going. **"What do you want now, Bob?"**	
My voice sounded strident. If only he'd back off, ease up on the full court press. I just wanted to get away, be by myself for awhile.	I hid the flowers behind my back. I'd surprise her.
	"Sharon?" I yelled. My voice echoed in the courtyard.
"Hold up a sec."	She paused and turned back. **"What do you want now, Bob?"**
I stood there, barely able to keep myself from bolting for my car. His boot heels stomped across the concrete, crunching bits of broken glass.	I felt my shoulders sag. Why had I bothered? *You're so pathetic— you just can't take no for an answer,* I heard my ex-wife's hectoring voice in my head. But I couldn't turn back now.
The flowers he held out were roses, shopworn, their heads already starting to droop. Pathetic, really. I suppressed a groan.	**"Hold up a sec."**
	I closed the space between us. Her eyes were hard, and there were lines of tension in her forehead. When I held out the flowers, her expression changed to pity.
	Should have known. Why the hell had I bothered?

In both versions, the same action takes place: Bob calls out; Sharon stops; he gives her flowers. The dialogue is identical. The differences in *internal dialogue* tell a very different story and create very different dynamics.

Writing and Selling Your Mystery Novel

NOW YOU TRY: Revise the narrator

Revise the scene between Sharon and Bob. Use only this dialogue:

    Bob: "Sharon?"
    Sharon: "What do you want now, Bob?"
    Bob: "Hold up a sec."

Communicate this with internal dialogue.

From Bob's point of view:

Bob is a private investigator, deliberately acting like a goofball so he can get close to Sharon without revealing his true identity.

From Sharon's point of view:

Sharon is madly in love with Bob but afraid to show her true feelings because he sees her as a friend.

MAKING A NARRATOR'S VOICE SING

If you were writing a memoir, the narrator's voice would be your own. You'd tell the story of the events in your life from your own perspective, sharing your thoughts and feelings along the way. Your language and word choice, jokes, cultural references, and metaphors would reflect who you are. The challenge of writing fiction is to tell a story in a voice that's not your own.

What does a strong voice look like? Linda Barnes fans instantly recognize the voice of cabbie/PI Carlotta Carlyle in these opening lines of *Deep Pockets*:

> I hate running errands. I put them off and put them off, and then one morning the cat's got no food, there are zero stamps on the roll, and I realize I own no underwear minus holes. I understand some people like to shop for clothes, do it for pure pleasure and entertainment, but I count it as one more damned errand. When the tasks mount up and I can't put it off any longer, I make a list and set forth to Harvard Square. There are less pricey areas, granted, but the Square has its own post office and lies within spitting distance of my house.
>
> I waited in line at the post office till my feet felt like they'd grow roots. I bought panties on sale at the Gap, mourned the passing of Sage's, where they always carried tons of my cat's favorite Fancy Feast, bought a few cans of an off-price substitute at the CVS instead. The wind tangled my hair, which helped me recall a shampoo shortage, and that led to cart-filling thoughts of toothpaste, soap, and lip balm.
>
> I first noticed him as I was waiting, along with thirty-five other assorted students, panhandlers, and shoppers, for the scramble light at the intersection of Brattle and Mass Ave.

Now, take a minute to reread and list *what happens* in this brief passage.

There's not much to list, right? Carlotta runs errands in Harvard Square, buys underwear at the Gap and sundries at CVS. She's waiting to cross Mass Ave. when she notices a man.

Read the passage again. This time make a list of what the passage *tells you about the narrator*.

This time, there is a lot to list, because the short passage is packed with information about Carlotta. We know she lives near Harvard Square, owns a cat, wears underwear until it wears out, hates shopping, watches her pennies . . . and those are just the facts, ma'am. In addition, we get plenty of *attitude*. We know Carlotta's a tough broad who disdains yuppies; has a dry, self-deprecating sense of humor; and already we suspect that she doesn't suffer fools and bristles at authority.

Notice Barnes doesn't come right out and tell you that Carlotta is impatient. Instead, she *shows* it: "I waited in line at the post office till my feet felt like they'd grow roots."

Now read these opening paragraphs from Alexander McCall Smith's *The Sunday Philosophy Club*. Think about what makes Isabel Dalhousie's voice so distinct from Carlotta Carlyle's.

> Isabel Dalhousie saw the young man fall from the edge of the upper circle, from the gods. His flight was so sudden and short, and it was for less than a second that she saw him, hair tousled, upside down, his shirt and jacket up around his chest so that his midriff was exposed. And then, striking the edge of the grand circle, he disappeared headfirst towards the stalls below.
>
> Her first thought, curiously, was of Auden's poem on the fall of Icarus. Such events, said Auden, occur against a background of people going about their ordinary business. They do not look up and see the boy falling from the sky. *I was talking to a friend*, she thought. *I was talking to a friend and the boy fell out of the sky.*

As narrators, Carlotta Carlyle and Isabel Dalhousie are a study in contrasts—Carlotta Carlyle brassy and street smart, Isabel Dalhousie reserved and refined. An analysis of the differences reveals some pointers on how to create your own strong narrator:

- **Directness.** Carlotta speaks in the first person, directly to the reader. Isabel is rendered in the third person, and while the story is told from her point of view, what happens is held at arm's length and examined dispassionately. Both approaches work. Pick a level of directness that suits your narrator and write to it.
- **Sentence structure.** Carlotta rat-a-tats, subject-verb-object. Her sentences are punchy and direct. The cultured Isabel's observations are rendered in complex sentences full of subordinate clauses. Structure your character's narration to match her background and personality. Some characters should talk in complete sentences, others in fragments, still others in convoluted, run-on monologues.
- **Word choices and analogies.** Carlotta talks about "zero stamps," "one more damned errand," and "spitting distance" and compares waiting to "growing tree roots." Isabel observes the young man with "tousled hair" falling as if "from the gods." She makes a literary reference to a poem by W.H. Auden. Different narrators choose different words and analogies to tell the story. Carefully choose the words and images you give your narrator.
- **Tone.** Carlotta's passage is full of humor and sass, while Isabel's is loaded with eloquence and polite reserve. Use tone to convey the personality of your narrator.

To create a strong narrative voice, incorporate all these elements into your prose: directness, sentence structure, word choice, and tone. Revise until you've developed a narrative voice that satisfies you. Try to keep that voice in your head and on the page as you continue writing, all the way to the end of the book.

ON YOUR OWN: Point of view

1. Scan through some of your favorite mysteries; examine the point-of-view choices the authors make:
   a. First person or third?
   b. Single or multiple points of view?

2. Open one of your favorite mysteries to scenes at the beginning, middle, and end of the book. In each scene, analyze how the author creates a distinct, compelling narrative voice. Look at each of the following:
   a. directness
   b. sentence structure
   c. word choice
   d. tone

3. Examine the scenes you've written so far, and make revisions as needed.
   a. Are you satisfied with your choice of first- or third-person narrative?
   b. Are you satisfied with the character(s) you picked to tell the story?
   c. Have you kept control of the point of view, or have you allowed it to slip and slide?

4. Continue writing. Keep in mind the character who's "telling" your story; continue making that narrative voice unique.

CHaPtEr 15:
writing dialogue

"Dialogue should be allowed to stand alone, pure and simple. Except when it shouldn't."

—LAWRENCE BLOCK
Telling Lies for Fun & Profit

Most authors have an Achilles' heel, something they need to work at. Mine is dialogue. I have to work to make each character's dialogue feel authentic, individual, and natural. It's probably related to the fact that I can never remember anyone's exact words. After a party, for example, ask me what was on the walls, what people wore, what food was served, and I can give you chapter and verse. But ask me what anyone said and I can only paraphrase. Paraphrasing isn't dialogue. Paraphrase and everyone else's speech sounds like your own, or even worse, like no one's in particular.

WRITING CONVINCING DIALOGUE

The guy who wrote the book on convincing dialogue is Elmore Leonard. Just about everything you need to know is illustrated in this brief, two-part excerpt from *LaBrava*:

> Cundo Rey said to Nobles, "Let me ask you something, okay? You ever see a snake eat a bat? Here is a wing sticking out of the snake's mouth, the wing, it's still moving, this little movement, like is trying to fly. The snake, he don't care. You know why? Because the other end of the bat is down in the snake turning to juice, man. Sure, the snake, he don't even have to move, just lay there and keep swallowing as long as it takes. He don't even have to chew," Cundo Rey said, watching Richard Nobles eating his Big Mac and poking fries in

his mouth a few at a time, dipped in ketchup. "Mmm-mmm, nice juicy bat."

. . .

He [Nobles] said, mouth full of hamburger, "I ate a snake. I've ate a few different kinds. You flour 'em, deep-fry 'em in some Crisco so the meat crackles, they're pretty good. But I never ate a bat. Time you skin it, what would you have?"

There—if the Cuban was trying to make him sick he was wasting his time.

Use these same techniques to give your characters authentic, unique voices:

• **Content and tone.** *You ever see a snake eat a bat?* What your character talks about and how he says it—that's the fundamental choice you make when you write dialogue. Here, there's something sinister, weird, and confrontational about Cundo Rey's little monologue about how a snake eats a bat. There's a not-so-veiled threat, and we get the sense of a ruthless, cold individual who gets his jollies watching another creature tortured.

• **Grammar and word choice.** *The snake, he don't care.* Use grammar to show the character's personality and background. Here, the grammatical error suggests a character who is tough and uneducated, perhaps not a native English speaker. You might choose other words to convey casual and hip ("That snake, he could care less") or painstakingly formal and correct ("From the snake's perspective, it matters not").

• **A little dialect goes a long way.** *You flour 'em, deep fry 'em . . .* Characters mispronounce words and talk with accents. Do you have to render what's said phonetically in order to make the character sound real? You can, but more than a touch of phonetically rendered dialect can be distracting and difficult to decipher. Not only that, dialect can turn character into caricature. Use the occasional phonetic version of a phrase to give the reader the flavor of how a character sounds, but do so sparingly. Trust the reader to mentally apply what you suggest to the remaining dialogue.

• **Simple attribution or none at all.** *Cundo Rey said . . .* New writers think they need to vary their choice of a verb to express speaking (chimed, chirped, responded, hissed, retorted, bellowed, queried). Equally egregious is when an author writes something like, *"Thanks," he grinned.* As if grinning had anything to do with speaking. (It's fine to say: *"Thanks," he said, grinning.* Or *"Thanks." He grinned.*) Yes, you can occasionally use *whispered* or *shouted*, if that's what the character did. But *said* and *asked* are perfectly sufficient, 98 percent of the time. In fact, often you can get away without any attribution at all if you make it clear to the reader who's talking.

• **Hold the adverbs.** *Cundo Rey said coldly . . . icily . . . scornfully.* You rarely find an adverb with *said* in Leonard's prose; nor should one show up in yours. Using adverbs in this way is a clunky way to tell the reader what's better shown through the dialogue itself and the character's behavior.

• **Dialogue/action combo.** *. . . watching Richard Nobles eating his Big Mac and poking fries in his mouth a few at a time, dipped in ketchup. "Mmmmmm. Nice juicy bat."* How do you convey the tenor of dialogue to the reader? Pack emotion into the words and the physical gestures and body language that accompany it. Combine dialogue with the right action, and the result is more than the sum of the parts—as the example shows with the combination of eating French fries with *"Mmmmmm. Nice juicy bat."*

• **Bring the characters' relationship to life.** *I ate a snake.* The thrust and parry of dialogue shows the relationship between the characters talking. When Nobles responds, the reader sees that these two guys are evenly matched for bravado.

• **Sprinkle lightly with internal dialogue.** *There—if the Cuban was trying to make him sick he was wasting his time.* During an exchange of dialogue, use internal dialogue to show your reader what's going on in the point-of-view character's head and to add an additional dimension to the interaction. Notice that internal dialogue need not sound or look like dialogue. Here, Nobles's thoughts are more grammatically correct, with less swagger and without the staccato sentences of this character's spoken dialogue. Notice also that internal dialogue doesn't require quotes, italics, or even *he thought* to cue the reader that these words are thoughts. Leonard maintains tense and point of view (here it's first person, past tense) and just writes the thought.

MAKING DIALOGUE SOUND AUTHENTIC

Good dialogue is not realistic conversation. People digress, pause, use the wrong words, repeat themselves, fail to clearly express themselves, or go on and on, boring everyone around them. If you write dialogue that's too realistic, your book will be a great sleeping aid but little else.

So how do you write authentic-sounding dialogue without making it too real? Take a cue from how real people talk. They speak in sentence fragments. They drop nouns and verbs. They use jargon, vernacular, and sometimes profanity. Edit out the meanderings, the repetitions, the digressions, get rid of the irrelevancies, and you've got something that approaches good dialogue. Remember, dialogue shouldn't call attention to itself. If it's too clever, get rid of it.

Here's an example. In this dialogue from S.J. Rozan's *Absent Friends*, notice how Zannoni drops words, uses sentence fragments, profanity, and police jargon, and comes off sounding like the tough, jaded, retired homicide detective he's supposed to be.

"I was a detective at the 124 then," he said. "Later got transferred to the Bronx. Christ what a schlep. Those days, right after the Knapp Commission—you heard of that?—they didn't have this community policing thing like now. They wanted you to live outside your precinct. Keep down graft. Pile of crap. Cops running all around the goddamn city, damn waste of time. I retired eight years ago."

To check whether your dialogue is working, read it aloud to yourself. Wooden dialogue jumps out at you when you hear it, more so than when you read it.

NOW YOU TRY: Analyze dialogue

Janet Evanovich writes funny, smart dialogue, and she gives each of her characters a unique voice. Analyze this dialogue among three characters in *Four to Score:*

Think about:

How is each character's dialogue made distinct and authentic? Consider:
- content
- grammar
- word choice
- dialect
- sentence structure
- profanity, vernacular
- internal dialogue and action combined with dialogue

Excerpt from *Four to Score*

"I still don't like this," Kuntz said. "Maxine is crazy. Who knows what she'll do. I'm gonna feel like a sitting duck out there."

Lula was standing behind me on Kuntz's porch. "Probably just another dumb-ass note taped to the bottom of the bench. Think you should stop your whining," she said to Kuntz, "on account of it makes you look like a wiener. And with a name like Kuntz you gotta be careful what you look like."

Eddie cut his eyes to Lula. "Who's this?"

"I'm her partner," Lula said. "Just like Starsky and Hutch, Cagney and Lacey, the Lone Ranger and What's-his-name."

Truth is, we were more like Laurel and Hardy, but I didn't want to share that information with Kuntz.

"We'll be in place ahead of time," I said. "Don't worry if you don't see us. We'll be there. All you have to do is show up and go sit on the bench and wait."

SHOWING EMOTIONS

Presencing is a term that a wonderful writing teacher, Arthur Edelstein, used when urging his students to write characters that seem physically present. For example, when a character is talking or listening, a bit of physical action gives the reader insight into the character's inner state.

This is why authors give characters props. What a character does with a drink while she's talking, for example, can alter how the reader perceives the dialogue delivered.

Here are two examples with identical dialogue:

> "Did you know him long?" I asked.
> She stirred her drink and stared into it. "Too long, and not long enough."

***

> "Did you know him long?" I asked.
> She knocked back her drink and slammed the empty glass down on the table. "Too long, and not long enough."

Just about anything in a scene—a cigarette, a tissue, a strand of hair, a necktie, a belt, shirt buttons, and so on—can be used, in combination with dialogue, to show different mental states. You don't even need props. A character can wring his hands, crack his knuckles, pick at a pimple, or take a quick intake of breath. Choose the action carefully and you effectively nuance the dialogue the character delivers.

NOW YOU TRY: Show emotions

Take this basic dialogue and, mixing and matching from the suggestions below, revise using different props and showing different emotions.

Dialogue	Action/prop	Emotions
"Did you know him long?" "Too long, and not long enough."	Smoking a cigarette Twirling a strand of hair Fiddling with a ring Adding sugar to coffee Crossing her legs and shifting position Doodling on a scrap of paper	Anger Resignation Disgust Sadness Ambivalence Grief Boredom

NOW YOU TRY: Write dialogue

1. Write a simple exchange of dialogue, ten or twelve back-and-forths between two characters. Just dialogue.

2. Make a list of what you want to show each character is feeling during this exchange (it could be boredom, anger, fear, sexual attraction, etc.).

3. Add body language, gestures, etc. to show the inner states.

4. To further illuminate, add some internal dialogue for the point-of-view character.

WHEN TO SUMMARIZE INSTEAD

Not everything your characters would say in a given situation belongs in dialogue. It's better to summarize and fast-forward through the necessary but unexciting bits than risk bogging down your story with trivial talk.

For instance, *He introduced himself and we shook hands* is fine instead of a lot of hello-and-how-are-you-ing—unless you're using the greetings to show the relationship between the two characters. If your character has to tell his partner about a visit to Nina's house, and that visit was dramatized a chapter earlier, then *I told him about my visit to Nina's house* is all you need.

Only use dialogue when it's dramatic, when it moves your story along, or when it develops characters and their relationships. Never force a character to deliver a speech about himself or another character, or why something is happening.

ON YOUR OWN: Writing dialogue

1. Pull out a few of your favorite novels. Skim for sections of dialogue. Read those sections carefully to see how the author uses dialogue to create drama, push the story forward, or develop the relationships between characters.

2. List the characters who deliver the bulk of the dialogue in your book. In order to give each one a distinctive voice, make notes for yourself describing how you want each one to sound. For example: direct or evasive; self-assured or uncertain; worldly or naïve; old or young. Add ethnicity, regional identity, and socioeconomic status.

3. Use the list you just developed and revise some dialogue you've written to make each character sound more unique and compelling.

4. Be on the lookout for dialogue in your novel that would be better summarized; look for summarized dialogue that would be better dramatized. Revise accordingly.

5. Read aloud passages of dialogue you've written. Revise so they sound natural and effective.

CHaPtEr 16:
creating a
sense of place

"In many cases, when a reader puts a story
aside because 'it got boring,' the boredom
arose because the writer grew enchanted with
his powers of description and lost sight of his
priority, which is to keep the ball rolling."

—STEPHEN KING
On Writing

Let's face it, mystery readers are looking for great plots and interesting characters. Too much detailed description of places and things and the reader is likely to skip ahead, looking for action.

Still, a strong sense of place can catapult your novel from good to great. Readers relish revisiting the settings as well as the characters in some of today's best-selling mystery fiction. Examples include Carl Hiaasen's Miami, Walter Mosley's Los Angeles, and Jim Fusilli's New York.

SETTING SCENES

A vivid glimpse of setting can be used to open a scene and provide a backdrop for the appearance of characters. Imagine being there. The smell of Los Angeles after a brush fire, the humidity of a Louisiana swamp, the colorful crush of people at a Mexican open market—use all your senses to make scenes come alive. Pick details that define the place and time.

Read this opening of Thomas Wheeler's *The Arcanum* and notice the techniques he uses to create a vivid setting:

> London—1919
>
> A September storm battered a sleeping London. Barrage after barrage of gusting sheets drummed on the

rooftops and loosened clapboards. Raindrops like silver dollars pelted the empty roads and forced families of pigeons into huddled clumps atop the gaslights.

Then it stopped.

The trees of Kensington Gardens swayed, and the city held its breath. It waited a few dripping moments, then relaxed.

Just as suddenly, a Model-T Ford swerved past Marble Arch in Hyde Park and buzzed around Speakers' Corner, peals of laughter following in its wake.

Inside the car, Daniel Bisbee held the steering wheel with one hand and patted Lizzie's plump thigh with the other.

Cinematically, it's as if a camera pans first from a distance and an omniscient narrator describes the setting. We feel the power of the rain, and then quiet descends upon London streets as the downpour stops. The camera comes in for a close-up of the Model-T, and the laughter of its occupants breaks the silence.

Here are some of the elements that make this passage so effective:

- **Place and time.** *London—1919.* Simple notations of place and year begin the scene.
- **Contrast.** *The storm battered a sleeping London.* The juxtaposition of the storm battering and London sleeping creates a mood for the scene.
- **Sensory impressions.** *Barrage after barrage of gusting sheets drummed on the rooftops and loosened clapboards.* This passage exploits the auditory and visual.
- **Comparison.** *Raindrops like silver dollars . . .* The use (but not overuse) of simile.
- **Details, not generalizations.** *. . . families of pigeons into huddled clumps atop the gaslights.* This single image is much more effective than "It was a dark and stormy night."
- **Drama.** *The trees of Kensington Gardens swayed, and the city held its breath. It waited a few dripping moments, then relaxed.* Endow the setting with human qualities. Here the rain becomes almost a character; rain stopping becomes a dramatic moment.

Notice what aren't in this list: adjectives and adverbs. We're taught in school that those are the parts of speech that carry descriptive power. But do they? Examine the passage again. Make a list of the adjectives and adverbs used.

I find only six: September, gusting, silver, empty, huddled, dripping, suddenly, and plump. Not a whole lot for a highly descriptive passage. Where does the descriptive power come from? Read the passage again and see if you can figure it out.

I think it's in the verbs: battered, drummed, pelted, swayed, swerved, and buzzed. In fact, notice that nearly half of the adjectives in this passage are verbs in disguise (gusting, huddled, dripping).

When you set a scene, use these tools: sensory impressions, details, comparisons and contrasts. Make your scene descriptions dramatic, and choose verbs for maximum impact.

NOW YOU TRY: Analyze a dramatic description of setting

Analyze the passage from Tony Hellerman's *Listening Woman* using the following questions as a guide.

Think about:

• How does the "camera" move?
• What are the contrasts?
• What sensory impressions are created; what senses are exploited?
• What details does Hillerman choose to make the scene come alive?
• How does Hillerman create drama without any human action or dialogue?
• Find the adjectives and adverbs. Now find the verbs. Which carry the descriptive power?

Excerpt from *Listening Woman*

The southwest wind picked up turbulence around the San Francisco peaks, howled across the emptiness of the Moenkopi plateau, and made a thousand strange sounds in the windows of the old Hopi villages of Shongopovi and Second Mesa. Two hundred vacant miles to the north and east, it sandblasted the stone sculptures of Monument Valley Navajo Tribal Park and whistled eastward across the maze of canyons on Utah-Arizona border. Over the arid immensity of the Nokaito Bench it filled the blank blue sky with a rushing sound. At the hogan of Hosteen Tso, at 3:17 P.M., it gusted and eddied, and formed a dust devil, which crossed the wagon track and raced with a swirling roar across Margaret Cigaret's old Dodge pickup truck and past the Tso brush arbor. The three people under the arbor huddled against the driven dust.

USES OF SETTING IN A MYSTERY NOVEL

Mystery writers never write "setting for setting's sake"—it's always *in support* of story and character. There are many ways setting functions to support story and character.

• **To orient the reader.** The most basic use of setting is to answer the question: Where are we now? This can be done at the beginning of a scene, as in this chapter opening from Chuck Hogan's *Prince of Thieves*:

Malden Center smelled like a village set on the shore of an ocean of hot coffee. With the coffee bean warehouse so close, sitting in Dunkin' Donuts was a little redundant, like chewing nicotine gum in a tobacco field. But that's what they were doing, Frank G. in a soft black sweatshirt, nursing a decaf, and Doug M. looking rumpled in a gray shirt with blue basketball-length sleeves, rolling a bottle of Mountain Dew between his hands.

• **To show time passing.** A character drives to work or waits on a park bench for an informant to show up—the author uses setting to show the passage of time. Here's an example from Raymond Chandler's *The High Window:*

> I pulled the phone over and looked at the number on the slip and called it. They said my package could be sent right over. I said I would wait for it.
>
> It was getting dark outside now. The rushing sound of the traffic had died a little and the air from the open window, not yet cool from the night, had that tired end-of-the-day smell of dust, automobile exhaust, sunlight rising from hot walls and sidewalks, the remote smell of food in a thousand restaurants, and perhaps, drifting down from the residential hills above Hollywood—if you had a nose like a hunting dog—a touch of that peculiar tomcat smell that eucalyptus trees give off in warm weather.
>
> I sat there smoking. Ten minutes later the door was knocked on . . .

Chandler uses a paragraph of pure atmospherics to kill ten minutes between the time that Marlowe calls for package delivery and when the package arrives. Talk about exploiting the senses. I grew up in Southern California and I know exactly that eucalyptus smell he's talking about.

• **To drive a suspense scene.** Setting can be used to build tension in a suspense scene. In this example from William G. Tapply's *Bitch Creek*, protagonist Stoney Calhoun stakes out the villain:

> The sun wasn't scheduled to rise for another hour, but already the black sky had begun to fade into a pewtery purple. Calhoun leaned forward so he could see through the bushes. He caught a shadowy movement on the far side of the parking area, then made out a dark shape easing along the edge of the opening, just inside the woods.

- **To give the reader a breather.** A paragraph or two of setting after a scene of high drama and action can be used to give your characters and the reader a chance to catch a breath.

SETTING: IT'S IN THE DETAILS

Setting can be applied in broad brushstrokes, as in the examples above. In addition, dabs of setting can be applied throughout a novel. You don't want to overdo it, but on virtually every page you have an opportunity to develop a sense of time and place. Here are just a few examples:

- How pedestrians cross the streets—do they wait for the green light or dart across against the red light when there's a break in traffic?
- Clothing—1950s women wear shirtwaist dresses; 1970s, microminis.
- Household effects—the furniture, household appliances, and accessories reflect time and place, poverty or wealth. An egg chair belongs in a 1960s suburban family room, just as a "Hoosier" cabinet belongs in a 1940s rural kitchen.
- Vegetation—does your character scramble down a hillside dense with bougainvilleas or Saguaro cacti?
- Dialect—when a character addresses two or more people, is it "You," "Y'all," or "Youze guys"?

How do details in this excerpt from our book *Delusion* convey setting?

> The place smelled great—coffee and bacon. A short or-
> der cook with a dishtowel wrapped around his waist was
> hard at work at the grill, flipping burgers and frying up
> a steak and cheese sub. I checked out the menu while
> I waited for Gratzenberg to show. The section labeled
> "Deep Fried Foods" confirmed that this place was
> caught in a time warp.
> The waitress was a brunette who reminded me of a
> girl I'd dated in college, an impression that disappeared
> the minute she leaned against the counter and shouted
> to the cook, "Ovah heah! Ovah heah!"

The smell of coffee, the dishtowel-wrapped cook at the grill, the menu—these are details that shout *greasy spoon*. And though this diner could be anywhere, when the waitress opens her mouth and shouts "Ovah heah!" it's pure Boston.

NOW YOU TRY: Write a diner of your own

Write a paragraph in which your character is sitting in a diner reading a menu in rural Vermont, Malibu, Tijuana, your own hometown, or the town where you've set your novel. Pick details that give that setting its own unique flavor.

Write a diner of your own.

NOW YOU TRY: Brainstorm your setting

Below are some aspects of life in metropolitan Boston we use in our Peter Zak series. Jot down your ideas for your own setting.

	Our setting PLACE: Metro Boston YEAR: The present SEASON: Early autumn	Your setting PLACE: YEAR: SEASON:
Weather	Cool crisp days, rain, shortening daylight	
Local events	"Head of the Charles" regatta, Halloween (pumpkins, dried corn stalks on front lawns)	
Locales	Harvard Square, Cambridge Courthouse, Charles River boathouse	
Landmarks	The Citgo sign in Kenmore Square, the Zakim bridge	

	Our setting PLACE: Metro Boston YEAR: The present SEASON: Early autumn	**Your setting** PLACE: YEAR: SEASON:
Food	Toscanini's ice cream, Italian food in the North End, dumplings from Chinatown	
Traffic	Rude Boston drivers talking on cell phones, traffic jams, rotaries, nowhere to park, The Big Dig	
Sports	The Red Sox, rowing on the Charles River, rollerblading along Memorial Drive	
Dialect/local lingo	Characters with Boston accents, drinking "tonic" (not soda or pop), "Mem" (not Memorial) Drive	
Vegetation	Maples and oaks turning color, willows turning bright yellow at the edge of the Charles River	
Architecture	Red-brick row houses, two-family houses and triple deckers, black glass Hancock tower	

ON YOUR OWN: Writing setting

1. Go to a place like the one where you're setting a scene in your book. Bring a notebook and jot down what you see and hear; tune into all the other sensory impressions and note the quirky details that define this particular place. Then write the scene. Remember, you want to evoke a place, not render it in painstaking detail.

2. Revise passages you've written that describe a setting. Try to:
   a. Replace generalizations (like a beautiful day) with specifics.
   b. Use a range of sensory images.
   c. Use contrasts.

3. Go back and add dabs of setting to scenes you've written.

CHaPtEr 17:

writing investigation:
clues, red herrings, and misdirection

> "Another clue! And this time a swell one!"
>
> —FRANKLIN W. DIXON
> —Joe to Frank in *The Tower Treasure*, the first Hardy Boys mystery

Investigation is the meat and potatoes of mystery fiction. The sleuth talks to people, does research, snoops around, and makes observations. Facts emerge. Maybe an eyewitness gives an account of what he saw. A wife has unexplained bruises on her face. The brother of a victim avoids eye contact with his questioner. A will leaves a millionaire's estate to an obscure charity. A bloody knife is found in a laundry bin. A love letter is discovered tucked into last week's newspaper.

Some facts will turn out to be clues that lead to the killer's true identity. Some will turn out to be red herrings—evidence that leads in a false direction. On top of that, a lot of the information your sleuth notes will turn out to be nothing more than the irrelevant minutiae of everyday life inserted into scenes to give a sense of realism and camouflage the clues.

THE INVESTIGATION: OBSERVING AND INTERROGATING

Asking questions and observing are any sleuth's main investigational activities. If your sleuth is a professional detective or police officer, investigating might include examining the crime scene, questioning witnesses, staking out suspects, pulling rap sheets, checking DMV records, and going undercover. If your sleuth is a medical examiner, we're talking autopsies and X rays, MRIs, and DNA analysis. If your character is an amateur sleuth, it's going to be about sneaking around, asking a lot of questions, and cozying up to the police.

How your sleuth investigates should reflect his skills and personality quirks. Take the extreme example of television sleuth Adrian Monk. A former star detective, Monk was traumatized after the murder of his wife. Now he has an extreme case of obsessive-compulsive disorder and is plagued by an abnormal fear of everything from germs to heights. His obsessions lend a comic touch to the stories, but his compulsive attention to detail is the hallmark of his investigative technique, enabling him to notice what police investigators miss.

Our character, Peter Zak, is a psychologist. He doesn't know beans about fingerprints or blood spatter. He knows behavior, so he's a keen observer of people, and psychological tests are part of his interrogation arsenal. Here's an example from *Amnesia* where Peter uses a "mental status test" to question Marie Whitson, a patient who is suffering delirium from a self-administered drug overdose. As you read the excerpt, think about how dialogue and observation fuel investigation, and try to spot the possible clues in the passage.

Think about:

- Dialogue—how are questions used to drive the scene?
- Observation—how do physical details, gestures, and body language add information?
- Clues—what sticks out as potential clues?

Excerpt from *Amnesia*

"Ms. Whitson? Could you put your right hand on top of your head?"

A hand floated upward and rested on top of her head. White lines scarred her wrist. Her head tilted sideways. She met my eyes. Then her gaze shifted to the faces of my colleagues and on to the flat, gray expanse of a window shade. The hand remained planted on top of her head.

"Ms. Whitson, could you wave your left hand and stick out your tongue?"

Now a definite smile appeared. Her lips parted and the tip of her tongue emerged. But the right hand on her head and the left one in her lap remained still.

I went through the other silly-sounding questions designed to take an instant picture of that mish-mash we refer to as mental status. Near the end, although I already knew the answer, I asked, "Have you ever thought about taking your own life?" This got her attention. She jerked slightly and then narrowed her eyes. I waited, wondering if she trusted me enough to answer.

Hesitantly, she nodded.

. . .

Finally, I asked her, "Do you feel safe here?"

Slowly and deliberately, she nodded. A smile tugged at the corners of her lips. It was an odd moment. I had the distinct impression that she was enjoying a little private joke.

This excerpt demonstrates some pointers to keep in mind as you write investigation:

- **Make interrogation physical as well as verbal.** Did you notice that Maria Whitson doesn't say much? Peter asks questions and notes her responses; more importantly, he observes her gestures, facial expressions, and demeanor. When your sleuth investigates, be sure to dramatize the body language he observes.
- **Don't spoon-feed the reader.** You don't have to explain the significance of every fact uncovered. For instance, Peter notices, *White lines scarred her wrist.* He doesn't give the reader the obvious news bulletin: This character has survived a suicide attempt. It's not necessary. Remember, your reader *wants* to solve the puzzle, too. So let the reader do some of the work.
- **Establish the to-be-connected dots.** There should be details that make your sleuth sit up and take notice but leave questions unanswered. For example, Maria nods when Peter asks if she feels safe. Then Peter thinks: *I had the distinct impression that she was enjoying a little private joke.* It's a tantalizing observation, and the reader and the sleuth tuck it away. Later, that observation pays off. So as your character investigates, establish the dots that you'll later connect.
- **Nip and tuck—summarize to avoid monotony.** Real psychological tests can take hours to administer. Notice how we summarized to shorten the testing scene: *I went through the other silly-sounding questions designed to take an instant picture of that mish-mash we refer to as mental status.* Many aspects of real investigations—crime scene examination, interrogations, stakeouts, fingerprint analysis, and so on—are painstaking and time-consuming. Abbreviate. Dramatize the interesting parts, and write only enough detail to make the investigation feel real.
- **Stay out of the future.** Notice that the point-of-view character stays in the moment. There's no sudden flash of 20/20 foresight: "If I'd known what was going to happen, I never would have left her alone in that room." Writers sometimes do this, thinking that it heightens suspense, but in fact it can rob a story of its surprise.

CREATING CHARACTER DYNAMICS IN THE Q&A

Whether your sleuth schmoozes over tea with the victim's neighbor, makes telephone calls to witnesses, formally interrogates a suspect, or huddles with colleagues to discuss blood spatter, your sleuth asks questions and gets answers. Talk, talk, talk. It can get pretty boring if all you're doing is conveying information. By creating a dynamic between the characters during the Q&A, your story continues to hold the reader's interest.

Take this example of investigation from Laura Lippman's *By a Spider's Thread.* PI Tess Monaghan questions her client.

"How much do you know about him if he didn't participate in the group?"

"Baltimore's Jews live in a small village, especially
those of us in the clothing business. There's lots of gossip
we keep to ourselves, so people in the city at large won't
cluck their tongues. It was shocking, seeing Nat go to
prison."

"Did you know him before he went in?"

"After a fashion." Rubin gave her a lopsided smile.
"The pun was intended."

"Only it wasn't really a pun," Tess said.

"Excuse me?"

"It was a play on words, but it wasn't a pun, which
involves changing a word in some way so it takes on a
double meaning." It was fun, correcting Rubin for once.
"You know, Mexican weather report—chili today—"

"Hot tamale. Groucho Marx." He moved his eye-
brows up and down, wiggling an imaginary stogie.

Interrogation becomes interesting when the relationship between the characters has some kind of electrical charge, some inner dynamic, as it does
here. Tess asks questions (*How much did you know about him..?*) Her client
gives evasive and misleading answers (*after a fashion*) because he's unwilling
to face certain truths himself. But what makes this scene work is the dynamic between the characters. There's mental sparring (*. . . it wasn't really
a pun . . .*) and humor (he imitates Groucho Marx) as their relationship shifts
at this point in the novel from adversarial to cautious, mutual appreciation.
It's all in the subtext. The relationship between characters makes this investigation dialogue interesting—the clues that get conveyed are a bonus.

The two examples below illustrate how body language can be used to
convey inner dynamics and show the relationship between the characters.
The highlighted dialogue in both passages is identical. Which Cassandra do
you think is more likely to be telling the truth?

Example 1	Example 2
I reached out and touched Cassandra's arm. **"Are you going to tell me what happened?"**	I pulled over a chair and pushed Cassandra down into it. **"Are you going to tell me what happened?"**
She looked away. **"Well—"** **"What did you see?"**	"Well—" She shrugged. Like what the hell.

Example 1	Example 2
She looked around, frantic for a moment, cornered, then resigned.	**"What did you see?"**
"I saw a car." She swallowed. **"Red. It was bearing down on me. I jumped out of the way."**	She gave me a sideways look, the flicker of a smile. **"I saw a car."** She stared down at her fingernails, picked at the peeling candy-apple red polish. **"Red. Coming fast. I got the hell out of the way."**

My intention was to make the reader think that Cassandra in Example 1 is telling the truth. By having her seem frantic, then resigned, and swallow before she says what she saw, I was trying to convey fear and reluctance and suggest that she may be telling the truth. Cassandra in Example 2 shrugs, doesn't seem to care, gives a flicker of a smile, then picks at her red nail polish before she says the car was red—maybe it's just occurring to her at that moment that red is a good color to pick. These details are designed to suggest that she's lying.

NOW YOU TRY: Put a charge in the Q&A

Combine physical gestures, internal dialogue, and body language with the dialogue below to develop one of these scenarios. Alter the word choice and add more dialogue to convey the dynamics of the scenario you pick.

Basic dialogue	Scenarios
"Are you going to tell me what happened?" "Well—" "What did you see?" "I saw a car. Red. It was bearing down on me. I jumped out of the way."	1. A PI questions a seven-year-old boy who's afraid if he admits what he saw, he's going to be punished. (He was supposed to be in school.) 2. A reporter questions the bereaved mother of the murder victim. 3. A police officer questions a local thug who, up to now, has denied he witnessed anything.

Write the Q&A adding physical gestures and body language to convey one of the scenarios.

MIXING UP THE CLUES AND RED HERRINGS

A clue can be just about anything: An object the sleuth discovers (a bloody glove). The way a character behaves (keeps his hands in his pockets). A revealing gesture (a woman straightens a man's collar). What someone says ("Julia Dalrymple deserved to die"). What someone wears (a locket stolen from the victim). An item that doesn't fit with the way the person presents himself or his history (a suspect's fingerprint lifted from a room that the suspect says she was never in).

Here are some techniques that enable you to play fair and, at the same time, keep the reader guessing:

- **Emphasize the unimportant; de-emphasize the clue.** The reader sees the clue but not what's important about it. For example, the sleuth investigates the value and provenance of a stolen painting and pays little attention to the identity of the woman who sat for the portrait.
- **Establish a clue before the reader can know its significance.** Introduce the key information before the reader has a context to fit it into. For example, the sleuth strolls by a character spraying her rose bushes before a neighbor is poisoned by a common herbicide.

- **Have your sleuth misinterpret the meaning of a clue.** Your sleuth can make a mistake that takes the investigation to a logical dead end. For example, the victim is found in a room with the window open. The sleuth thinks that's how the killer escaped and goes looking for a witness who saw someone climbing down the side of the house. In fact, the window was opened to let out tell-tale fumes.
- **Have the clue turn out to be what *isn't* there.** The sleuth painstakingly elucidates what happened, failing to notice what should have happened but didn't. The most famous example is from the Sherlock Holmes story "Silver Blaze." Holmes deduces there could not have been an intruder because the dog didn't bark.
- **Scatter pieces of the clue in different places and mix up the logical order.** Challenge your reader by revealing only part of a clue at a time. For instance, a canary cage with a broken door might be found in the basement along with other detritus; later the sleuth has a "wait a minute!" realization when he discovers the dead canary with its neck wrung.
- **Hide the clue in plain sight.** Tuck the clue among so many other possible clues that it doesn't stand out. For example, the nylon stocking that was the murder weapon might be neatly laundered and folded in the victim's lingerie drawer. Or the sleuth focuses on the water bottle, unopened mail, pine needles, and gas station receipt on the floor of the victim's car and fails to recognize the significance of a telephone number written in the margin of the map.
- **Draw attention elsewhere.** Have multiple plausible alternatives vying for the reader's attention. For example, the sleuth knows patients are being poisoned. He focuses on a doctor who gives injections and fails to notice the medic who administers oxygen (toxic germs can be administered in a nebulizer attached to an oxygen tank).
- **Create a time problem.** Manipulate time to your own advantage. For example, suppose the prime suspect has an alibi for the time of the murder. Later the sleuth discovers that the time of the alibi or the time of death is wrong.
- **Put the real clue right before a false one.** People tend to remember what was presented to them last. For example, your sleuth notices that the stove doesn't go on properly, and immediately after that discovers an empty bottle marked "poison" wrapped in newspaper stuffed in with the trash. Readers (and your sleuth) are more likely to remember the hidden poison bottle than the malfunctioning stove that preceded it.
- **Camouflage a clue with action.** If you show the reader a clue, have some extraneous action happen at the same time to distract attention. For example, your sleuth gets mugged while reading a flyer posted on a lamppost; the mugging turns out to be irrelevant, but the flyer turns out to contain an important clue.

NOW YOU TRY: Mix up clues and red herrings

Write a few paragraphs in which your sleuth does one of the following:

- inspects a murder scene
- searches a victim's bedroom
- examines a suspect's car

Have your sleuth find at least one real clue that implicates the villain; camouflage it among false clues and extraneous details of everyday life.

> (!)
>
> ---
>
> Write an investigation that mixes up clues and red herrings.

DON'T CHEAT

You can't withhold from the reader information that a point-of-view character knows. The reader and the sleuth should realize the identity of the culprit at the same time. So how do you keep the mystery from unraveling before the end of your story?

Along the way, your sleuth can be bamboozled, blindsided, only partially informed, or flat-out wrong. What I find infuriating is when an author withholds, even temporarily, some important piece of information that the point-of-view character knows.

Here's an example:

> Sharon's cell phone rang.
>
> "Sorry," she told Bob. "This could be important."
>
> She flipped the phone open and pressed it to her ear. "Hello?"
>
> Sharon recognized the caller's voice, the last person she'd expect after all that had happened.

> "What's up?" she said, trying not to sound
> surprised.
> "You need to know this—" the caller began.
> As she listened, she found herself pressing against
> the car door, trying to insert a few extra inches between
> herself and Bob. Bob was eyeing her closely, and his un-
> concerned look suddenly seemed no more than a thin
> veneer.

The chapter ends and the reader doesn't discover for twenty pages the identity of the caller, or what troubling information that person imparted. Never
mind that we've been hanging out in Sharon's head for the last hundred
pages and she's been blabbering about everything she sees, hears, feels, and
thinks. Now all of a sudden she plays coy with this critical tidbit.

Why do authors do it? To create suspense. But it's cheating. Not only that,
it breaks character as the author intrudes by withholding information. I know,
I know, mystery authors get away with this kind of shtick all the time and
laugh all the way to the bank. But it's a cheap trick, and my advice: Don't
succumb.

This is why guilty narrators are problematic in a mystery. They know too
much. Some mystery writers manage to pull off a guilty narrator by keeping
the character's identity hidden. For example, this excerpt from Peter Clement's *The Inquisitor* is written from the point of view of a particularly chilling
villain who gets his jollies bringing terminal patients near death:

> "Can you hear me?" I whispered, holding back on the
> plunger of my syringe.
> "Yes." Her eyes remained shut.
> I leaned over and brought my mouth to her ear. "Any
> more pain?"
> "No. It's gone."
> "Do you see anything?"
> "Only blackness." Her whispers rasped against the
> back of her throat.
> "Look harder! Now tell me what's there." I swallowed
> to keep from gagging. Her breath stank.
> "You're not my doctor."
> "No, I'm replacing him tonight."

Notice that by writing this passage in the first person, Clement not only
conceals the villain's identity but also the villain's gender. This subterfuge
leaves the author free to cast suspicion on both male and female characters.

But it's cheating to spend chapter after chapter in a character's head, only
to reveal in a final climactic scene that she's been hiding one small detail: She
did it. You might get away with it if the character turns out to be an *unreliable*

narrator who can't remember (amnesia?), doesn't realize (delusional? naïve? simple minded?), or refuses to admit even to herself that she's guilty.

CONFUSION: INTEREST KILLER

Your goal is to misdirect, but never to confuse. Lead the reader down a series of perfectly logical primrose paths—your reader must always feel grounded, even if it's on a false path. Set too many different possible scenarios spinning at once, or overwhelm your reader with a cacophony of clues, red herrings, and background noise, and your baffled reader will get frustrated and set the book aside . . . permanently.

As you write, keep track of the different scenarios and the clues that implicate and exonerate each suspect. Also, be sure to keep track of who knows what—particularly if you're writing from multiple viewpoints.

COINCIDENCE: CREDIBILITY KILLER

All of us are tempted, from time to time, to insert a coincidence into a story line. Wouldn't it be cool, you say to yourself, to have a character happen to run into the twin sister she never knew she had in a hall of mirrors at a county fair? Dramatic, yes. Credible, no.

Never mind that Agatha Christie wrote a story that turns on a similar coincidence: A man runs into his unknown twin brother coming out of a drugstore; the evil twin then commits a murder and implicates his brother. Never mind that you once read a newspaper article about separated twins who ran into each other in a supermarket. Life is full of bizarre coincidences. You can't put a coincidence like that in a mystery novel today and expect your work to be taken seriously.

Coincidence is most likely to creep in when you find yourself having to maneuver your character into position in order discover some piece of information your plot requires. Maybe your character needs to find out when and where a crime is going to occur—so you have him happen to find that information in a letter someone drops on the sidewalk. Or maybe your character needs to find a buried clue—so you have her get the urge to plant petunias and dig in just the right spot. Or maybe your character needs to know the scheme two characters are hatching—so he happens to pick up the phone extension and overhears them planning.

It may be more difficult, but it's much more satisfying if you come up with logical ways to maneuver your character into position to find the clues and red herrings your plot requires. Repeat after me: *Thou shalt not resort to coincidence, intuition, clairvoyance, or divine intervention.* In a mystery, logic rules.

If you do put coincidence in your story, at least have your point-of-view character comment on the absurdity of the coincidence. I don't think that gets you off the hook, but at least it will keep the reader from dismissing you as a hack.

ON YOUR OWN: Writing investigation

1. Check out a how-to book about magic. Mystery authors would do well to take a few pages from magicians, who perfected the art of misdirection. My favorite is the classic by Henning Nelms, *Magic and Showmanship*. Take to heart his distinction between diversion (good showmanship) and distraction (poor showmanship).

2. Write a scene in your novel in which your sleuth questions one of the other characters. Show the dynamic between the characters.

3. Keep track of your clues. As you write your novel, keep track of these key pieces of information you reveal through the investigation of the crime:
   a. the clue
   b. who knows it
   c. whom it implicates

CHaPtEr 18:
writing suspense

A character who unknowingly carries a bomb around as if it were an ordinary package is bound to work up great suspense in the audience.

—ALFRED HITCHCOCK

Suspense happens when a scene becomes charged with anticipation. It's the possibility of what *might* happen that keeps the reader on the edge of her chair.

Think of the classic suspense scene in the Alfred Hitchcock movie *Suspicion*. The Joan Fontaine character believes that her charming, wastrel husband, played by Cary Grant, is an embezzler and a murderer who is now out to poison her. There's a long shot as Grant mounts the stairs, and then the camera focuses on the nightly glass of milk he carries up to her. Everyone in the audience is wondering: Is it poisoned? To heighten the threat and foreboding, Hitchcock had a light bulb placed in the glass to give it an eerie glow.

To create suspense, your job is to do the literary equivalent of what director Hitchcock did by putting that light bulb in the milk: Build dramatic tension by making the ordinary seem menacing. The writer's tools for achieving this are *sensory detail* and *the slowing down of time*.

TURN UP THE SENSORY DETAIL

By focusing on the right sensory detail, you can heighten the sense of potential menace in everyday objects.

Read this example from our first Peter Zak novel, *Amnesia*. Peter Zak and Annie Squires approach a house where they suspect one of Peter's patients is being held captive.

Tall bushes shrouded a shadowy front porch. Only a sliver of light between drawn drapes suggested anyone was home.

Someone had made an effort to dress up the house for Halloween. On the small lawn, dried cornstalks were teepeed around a lamppost. A pumpkin grinned from the top of a wheelchair ramp. Opposite the pumpkin was a little barrel of chrysanthemums. Beside the front door, barely visible in the shadow, a scarecrow dummy wearing a cowboy hat was slumped in a chair. I exhaled, realizing I'd been holding my breath.

. . .

Annie got out and eased the car door shut. I did the same.

We moved up the side of the house, crouching as we passed under the dark windows. I was conscious of every sound—my own breathing, traffic whooshing up and down the adjacent streets, the far-off pulsing wail of a siren. At every step, the sound of leaves crunching underfoot seemed thunderous.

Traditional trappings of a New England autumn, like a pumpkin and a scarecrow dummy, seem ordinary and ominous at the same time. Taking apart the pieces, here's what happens, and the sensory details that are used to create the suspense:

What happens	Sensory details to create suspense
Annie and Peter look at the house, get out of the car, and creep along the side of the house.	Bushes shroud the porch
	Sliver of light between front curtains
	Grinning pumpkin
	Scarecrow dummy slumped in the shadows
	Peter holds his breath
	Peter hears his own breathing, traffic whooshing, leaves crunching

By making your character hyperaware of sensations and sounds, you ratchet up the dramatic tension. It all adds up to a feeling of impending danger, though it isn't clear from what.

Suspense is sustained by the absence of anything terrible happening and the continued focus on detail. When you write suspense, remember your goal is to heighten anticipation.

Here are some useful devices for creating suspense:

- **Weather.** Building storm clouds, a flash of lightning, or distant thunder suggest something bad is about to happen, even if they are a bit cliché.
- **Objects that cover other objects.** Create the suggestion of hidden menace with closed curtains, a tarp covering something, a folding screen set up in the corner of a room, a closed (or just barely ajar) door, a shadow, and so on.
- **Internal sensations.** Show that your character feels the anticipation, too. Your character might pull up her coat collar, pat her pocket to be sure she's got her mace, or feel her scalp prickle.
- **Something that's not quite right.** A telephone off the hook, a broken window, a single high-heeled shoe discarded on a front walk, water left running in a kitchen sink—these kinds of not-quite-right details create suspense.

TURN DOWN THE VELOCITY

Slowing down time increases suspense. I deliberately drew out the moment Peter and Annie spend in the car looking at that house so it seemed longer than it would have if they were just arriving to deliver a package.

Here are some ways to slow things down:

- **Complex sentences.** To create a feeling of apprehension about what might happen next, use longer, more complex sentences rather than rat-a-tat, subject-verb-object.
- **Internal dialogue.** Let the reader hear your character's thoughts.
- **Camera close-ups.** You want the reader as close in as possible, experiencing the tension of your suspense sequence firsthand.
- **Quiet and darkness.** Stillness and shadows suggest hidden menace.

MODULATING SUSPENSE

Building suspense takes time. The reader will lose interest if all you do is pile on descriptive paragraph after descriptive paragraph, no matter how much menace there is in your descriptions. Break the tension by having something happen that advances the plot or provides a moment of comic relief.

There are many ways to insert a pause into suspense. The telephone rings. One of the characters cracks a joke—in real life, we all use humor to get through tense times. Or something that seemed menacing is revealed to be ordinary: A scary shape turns out to be the shadow of a moonlit tree; a hand placed on your protagonist's shoulder turns out to be his best buddy, come to help; boot heels stomping across a deserted parking lot turn out to belong to a man carrying a child on his shoulders.

For example, that excerpted scene from *Amnesia* continues for four pages as Peter and Annie circle to the back of the house and check out the yard. They find a boat and a sodden hooded sweatshirt, both of which advance the plot. Then:

> A nearby branch snapped and we both hunkered down
> beside the boat. In the darkness, all I could see were
> little white paws mincing toward me and the white tip
> of a tail held aloft.

The innocuous pussycat provides a momentary release, a false payoff. The reader says *phew*, and relaxes. Use this technique of inserting a brief respite or comic relief into a suspenseful scene to give readers a break, then continue to ratchet up the suspense to keep them hooked.

FORESHADOWING VS. TELEGRAPHING

Creating a suspense sequence that ends harmlessly is a good way to foreshadow something more sinister that happens later in your novel. For example, in chapter three your protagonist goes into a dark, dank basement and emerges, joking about things that go bump in the night. In chapter twenty-three, she goes down into that same basement, and this time she finds the villain waiting for her. Just be careful you foreshadow and don't telegraph—giving away too much too soon is guaranteed to ruin the suspense.

The line between foreshadowing and telegraphing is a subtle one. Let's say your female sleuth meets a man who turns out to be a serial rapist/murderer who preys on young businesswomen whom he picks up at yuppie bars. What would be foreshadowing, and what would be telegraphing? Consider this list of possibilities. Where would you draw the line?

1. The man is charming; his nails are manicured, and he smells of expensive aftershave. She finds herself feeling a bit uneasy around him, but she can't put her finger on why.
2. The man's eyes linger on her chest when they're introduced.
3. When the man shakes her hand, he places his other hand on the small of her back.
4. When she gets ready to leave, he offers to walk her to her car, saying there have been some muggings in the neighborhood.
5. She finds his direct, penetrating blue eyes unnerving.
6. She notices a scratch on his face; he notices her noticing, and says his cat scratched him.
7. She's repelled by the man. He reminds her of the college football player who tried to rape her years earlier.
8. The man opens his briefcase; she notices a copy of *Hustler* magazine tucked inside.

9. The man opens his briefcase; she notices that the briefcase contains a roll of duct tape and handcuffs.
10. The man's name is Vlad Raptor.

For me, items one through six are foreshadowing. Seven through ten telegraph to the reader that this guy is, at the very least, a pretty dodgy character.

When you insert a hint of what's to come, look at it critically and decide whether it's something the reader will glide right by but remember later with an *Aha!* That's foreshadowing. If instead the reader groans and guesses what's coming, you've telegraphed. Ultimately, the line between foreshadowing and telegraphing is in the eye of the beholder. I depend on my writing group to help me ferret out and tone down telegraphed clues. (See chapter twenty-five for a discussion of writing groups.)

END SUSPENSE WITH A PAYOFF

You can have a suspense sequence early in your novel that ends with nothing more than a harmless tabby padding off into the night. But as you near one of your novel's end-of-act climaxes, the suspense sequence should pay off.

The payoff can be an unsettling discovery of evidence of a crime—finding a dead body, bloodstained clothing, a weapons cache, or that the floor of a basement has been dug up. The discovery might reveal a character's secret. Finding love letters or a personal diary might reveal a hidden relationship between two characters. Finding drug paraphernalia in a car might suggest that a suburban matron has a secret life.

Or the payoff can be a plot twist: The bad guy confesses; the sleuth gets attacked, or locked in a basement, or lost in a cave; or the police show up and arrest the sleuth.

Here's how the suspense sequence from *Amnesia* pays off a few pages later, after Peter and Annie break into the garage alongside the house. It's pitch-black inside, and Annie turns on a penlight and shines it along the fender of a red Firebird:

> "Do you see what I see?" she asked, indicating a dent and a streak of dark green paint.
>
> I started to answer when Annie put her finger to her lips and doused the light.
>
> The door to the house on the opposite side of the garage opened. I crouched. Footsteps were barely audible, rubber soles crossing the garage's empty bay. As my eyes got accustomed to the dark, I began to make out a pale round shape, floating, suspended in the shadows at about head height.

There was a click and the room sprang to light. I blinked away the brightness. Angelo di Benedetti stood facing me.

"Well, if it isn't the expert witness," he said, sneering.

He wore a black turtleneck and baggy black pants, rolled at the ankle above combat boots. His handsome face was hard and a vein pulsed in his forehead. He had his hands in his pockets. I wondered where Annie was, but I didn't dare look at the spot where I knew she'd been not more than ten seconds earlier. Another instinct told me not to move suddenly.

The payoff here is the appearance of the villain. But there's a surprise, too— Annie disappears. Peter knows she can't have gone far. So suspense continues as Peter confronts the villain, and all the while, Peter (and the reader) worry that Annie's whereabouts will be discovered.

NOW YOU TRY: Analyze suspense

Analyze this passage from Michael Connelly's *The Narrows*:

I turned my attention back to the house. There was a full porch off the rear. There were no gutters on the roof here and the rain was coming off in sheets, so heavy that it obscured everything within. Backus could've been sitting in a rocker on the porch and I wouldn't have seen him. The line of bougainvilleas carried along the porch railing. I ducked below the sight line and moved quickly to the steps. I took the three steps up in one stride and was in out of the rain. My eyes and ears took a moment to adjust and that was when I saw it. There was a white rattan couch on the right side of the porch. On it a blanket covered an unmistakable shape of a human form sitting upright but slumped against the left arm. Dropping to a crouch I moved closer and reached for a corner of the blanket on the floor. I slowly pulled it off the form.

It was an old man. He looked like he had been dead at least a day. The odor was just starting.

_____

What happens:

_____

Sensory details to create suspense:

_____

Payoff:

NOW YOU TRY: Create suspense

Here's a simple scene description. Make a list of sensory details you might use to create suspense. Try to use details from all the senses. Decide what the payoff will be. Then write the scene.

What happens

Janie Mangiano locks the door to her office building and walks across the parking lot to her car. As she gets nearer, she realizes her car window is partly open (didn't she remember to close it?) and she catches a glimpse of a dark shape in the back seat.

_____

Sensory details to create suspense:

_____

Payoff:

_____

Write the Scene:

Now repeat the exercise with a suspense sequence from your own novel.

(!)

What happens:

Sensory details to create suspense:

Payoff:

Write the Scene:

ON YOUR OWN: Writing suspense

1. Pick a novel you've read in which there was a lot of suspense. If you can't recall one, pick any of Jeffery Deaver's novels. Skim the last third until you find a scene with rising suspense. Examine how the author creates dramatic tension and the sense of anticipation. Does the author provide moments of respite, and how? What's the payoff?

2. Write (or rewrite) a suspense sequence from your outline, focusing on sensory detail and slowing down time to create rising tension.

3. Continue writing. Use this suspense checklist to guide your work:

— Use sensory detail to make everyday objects seem menacing.

— Consider using the weather, objects covering other objects, or your character's internal sensations.

— Don't rush. Use description, internal dialogue, and complex sentences to slow the pace.

— Pull the camera in close.

— End suspense with a payoff.

— Foreshadow, don't telegraph.

CHaPtEr 19:
writing action

"You have to open yourself to fully imagining action if you want it to feel authentic. I once toyed with the idea of asking my husband to tie me up and drive me around the block in the trunk of the car and then decided that was too weird."

—KATE FLORA

Every mystery novel has action sequences. An action sequence can be a getaway, a chase, or just hurrying to make a plane. It can be a confrontation: an attack, a fistfight, or a gun battle. Your character could get tied up, thrown in a trunk and taken for a ride, or stumble through a forest in the dead of the night while being tracked by attack dogs. To make it work, you have to write convincing physical action.

In the hands of a master, writing action seems simple. Take this passage from Lee Child's *The Enemy*:

> I stood up and raced the last ten feet and hauled Marshall around to the passenger side and opened the door and crammed him into the front. Then I climbed right in over him and dumped myself into the driver's seat. Hit that big red button and fired it up. Shoved it into gear and stamped on the gas so hard the acceleration slammed the door shut. Then I turned the lights full on and put my foot to the floor and charged. Summer would have been proud of me. I drove straight for the line of tanks. Two hundred yards. One hundred yards. I picked my spot and aimed carefully and burst through the gap between two main battle tanks doing more than eighty miles an hour.

This paragraph leaves the reader breathless, as an action sequence should. Take a minute to analyze Child's word choice and sentence structure.

Here are some of the things I notice that make it work:

- **And, and, and . . .** *I stood up **and** raced the last ten feet **and** hauled Marshal around to the passenger side **and** opened the door **and** crammed him in the front.* A run-on sentence of short action statements connected by *ands* creates a sense of urgency and a drumbeat rhythm.
- **Sentence fragments.** *Hit that red button . . . Shoved it into gear . . .* Sentence fragments starting with the verb suggest quick actions.
- **Powerful action verbs.** *Stood, raced, hauled, crammed, climbed, dumped, hit, shoved . . .* The sentences aren't freighted with complex phrases, descriptions, adjectives, or adverbs; the verbs do all the heavy lifting.
- **Actions and reactions.** *. . . stamped on the gas so hard the acceleration slammed the door shut.* Just like in the real world, when something violent happens, there's a reaction.
- **A moment of introspection.** *Summer would have been proud of me.* Use internal dialogue to let the reader catch a breath in the middle.
- **The countdown.** *One hundred yards. Two hundred yards. I picked my spot and aimed carefully . . .* Internal dialogue like this puts the reader right there, moving forward, closing in.

Here's how Lee Child explains his approach to writing this action sequence:

> There's a lot of visualization. I used to be a TV director and all this stuff is choreographed in my head, like I'm watching a phantom screen.
>
> Also I try to pre-explain anything that would slow the scene in question. Much earlier in the book I established that Humvees are low and wide inside, so it seemed okay that Reacher could be shown climbing over Marshall and diving for his own seat. And earlier in that Reacher/Marshall scene I had established the big red button instead of a regular key. That was quasi-researched inasmuch as I'm pretty sure I read it somewhere. I think it's accurate. But even if it's not, it sounds right, which is 99 percent of my research process.

How many revisions did it take Lee Child to get to an action sequence of this quality? I nearly cried when he gave me his answer: "With climax pieces like that one, I always use the first draft. No revision at all. I'm usually in a zone by then, and that makes the first pass the best."

What I wouldn't give to get a ticket to whatever "zone" he's talking about. For me, and for most writers I know, it takes quite a few rewrites to get action that's this spare and effective.

Read this action sequence from Kate Flora's *Liberty or Death*. List the ways Flora uses the language and sentence structure to convey action. Notice also how she conveys heroine Thea Kozak's complete exhaustion, despite the action that's going on.

Excerpt from *Liberty or Death*	How language and sentence structure convey action
I took some quick steps forward, raised my gun, supporting it in two hands as I'd been taught, and fired. I kept it pointed toward Belcher and kept on firing until the gun was empty. Fired at his back. Fired at his side, fired as he turned to face me. Fired as he took a step forward and brought his gun the rest of the way up. I fired until he fell onto the ground and lay still. If I'd had more ammunition, I would have gone right on firing.	1. 2. 3.
I sat down then, a surprised collapse, the sudden boneless fall of a baby just learning to walk. Still holding the gun, I brought my knees to my chest, and rested my head on them.	4. 5.

VISUALIZATION IN ADVANCE

A first step in writing an action sequence is to visualize what you want to happen. Some people can visualize the whole scene from start to finish. Usually I can see what's going to happen at the beginning and how it's going to end, but the middle is a blur. I have to write my way into the action in spurts.

Action sequences are about action and reaction, action and response. A useful approach is to map out an action before you write it—choreograph it in your head and then list the main points:
- where the action takes place

- what happens
- step-by-step, what the characters do in relationship to one another

For example, here's how Flora's action sequence might be mapped out.

Who: Thea Kozak and Roy Belcher
Where: In a field behind the house
What happens: Thea shoots Belcher

Thea's actions	Belcher's actions
1. She raises gun, takes a stance, and fires.	2. He turns to face her.
3. She fires again.	4. He raises his gun.
5. She keeps firing.	6. He goes down.
7. She runs out of ammunition.	8. He stops moving.
9. She collapses.	

Mapping out the action in advance helps you wrap your mind around what your characters are going to do before you try to dramatize it in writing.

NOW YOU TRY: Mapping out the action

1. Record a two-character action sequence from a television program.
2. Play one minute or so of it back with the sound turned off, and replay it as many times as necessary to map out the sequence below.

Who:

Where:

What happens:

Character One's actions	Character Two's actions
1.	2.
3.	4.
5.	6.
7.	8.
9.	

SPEEDING IT UP, SLOWING IT DOWN

Sometimes you'll want to speed up an action sequence and compact time. Other times you'll want to slow the action down and make it seem surreal. Both techniques can be riveting.

In Lee Child's previous tank scene, he speeds up the action. He keeps the camera in close and lets the action go rapid-fire. His goal is to get his character the hell out of Dodge and leave the reader panting for breath.

In Kate Flora's shootout, she slows down the action. Her character is exhausted, on the brink of collapse. By pulling the camera back and slowing the sequence down, she gives the sequence an almost dreamlike quality.

Here's a guide to how to modulate the time:

To speed up the action	To slow down the action
Focus, pull the camera in close.	Pull the camera back.
Limit extraneous detail.	Provide descriptive detail.
Keep sentences short and direct, drop the pronouns.	Use longer, more complex sentences.
Minimize internal dialogue.	Convey some introspection.

MAKING ACTION BELIEVABLE

For an action sequence to work, the reader has to find it believable. Lapses in realism are like tears in the canvas of a painting. They distract the reader from the drama you're trying to create.

If your action has guns in it, know what you're talking about. Are you talking handguns, rifles, or shotguns? If it's a handgun, is it a revolver or a semiautomatic pistol? I don't know Glocks from Mausers, but if you're writing about them, you should. You need to know how to load, aim, and fire, what the recoil feels like, what happens to the spent shell casing, and most importantly, whether your character could handle that particular weapon.

Kate Flora told me how she learned about guns:

> One day I was sitting in a police station talking with an officer who was a good friend. When I mentioned that I had never shot a handgun, he looked at his watch, shook his head, and said, "We'll have to fix that."
>
> He then took me to a shooting range in the basement of the department and walked me through the process of shooting. He taught me about how to hold the gun and the proper stance for shooting and bracing for recoil and then I squeezed the trigger (not pulled) and everything I'd ever seen on TV or read about guns was literally blown away.
>
> It was a big gun with a big jump and a flash of flame and a thunderous noise followed by a gust of smoke, the air filled the smell of exploding gunpowder, the ejected shell flying back at me, and it left me stunned, shaken, and rubber-limbed. Shooting a gun is not a small thing.

If guns play a major role in your book and you don't have a friendly cop who'll take you to a firing range, take a firearms class.

Writing a physical fight requires some know-how, as well. If you're like me and you've survived this long by fleeing not fighting, you need to do some research. There are many books and handbooks on the subject. For instance, the U.S. Army has an inexpensive official training manual on hand-to-hand combat that covers different moves such as choke holds, throws, kicks, and blocks. Rent a hand-to-hand combat video. Or better yet, take a self-defense class—many community police departments sponsor them.

Get the medical detail in your action sequence correct, too. Ask any doctor and you'll discover that a single blow to the head is almost never fatal. Rarely is death instantaneous from a stab or gunshot wound, either. The pool of blood around a corpse shouldn't be growing. Dead men don't bleed.

A good source for this kind of information is *Murder and Mayhem: A Doctor Answers Medical and Forensic Questions for Mystery Writers* by D.P. Lyle, M.D. (Thomas Dunne Books, 2003).

So do your homework, get the details right, but don't show off. One guaranteed way to kill a gun battle is to dump everything you've learned about semiautomatic pistols right into the middle of it. Another way to kill an action sequence is to describe the action with excruciating detail.

Here's an example of what *not* to do:

> He took three steps forward and stood facing me, inches
> away. His breath smelled like he'd been chewing on old
> tires. I averted my face, a quarter turn to the right, and
> pressed my left index finger in the middle of his chest.
> He stepped back six inches, tilted his head twenty de-
> grees, and batted away my hand.

I know, this is an exaggeration, but you get the idea. The only detail I like in this passage is the bit about bad breath. Little red flags should go up if you find yourself writing about quarters and halves, left and right, inches and degrees. Yes, this describes action. But all that measurement and detail bring it to its knees.

If you find yourself explaining something in the middle of an action sequence, another little red flag should go up. For instance, your character is chased along the edge of a cliff to a particularly dangerous spot, and you find yourself having to explain to the reader how high it is, how the waves crash on jagged rocks a hundred feet below, and . . . Whoa. Don't dump explanation into the action sequence unless you want to deliberately drag down the forward momentum. Establish earlier that this particularly dangerous spot exists along the cliff edge—maybe have your character take a walk there while he's thinking through the clues or searching for evidence. When you get to the action sequence, you can let 'er rip.

In an action sequence, less is more. Provide just enough detail to show the reader what's going on using simple sentences and powerful verbs. Establish anything you need to in advance. Trust the reader to fill in what you judiciously leave out.

NOW YOU TRY: Write an action sequence

Take the action sequence you mapped out earlier in this chapter and write it. When you've finished:

1. Underline all your verbs. Are they strong enough? Replace the ones you feel need strengthening.

2. Examine your sentence structure. Is it appropriate to the feeling you're trying to convey—simple, straightforward if you want the scene to move fast; more complex if you want it to slow down?

3. Are you writing with the camera as close in as you need to? Remember, zooming the camera in heightens intensity and speeds up action; drawing back gives more of a dreamlike feel and slows things down.

4. Is the writing clear and lean?

5. Is there anything in this scene that needs to be established earlier in

the novel? Make a note in your outline to establish that information where you think it belongs.

ON YOUR OWN: Making action

1. Pick a novel you've read in which there was a lot of action. If you can't recall one, pick anything by Michael Connelly or Lisa Scottoline. Skim the last third for an action sequence. Read and analyze it. What's the overall effect of the scene and how does the writer achieve it?

2. Make a plan to learn what you need to in order to write the action sequences in your book. Your plan might include taking a firearms class or observing a class in self-defense.

3. Write action sequences, mapping them out in advance if you like. Use this checklist to guide your work.

__ Use powerful verbs.

__ Use active voice.

__ Use simple sentences.

__ Keep introspection to a minimum unless you're deliberately slowing the action down.

__ Keep description to a minimum unless you're deliberately slowing the action down.

__ Make all actions have reactions.

__ Establish in advance anything that will bog down the scene.

CHaPtEr 20:
puzzling it out:
writing reflection

"In mysteries, the penny-drop comes when the
sleuth hears, sees, tastes, smells, touches, or
otherwise experiences something that when combined (usually mentally) with a fact or facts
gleaned earlier tells the detective that 'til
now, everyone has been following false leads."

—TOM SAWYER
head writer/producer of *Murder, She Wrote*

A mystery is about solving a puzzle. Puzzle solving requires *thinking*. So
throughout your novel, especially after suspense and action sequences,
take time to pause, turn down the heat, and let your character (and the
reader) think about what's happened so far and put together the clues.

It's all about getting to the *Aha! moment* when the sleuth realizes the
significance of something which, up to that point, has seemed unimportant.
For example, the *Aha! moment* might be the revelation of a secret that estab-
lishes a character's motive for murder, or it might be the discovery of evidence that explains how a crime was committed. When the metaphorical
bulb lights up inside the sleuth's head, facts and events snap into focus and
the story is propelled forward.

You have two tools for dramatizing reflection. One is through dialogue—
characters discuss what happened and think aloud. Here's where your sidekick and supporting cast become sounding boards for the sleuth. A second
way to dramatize reflection is through internal dialogue—making the reader
privy to your character's thoughts.

REFLECTION IN DIALOGUE

One of the main reasons Sherlock Holmes needs Watson is so he can discuss the case and astound Watson with his mental acumen. Holmes, the master detective and wizard of discernment, appears even more so alongside dense-as-a-stump Watson.

Here's an example of how it works. This conversation between Holmes and Watson occurs near the end of "The Speckled Band":

> "Well, there is at least the curious coincidence of the dates. A ventilator is made, a cord is hung, and a lady who sleeps in the bed dies. Does that not strike you?"
>
> "I cannot as yet see any connection."
>
> "Did you observe anything very peculiar about that bed?"
>
> "No."
>
> "It was clamped to the floor. Did you ever see a bed fastened like that before?"
>
> "I cannot say that I have."
>
> "The lady could not move her bed. It must always be in the same relative position to the ventilator and to the rope—for so we may call it since it was clearly never meant for a bell-pull."
>
> "Holmes," I cried. "I seem to see dimly what you are hinting at. We are only just in time to prevent some subtle and horrible crime."
>
> "Subtle enough, and horrible enough. When a doctor does go wrong, he is the first of criminals. He has nerve and he has knowledge. Palmer and Pritchard were among the heads of their profession. This man strikes deeper still. But we shall have horrors enough before the night is over; for goodness' sake let us have a quiet pipe, and turn our minds for a few hours to something more cheerful."

Though this passage feels a bit wooden by today's standards, every good mystery needs sequences of reflection like this to move the plot forward. Here's what this bit of dialogue accomplishes:

- **Reviewing what happened.** In case the reader missed anything in the preceding tumult, the characters highlight the clues (some may turn out to be red herrings). Here, Holmes points out the coincidence of the dates, the nailed-down bed, and the rope that's not a bell pull.
- **The *Aha!* moment.** The sleuth realizes the significance of a clue. Holmes concludes that the bedroom was arranged in that very peculiar way in order to facilitate a murder.

- **Reacting.** The characters sense the gravity of the implications. Even Watson gets it: *We are only just in time to prevent some subtle and horrible crime.*
- **Raising questions.** Unanswered questions propel the story forward. In this example, the reader wonders about that sinister rope hanging from the ceiling—how was it used to commit a crime? And what "horrors enough" lie ahead?

Create opportunities for your sleuth to discuss the case and draw conclusions after turning points in the story.

NOW YOU TRY: Analyze reflection in dialogue

In this passage from Jonathan Kellerman's *Twisted*, analyze how Detective Petra Connor and intern Isaac Gomez puzzle out the pattern behind a series of killings.

Think about:

- What clues are explained?
- The *Aha!* moment—what conclusions are drawn?
- Reacting—how does Isaac show his emotional reaction to this train of thought?
- Raising questions—what unanswered questions propel the story forward?

Excerpt from *Twisted*

"There's another discrepancy between Marta and the others. They were beaten to the ground and left there. She was killed on the street but placed in her car. You could look at that as her being treated with a bit more respect. Which would also fit with a killer who knew her well."

He grimaced. "I should have thought of that."

. . .

"That's why it's good to brainstorm," said Petra. They reached Santa Monica Boulevard. Traffic, noise, pedestrians, gay hustlers loitering on corners.

Petra said, "Here's another distinction for Doebbler: She was the first. When Detective Ballou told me he thought Kurt Doebbler's reaction was off, and then after I met Kurt, it got me thinking: What if the bad guy never set out to commit a string of murders. What if he killed Marta for a personal reason and found out he *liked* it? Got himself a hobby. Which brings us back to Kurt."

"A once-a-year hobby," said Isaac.

"An anniversary," she said. "What if June 28 is significant to Kurt because he happened to kill Marta on that day? So he relives it."

He stared at her. "That's brilliant."

REFLECTION IN INTERNAL DIALOGUE

Reflection can also be expressed through internal dialogue. For example, in this passage from Jan Brogan's *A Confidential Source*, reporter Hallie Ahern reflects while she tries to write a news story about a convenience store shooting she witnessed:

> I forced myself to reread my paragraph as an editor might. *Almost instantly*, what did that mean? I erased *almost*, began the next sentence, and halted. Who cared whether it was instantly or almost instantly; Barry was dead. An image flashed in my head: his eyes, frozen in alarm. The handgun on the floor. My fingers retracted from the keyboard, my hands balled into fists.
>
> Another picture, this time: the big man in the khaki parka. The ugly look on his face when I'd apologized for scaring him. He would have killed me if I'd been at the cash register. He'd want to kill me even more if he read my byline, realized I'd been there. That I was the one who had called the police.
>
> The shiver again. This time from lower in my spine. I wondered about the guy in the old navy jacket and gray cap, the hairy guy who'd never turned around. I wasn't entirely sure the two had even been together.

The same goals accomplished with dialogue are accomplished with internal dialogue:

- **Reviewing what happened.** *An image flashed in my head . . .* Ahern remembers the face of the killer, the gun, the man in the khaki parka. Your characters have all their senses at their disposal and can remember sounds, dialogue, smells, tastes, sensations, or emotions.
- **The *Aha!* moment.** *He would have killed me . . .* Ahern realizes how she could easily have been killed and that she's continuing to put herself in danger by writing the eyewitness account. Here's where your character gets to put together the clues and make sense of what happened.
- **Reacting.** *My fingers retracted from the keyboard, my hands balled into fists.* Ahern doesn't have to say, "I was afraid." The reader can see from how she behaves that she is. As your character reflects, allow the memories to trigger an emotional response that you can show the reader.
- **Raising questions.** *I wondered about the guy in the old navy jacket and gray cap . . .* Using internal dialogue to reflect on what has happened provides your reader with more than a summary. Moving point by point, frame by frame, raising questions, and reaching a logical and surprising conclusion should send the investigation forward in a new direction.

ADDING SPICE TO REFLECTION: CONFLICT

Conflict adds an additional dimension to reflection. Conflict can be played out in dialogue (argument, debate) or internal dialogue (disbelief, self-doubt).

Here's an example from Lynne Heitman's *First Class Killing*. PI Alex Shanahan wants to continue with her investigation into a prostitution ring, but her boss pushes back:

> "Please do not suggest to me that you want to open a new front on this investigation."
>
> "No, I want to finish this one. What I learned last night was that Angel has a business problem."
>
> "It would seem so."
>
> "People with business problems need business strategies to solve them."
>
> "Ideally."
>
> "Where do you get a strategy if you can't think one up yourself?"
>
> "Consultants."
>
> "Exactly." I stopped and presented myself for inspection. "You're looking at Angel's new management consultant."
>
> "Oh." He leaned all the way back in his chair. "Oh my."

The source of the disagreement in this example is twofold. First, Shanahan and her boss are opposites—she's a rookie PI and impulsive, he's seasoned and cautious. They also have opposite goals. He wants to get answers as quickly as possible, satisfy his client, and get paid. She wants to close down the prostitution ring operating in the airline where she works.

Here are some examples of the different kinds of conflict you can inject into reflection:

- **Odd couple.** Characters with opposite personalities have different takes on the same evidence. For instance, the older, jaded, male homicide detective pressures the less experienced but smart female medical examiner to highlight evidence that supports his theory about the murder; she points out all the inconsistencies.
- **Opposing desires/pressures.** One character wants to move ahead with the investigation while another character wants to hold back. For instance, a reporter is eager to investigate a recent death that police have labeled a suicide; her editor wants her to stick to covering town politics.
- **Credibility.** Characters argue over the existence of evidence. For instance, an innkeeper hears a scream outside in the middle of the night and sees shadowy shapes moving about in the field; the police officer who finds no evidence of a crime wonders if the innkeeper is dotty.

- **Self-doubt.** The character saw or felt something, then questions his own senses and wonders if he's overreacting, embellishing, or making it up.
- **Deadlines.** A ticking clock adds urgency. The characters argue about whether there's enough time (before the killer strikes again . . . before a kidnapper's deadline runs out . . . before an innocent person is executed).
- **The war within.** The character chokes on a decision he has to make in order to move forward. For example, an attorney has to decide whether violating attorney-client privilege is ever justified, even to catch a killer.
- **Withholding information.** One character tells another what happened but lies or withholds some information. For example, a character might tell her father what's happening in a case but leave out the parts that would make her father worry about her safety; he's no pushover, so he calls her on it.

NOW YOU TRY: Write introspection

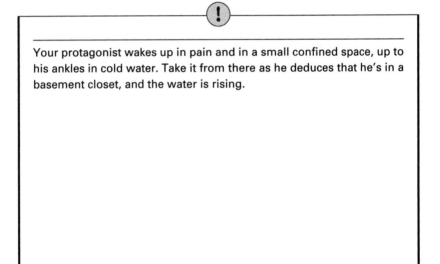

Your protagonist wakes up in pain and in a small confined space, up to his ankles in cold water. Take it from there as he deduces that he's in a basement closet, and the water is rising.

NOW YOU TRY: Plan and write reflection

Review your outline and pick a place where your characters will need to stand back and reflect. Decide how you're going to write that passage:

- Will you use dialogue or internal dialogue?
- Will there be conflict? And if so, what's its source?
- What's the *Aha!* moment?
- What's your point-of-view character's emotion, and how are you going to show it to the reader?
- What unanswered question will propel the reader forward?

!

Now write that scene.

ON YOUR OWN: Time out—writing reflection

1. Pull out a few of your favorite mystery novels and skim for action and suspense sequences. After each one, does the author take time out to let the characters think? Can you find an *Aha!* moment in each reflection sequence?

2. Go through your outline and flag each place you think it would be a good time to have your character sit back and reflect about what happened.

3. Continue writing. Whenever you write a reflection sequence, use this checklist to guide your work:

   __ Use sensory images to bring the memory alive.
   __ Show your character's emotional response.
   __ Write the *Aha!* moment where your character realizes the significance of a clue or impending danger.

   __ End with an open question that propels the reader forward.
   __ Inject conflict (self-doubt, argument) wherever it makes sense.

CHaPtEr 21:
layering in backstory

Suppose you're writing a novel that starts with a brutal rape and murder. In the opening scene, Medical Examiner Renata Ruiz examines the body. The reader doesn't know that Renata grew up dirt poor on a farm in central California, put herself through college, modeled for the *Playboy* college issue to make ends meet, and most important, was the victim of a brutal rapist who also raped and murdered her roommate and best friend. You want to convey all these aspects of her background because, by the end of the novel, you want Renata to triumph on two levels—first, putting this sexual pervert in jail, and second, coming to terms with her own "survivor's guilt."

So, when do you reveal Renata's backstory?

Tell it a little at a time. Too much backstory in the beginning can bog down your novel before you get it off the ground. Initially, your reader may need to know only that Renata is an experienced medical examiner. Then, once you're airborne, slip in more at opportune moments.

The really dramatic information that resonates with this investigation—that Renata was herself a rape victim and her best friend was murdered by the rapist—is best revealed in layers as part of the unfolding drama. You might slip in, early on, that Renata was a crime victim. Later, that she was raped. Later still, that her best friend was raped and murdered. At a major turning point in the novel, perhaps when Renata is about to confront the villain, you might write a vivid flashback that dramatizes the rape or her friend's funeral.

The stronger and more compelling your front story, the more backstory it can hold. Here are three rules of thumb to keep in mind:

- Hold the backstory until your novel is launched.
- Gradually layer in backstory wherever it resonates with your main story, letting the past drama reinforce the drama in the present.
- Tell the backstory in a variety of ways.

There are a number of different strategies for telling that backstory.

BACKSTORY: FIRST-PERSON NARRATOR TELLS ALL

A first-person narrator can break the "fourth wall"—that imaginary barrier between the characters and the audience—and tell the reader about his past. In this an example from Kathy Reichs's *Monday Mourning*, Temperance Brennan enters a courtroom. As she walks up the center aisle she talks to the reader:

> I have testified many times. I have faced men and
> women accused of monstrous crimes. Murder. Rape.
> Torture. Dismemberment. I am always underwhelmed
> by the accused.

Voilà. For the reader who hasn't read the earlier half-dozen or so Temperance Brennan novels, here's a snapshot of her background as an expert witness. Talking directly to the reader like this is an easy and economical way to convey a first-person narrator's background. It's an efficient way to convey facts or downplay some information that will become important later on. But keep in mind, it can be emotionally flat and lack dramatic impact.

BACKSTORY: THIRD-PERSON NARRATOR TELLS ALL

Another simple, straightforward way to tell backstory is to have a third-person narrator tell the reader. Here's an example from Gary Braver's *Elixir*:

> Chris had been as good as his vow. For six years only
> one other person at Darby Pharms knew of his re-
> search. They had worked on the sly—nights and week-
> ends—isolating, purifying, synthesizing, then testing
> the flower extract. And Chris got away with it because

as senior researcher he had complete autonomy in the
lab and could mask requisitions for material and
animals.

The novel continues for several pages, explaining the main character's research to find an antiaging drug. This backstory is delivered in the third
chapter, after Braver has set up and launched his story.

Having a third-person narrator give the reader backstory is effective and
efficient, though not dramatic; it's a good approach to use in small doses
after your story is launched.

BACKSTORY: SLIPPING IT INTO DIALOGUE

An equally simple, somewhat more artful way of layering in backstory is
through dialogue. In this example from *Mansions of the Dead*, Sarah Stewart
Taylor uses dialogue to let her reader know that the protagonist is an expert
on mourning jewelry:

> "Sweeney?" Mrs. Pitman's hesitant voice came over the
> phone. "This is kind of strange, but the Cambridge po-
> lice just called. A Detective Quinn. They need to talk to
> someone who knows about mourning jewelry. I thought
> of you, of course, and they said they want to talk to you
> as soon as possible."

Done well, dialogue that delivers information like this slides by easily. Done
clumsily, it sounds stagy and artificial, as in the excerpt that I made up
below to demonstrate the point:

> "Here's something right up your alley, Digby," Prothero
> said, jabbing his finger at a newspaper article. "You
> know all about poisons. Wasn't your brother killed
> eating poisonous mushrooms? I heard that's why you
> became an expert and wrote that definitive pamphlet
> for the Poison Control Center."
> Digby scanned the story. "Dr. Willem Banks. Died
> of strychnine poisoning. Isn't he that old codger who
> lives in that huge mansion I wanted to buy a few years
> back? Maybe one of my three sisters knew him."

Yes, we get tons of backstory. There it is, in all its glory, wedged into
wooden dialogue. Never force words into a character's mouths like this.
Use dialogue to convey backstory only when it feels natural and works
dramatically.

(!)

Jot down some aspects of your character's life history or professional background that you want to convey to the reader early on in your novel.

Write it as first- or third-person narration.

Write it as dialogue between two characters.

BACKSTORY: FICTIONAL DOCUMENTS

Another way to deliver backstory is through fictional documents—wills, newspaper articles, photographs, letters, school yearbooks, and so on. You can reproduce the "document" or have one of the characters summarize what's in it.

For example, your main character might receive a letter from an old friend, reminiscing about when they were in school together, asking after the main character's family, and reminding the character that the friend once saved his life. Now the friend is calling in his chips and asking a favor.

The letter effectively moves the story along while delivering information about the main character's past.

It's a commonly held belief that mystery readers skip over the fictional documents in mystery novels. They skip the letter, will, or newspaper article in order to get to whatever is happening in the scene. I have no idea if this is true or not, but I've heard it often enough that I offer this word of caution: Keep those fictional documents short, and don't put anything the reader really needs to know in a fictional document and nowhere else.

BACKSTORY: MEMORIES

A dramatic way to tell backstory is as a memory. In this an example from Luiz Alfredo Garcia-Roza's *A Window in Copacabana*, Inspector Espinosa remembers his grandmother:

> He dedicated the following two hours to examining a book that, along with a few hundred others, he'd inherited from his grandmother. Every once in a while his grandmother had felt the need to purge some of the thousands of books piled in two rooms of her apartment, and these were destined for her grandson, who also inherited her habit of stockpiling books. Their styles were different: hers were anarchic piles, his orderly stacks against the wall. They shared a disdain for shelving.

Looking at a book triggers a memory of Espinosa's grandmother. This memory is not essential to the plot but gives the reader insight into Espinosa's character, revealing a contemplative, literate side to this tough police inspector. The "orderly stacks" suggest an orderly mind, and a "disdain for shelving" suggests a man who lives alone and feels no need to conform to conventions.

Here are some examples of what might trigger a memory:

- **What a character says.** *He sounded just like Red, my mentor at the police academy who* . . .
- **How a character looks.** *She had that same look on her face as my first wife, right before she slapped me with divorce papers.*
- **A dream.** *I dreamed I was back in elementary school, fourth grade, Mrs. Joffey standing there, glaring at me bug-eyed, like I had the IQ of a frog* . . .
- **An object.** *Whenever I saw that photograph, I thought of Joe and the day we* . . .
- **A song.** *That was our song. I remember the first time* . . .

Memories conveyed in a sentence to a few paragraphs, strategically sprinkled throughout your novel, enable you to reveal layer after layer of your characters' backstories.

BACKSTORY: EXTENDED FLASHBACK

Another strategy for delivering backstory is to insert an extended flashback. An extended flashback can show how a character's past experience compels him to behave the way he does in the present or to build understanding of how a situation got to be the way it is now.

Here's how William G. Tapply starts a four-page flashback in the second chapter of *Bitch Creek*:

> An hour before sunup on a June morning almost ex-
> actly five years earlier, Calhoun had been creeping
> along the muddy bank of a little tidal creek that emptied
> into Casco Bay just north of Portland. A blush of pink
> had begun to bleed into the pewter sky toward the east.
> The tide was about halfway out, and the water against
> the banks lay as flat and dark as a mug of camp coffee.
> A blanket of fog hung . . .

A tricky part of writing a flashback is handling the time-and-space shift. Notice Tapply does it simply.
- the time shift: *almost exactly five years earlier*
- the space shift: *along the muddy bank of a little tidal creek*

A second tricky part is handling verb tense. If the main part of your novel is written in the present tense (*he "pulls" the trigger . . .*), a flashback is written in the past tense (*he once "killed" a man . . .*). That's easy. But what if the body of your novel is written in the past tense? Logic dictates that the flashback would be written in the past perfect (*he once "had killed" a man . . .*). Notice that the flashback in the example from *Bitch Creek* begins like that, in the past-perfect tense:
- *Calhoun "had" been creeping . . .*
- *A blush of pink "had" begun to bleed . . .*

Had, had, had . . . Past perfect quickly gets cumbersome, and the good news is once you've launched your flashback and oriented the reader by using past perfect a few times, you can revert to the regular past tense, as Tapply does in the excerpt:
- *The tide "was" about halfway out . . .*

At the end of a flashback, once again you need to cue the reader: Back to the present! To show the transition, insert the past perfect a time or two at the end of the flashback; when you're out of the flashback and back in the main story, revert to past tense.

Here's an example of a sentence that signals a transition back:

> She *had* never called him. At the time, he *had* thought it
> was odd. Now he *wasn't* so sure. He *got up* and *headed . . .*

An extended flashback is a dramatic way to tell the reader about past events, but it interrupts the narrative flow of your main story. Delivered at the wrong time, a flashback can derail the current action and waste any momentum you've gathered. Delivered at the right dramatic moment, a flashback enhances and deepens your story.

NOW YOU TRY: Put backstory into a memory or flashback

(**!**)

Jot down an event in your character's past that you want to convey dramatically to the reader.

Write the flashback as internal dialogue—a memory, triggered by something in the present. Write the trigger, then the memory.

Write an extended flashback. Remember to orient the reader to the time-and-place shift, shift verb tense (present to past; past to past perfect), and segue back to the main story at the end.

ON YOUR OWN: Layering in backstory

1. Read the first three chapters of a popular mystery novel. Make a list of the backstory elements, and notice how the writer chooses to convey each.

2. Each time you layer in some backstory, remember that the stronger and more compelling your front story, the more backstory it can tolerate. Make a conscious decision about how you're going to tell each layer of backstory:
   a. narrator tells (internal dialogue)
   b. dialogue
   c. a fictional document
   d. a burst of memory
   e. an extended flashback

3. Continue writing. Whenever you tell backstory, use this checklist to guide your work:

__ Be sure this is the dramatically appropriate spot to deliver this layer of backstory.

__ Pick the most appropriate method to deliver the backstory (narrator tells, fictional document, dialogue, short memory, or extended flashback).

__ Trigger memories with something in the present (the sound of a car backfiring: the memory of gunshots; the sight of a woman arguing with her husband: the memory of arguments with an ex-wife; the smell of cotton candy: the memory of a childhood trip to a carnival).

__ For flashbacks: Orient the reader to the time-and-place shift; shift verb tense (present to past; past to past-perfect); segue back to the main story at the end.

CHaPtEr 22:
writing the coda

"One of the pleasures of a mystery is the contest between the reader and the sleuth as to who will solve the puzzle first. The reader wants to lose this game, but he doesn't want to find out he was duped by not being given all the information along with the detective."

—JUDITH GREBER
(aka Gillian Roberts)

Mystery novels usually end with a coda, a final scene that's primarily reflection. This is the denouement, which contains the final resolution or clarification of the plot. Coming after the book's final exciting climax, the coda is like a cleansing breath after vigorous exercise. It's a chance to tie up loose ends.

The coda might be nothing more than dialogue between two characters, talking about what happened. It might be an extended internal dialogue in which your main character thinks about what happened. It might include a lighthearted scene between your protagonist and the love interest. By the end of the coda, all of your plot's puzzle pieces should fit snugly together.

THE FINAL CODA: AN EXAMPLE

Here's part of the ending of Raymond Chandler's *The Big Sleep*, a novel about pornography and blackmail and one of the first classics of the "hard-boiled" genre. As you read, think about how the main character's introspection puts the story in perspective and provides a sense of ending.

> I got into my car and drove off down the hill.
>> What did it matter where you lay once you were dead?
>> In a dirty sump or in a marble tower on top of a high hill?
>> You were dead, you were sleeping the big sleep, you were

not bothered by things like that. Oil and water were the same as wind and air to you. You just slept the big sleep, not caring about the nastiness of how you died or where you fell. Me, I was part of the nastiness now. Far more a part of it than Rusty Regan was. But the old man didn't have to be. He could lie quiet in his canopied bed, with his bloodless hands folded on the sheet, waiting. His heart was a brief, uncertain murmur. His thoughts were as gray as ashes. And in a little while he too, like Rusty Regan, would be sleeping the big sleep.

On the way downtown I stopped at a bar and had a couple of double Scotches. They didn't do me any good. All they did was make me think of Silver-Wig, and I never saw her again.

Not much happens here. Detective Philip Marlowe walks out of a house, drives to a bar, and has a couple of drinks. The action itself is irrelevant, except to provide a foil for Marlowe's final bitter reflections.

But these paragraphs provide an elegiac coda as Marlowe leaves the story behind, figuratively and literally (*I got in my car . . .*). He contemplates "the big sleep" to which fellow characters have gone and ruminates about the meaning of death (*What did it matter where you lay . . .*) and how he's become tainted by what's happened (*I was part of the nastiness now . . .*). He stops at a bar for two double scotches and remembers "Silver-Wig," the girl who helped him dodge the big sleep (*. . . and I never saw her again*).

PURPOSE OF THE CODA

The final coda should not be a long scene, belaboring every point in the story or giving a cumbersome synopsis. Three to five pages is usually sufficient. No new plot strands; no new characters. Here are some of the purposes it can serve:

- **Resolve the major conflicts.** Resolve the internal conflicts—the dilemmas your main character had to deal with, perhaps reconciling something from the past. Resolve external conflicts—the obstacles your protagonist had to overcome in order to find the killer.
- **Account for the facts.** This is your last chance to make sure all the important facts are accounted for—for example, why the villain did what he did and who was hiding what secrets.
- **Tell what happened next.** Let the reader in on what's happened since the book's climactic action sequence. Did the protagonist survive the wounds he suffered in the final shootout? Has the villain been arraigned? Were the stolen jewels returned to the museum?

- **Resolve the subplots . . .** The coda is a good place to put the finishing touches on any subplots, such as a romance or character rivalry.
- **. . . or leave a subplot dangling.** You may want to leave a subplot involving your cast of supporting characters dangling. For example, you might have left the detective on the brink of connecting with a love interest, or you might have left the sleuth relegated to desk duty, fighting charges of insubordination at work. Dangling subplots can be carried forward into the next series novel.
- **Get the sleuth's take on the case.** Is she satisfied, dissatisfied? Does she feel justice was served? Does this change her in any fundamental way—show that there is hope in this world, or only despair?
- **Sail off into the sunset . . .** The final scene can be a happily-ever-after ending with your characters setting out into a world that's safer because evil has been defeated.
- **. . . or leave your hero off balance . . .** The final scene can leave your protagonist feeling unsettled, with issues to be resolved (in the next book!). Maybe the killer was captured, but the person who put him up to it got away. Maybe your hero did something questionable that he's going to have to live with (killed someone, told lies, slept with the enemy).
- **. . . or a final shocker.** You save a final plot twist for the coda. In *Delusion*, that's where we revealed the identity of the murder victim's lover.
- **Leave the reader satisfied.** The ending need not be a happy one, but it should be satisfying.

FINAL WORDS

The last lines of your book should provide closure. One way of doing this is to show your protagonist looking back and looking forward, like the two-faced Janus from Roman mythology, putting the past to rest and moving on.

Here are examples of final lines from best-selling mysteries that show the protagonist moving on:

> With a deep sigh, George put his car in gear and slowly edged back on to the Scardale road. No matter what the future might hold, it was time to take the first step on the road to burying the past, this time forever. (*A Place of Execution* by Val McDermid)

> Overhead, the sky was a brilliant blue. The hot Miami sun warmed hearts and minds and points south. A late-afternoon breeze rattled in the palms and caused the water of Biscayne Bay to gently lap against the boat hull. Life was good in Florida. And okay, so I was going back to working on cars. Truth is, I was pretty happy with it. I was looking forward to working on Hooker's

equipment. I'd seen his undercarriage and it was damn sweet. (*Metro Girl* by Janet Evanovich)

She walked away from that building of captive souls. Ahead was her car, and the road home. She did not look back. (*Body Double* by Tess Gerritsen)

Spend time crafting your final sentences. Make them memorable, and leave readers looking forward to your next book.

NOW YOU TRY: Plan the final coda

A final coda is a workhorse of a scene, so a little housekeeping is needed to make sure it has everything needed to provide a satisfying conclusion to your novel. Make a list of everything you want the ending to accomplish:

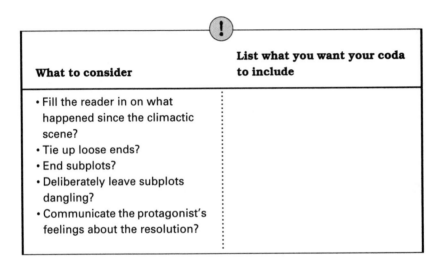

What to consider	List what you want your coda to include
• Fill the reader in on what happened since the climactic scene? • Tie up loose ends? • End subplots? • Deliberately leave subplots dangling? • Communicate the protagonist's feelings about the resolution?	

ON YOUR OWN: The final coda

1. Decide the backdrop for the coda—what action will take place while your characters reflect on what happened?

2. Write the coda. Use this checklist to guide you:

— Tell what's happened since the last climactic scene.

— Summarize the resolution, and communicate the protagonist's feelings about it.

— Resolve all plots and subplots.

— Tell what happened since the climactic final scene.

— Make the final lines sing.

PaRt 3:
revising

Introduction

"What's nice about writing is that nothing's
set in stone till it's finished. It's only then
that you hang yourself out to dry."

—EVAN HUNTER
(aka Ed McBain)

When I type *The End* on a first draft, I go out and celebrate. The hard part is over, and now the fun begins.

Not everyone shares my enthusiasm for revision. But whether you love it, loath it, or something in between, one thing we can all agree upon: No one writes a publishable first draft. Plot and characterization are bound to need fixing; word choice, spelling, and grammar will surely need tweaks.

So when you've finished the manuscript, take a moment to pat yourself on the back. You finished the first draft. Take a week or two off to recuperate.

Then begin to revise. There's no point to line editing what you're going to cut, so work from large to small. Make the big changes first, the ones that cut across the manuscript; then polish the small stuff.

Here's a revision strategy:

1. Prepare to slash and burn: Create an "Out" file. It can be hard to "murder your darlings"—to delete those cherished words you labored over. So make it easier. Instead of throwing words away, set them aside for safekeeping. Create a file where you can paste the sentences and paragraphs you cut from your manuscript. Change your mind later and you'll know where to find them. Don't be surprised when your Out file starts to grow—my Out file for *Guilt* was 140 pages long by the time I finished the 310-page manuscript.

2. Take a break. You've run the spell checker, fussed with the margins, and altered the font to see how that changes the page count. One day you love it, the next day all you see are flaws. You know the truth lies somewhere in between. In order to revise effectively, you need perspective, so print the whole thing out and take a break. For a week or two at least, go fishing, build a birdhouse, take a trip to New Jersey—anything to keep you from picking at the manuscript.

3. Fly high over your manuscript; identify the big changes needed. Re-read the manuscript and get feedback from some trusted readers. Compile a list of major revisions needed such as plot shifts, character adjustments, cutting in the dull spots.

4. Make the big fixes. Rewrite, handling the biggest issues first and working your way down to smaller ones.

5. Fly low over your manuscript; identify the small changes needed. Read your revision and do a careful line edit. Blue-pencil errors in spelling, grammar, and punctuation; improve your word choices; tweak dialogue; clarify ambiguities.

6. Make the small fixes. Revise, from page one to the end, making the small fixes needed.

How long should you spend on revision? We spent a year completing a draft of our first mystery novel, *Amnesia*, then a year revising it to get it good enough to send out to agents. In between agent and publisher rejections, we spent another year revising. All in all, the novel went through at least twenty revisions, each of which involved at least one major change, and we both had full-time day jobs at the time. We were thrilled when, at around the time we were ready to throw in the towel, St. Martin's offered us a two-book contract. Then we freaked out when we realized: We had only one year to write and revise the second book.

These days it takes us about two months to plan and five months to write a three-hundred-page first draft, then another two months to revise it so it's good to go. Like most series authors, we've been on a-book-a-year treadmill.

How do you know when a manuscript is finished? I rely on Don's and my gut feelings about whether it's as good as we can get it. Then I ask other writers I trust to read the manuscript. For our first two series novels, we hired a freelance editor to go through it as well.

We don't give the manuscript to our agent until it's been thoroughly revised, and it doesn't go to our editor until we've done the revisions our agent suggests.

Is there such a thing as too much revision? There's certainly such a thing as revising the wrong stuff. That's what happens when you hear a writer say, *I rewrote it and sucked the life out of it.* At one point while we were revising *Amnesia*, we eliminated Peter's mother from the book—an agent who had rejected the book hated her. Louise Quayle, the agent who took us on, pitched a fit. Turned out Mom was her favorite character. So we put her back in (thank goodness for that Out file) but sanded her rough edges. Louise was right. Mom has turned out to be one of the strengths of the series.

The trick is to figure out what's not working and fix it, figure out what is working and don't mess with it. The chapters in this section provide advice for how to thoroughly revise your manuscript so it's ready to be launched down streets far meaner than any conjured in a mystery novel.

CHaPtEr 23

flying high:
fixing plot and character

"Revision is what separates the pros from
those who always wanted to write if only they
had the time."

—CAROLYN WHEAT

It's tempting to open up your document and start editing, tweaking word
choices and punching up sentences.

Sure, you could do that, or you could take a more strategic approach
and look first at the big picture. Looking at the big picture is not an easy
task when we're talking about a 250- to 350-page manuscript. This chapter
suggests ways to help you by flying high over your manuscript, doing a surface check, then diving down successive times, focusing on different aspects
of the novel.

After that you'll be ready to make the big revisions your manuscript
needs. I recommend three techniques to doing this:

- Reread from start to finish, examining the main plot and central
  character.
- Create a scene-by-scene outline and analyze the chronology and
  pacing.
- Take multiple, selective read-throughs, leapfrogging through your
  manuscript looking at subplots and characters.

REREAD FROM START TO FINISH: EXAMINE
THE PLOT AND CHARACTERS

After you've let your manuscript cool for a few weeks, reread it from start to
finish. During the read-through, write notes to yourself and keep a running
list of suggestions for changes. Pay special attention to these aspects of your
novel:

THE MAIN PLOT

1. Does your plot unfold logically, without resorting to coincidence or the supernatural?
2. Are there at least two major plot twists where attention is diverted to an innocent suspect or where the murder seems to be something that it was not?
3. Have you planted all the clues in the story so the solution is plausible?
4. Have you camouflaged the clues well, and distracted the reader's attention with red herrings, so the ending is a surprise?
5. Have you played fair with the reader and shared what your point-of-view character knows?
6. By the final page, have you explained whodunit, why, and how, and tied up all the loose ends?

POINT OF VIEW

1. Whether you've chosen to write in the first person or third, from single or multiple points of view, have you adhered consistently to your choices?
2. Can you strengthen your narrator's voice and make it more consistent throughout the novel?

THE MAIN CHARACTER

1. Have you established why solving this particular crime matters to this character (without a backstory dump in the first act)?
2. By the end, have you resolved your character's inner journey as well as solved the mystery?
3. Does your character actively do the detecting to solve the mystery?
4. Near the end, is there a satisfying confrontation in which the protagonist defeats the villain?
5. Have you given your character a sufficiently rich inner life, so the reader knows both how she behaves and also what she thinks?
6. Are your character's dialogue, inner dialogue, and behavior throughout the book consistent with his personality?
7. Are all the heroics on your character's part consistent with who he is?

THE VILLAIN

1. Have you established a convincing reason why the villain committed this crime?
2. Have you given the villain a sufficiently major role in the novel?
3. Did you make the villain seem innocent through most of the novel, so the revelation of guilt came as a surprise?
4. Did you lay the groundwork for guilt so the revelation seems plausible?

CHRONOLOGY CHECK USING A
SCENE-BY-SCENE OUTLINE

A scene-by-scene outline is a useful tool for looking at the big picture. While I'm rereading my manuscript, I put together this outline. It contains brief descriptions of the major plot points in each scene, plus the basic chronology of the story.

The example below is the beginning of the final scene-by-scene outline for *Delusion*.

Chapter	Scene	Elapsed time	Season/ day/time	Main plot points
1	1	Week 1 Day 1	Sunday early (late summer)	Annie & Peter in bed; phone call from Chip asking for Peter's help
2	2		Continued	Drive to Weston; meet Nick Babikian; find Lisa Babikian murdered; call police
3	3		Continued	Police arrive; Det. Boley questions Nick
	4		3:00	Annie & Peter leave Nick's house; newspaper photo taken
4	5	Week 1 Day 3	Tuesday late morning	Jail—interview 1 with Nick; Peter thinks he sees his wife's murderer Ralston Bridges
5	6		Tuesday evening	Meet Chip and Annie at Inman Lounge; Annie finds flyer in bathroom
	7		Hour later	Peter goes home— mother freaked out; she tells Peter she got 'package' a few weeks earlier
6	8	Week 1 Day 4	Wednesday morning	Interview Teitlebaum; see duck boots, newly planted bushes

Keep your final scene-by-scene outline spare. Too much detail and you defeat the purpose of this tool, which is to give you a bird's-eye view of your novel.

Once you've laid out your entire book in this table, problems with your novel's timeline will pop out at you. For example, if you've written a scene that takes place on a "Monday," and "the next day" your character is reading the comics in the Sunday paper, you know you've got a problem.

Here are some different kinds of chronology issues to check for:

- **Continuity errors.** Check that your novel's clock and calendar are logical and consistent from scene to scene. At the end of the book, your hero looks back and remembers the murder that took place in the opening chapter was "six weeks ago"; check how long ago it really was.
- **Cluttered days.** Be sure you haven't packed twenty hours worth of events between sunrise and sunset. If you've overfilled time, revise to spread out the events.
- **Snowing in summer.** Make sure the weather is right for that time of year and geographic location. If your characters are running around Phoenix in August, be sure they're kvetching about the heat.
- **Sunrise/sunset.** Check that the sun goes down and comes up when it should. If your character is coming home at 6:30 P.M. in February in the northern hemisphere, it's dark out.
- **The domino effect.** A chronology fix in one scene may require you to fix the chronology in surrounding scenes.

PACING CHECK USING A SCENE-BY-SCENE OUTLINE

Does the novel bog down in places, or does nonstop action go on for pages on end, leaving your reader numb? Analyze your scene-by-scene outline to pinpoint the source of these pacing issues.

Get a pink, a yellow, and a blue highlighting marker. Then highlight the main plot points in the outline to indicate the intensity of the scene:

- blue for primarily narrative, basic investigation, and reflection
- yellow for rising suspense
- pink for action and plot twists

Then stand back and see what you've got. A well-paced novel has rising and falling tension; scenes with high suspense and action are modulated by scenes of investigation and reflection. Plot twists are spaced out.

If you have scene after scene coded blue, you may want to look at ratcheting up the suspense somewhere in there. If you have scene after scene coded yellow, you may want to modulate the pace by inserting a scene or two of reflection. If all your pink moments are bunched up together, you might want to think about restructuring your novel to space them out.

SELECTIVE READ-THROUGHS

A selective read-through is where you leapfrog through your manuscript, reading and evaluating related passages. It's a good way to help you differentiate plot issues from character issues.

Your scene-by-scene outline provides a useful guide for selecting scenes to reread, each time through.

• **Read through by subplot.** Start with the largest subplot and move on to smaller ones. Look at these issues:
- Check that each subplot has a beginning, middle, and end.
- Each subplot should be either resolved or deliberately left unresolved.
- Consider whether each subplot can be eliminated without damaging the rest of the story; if so, delete it.

• **Read through by character.** Start with the character that has the largest role in your novel, and move on to the ones that play more secondary roles. Look at these issues:
- Does the character have a distinctive look and feel? How can you shade the character's dialogue and mannerisms to make the character more vivid without creating a cliché?
- Is the character too much of a stereotype? How can you sand the character's edges to make the character more three-dimensional?
- Does this character change? How can you show the change more effectively?
- Is this character hiding something? How can you reveal it more effectively?
- Can any character be eliminated without damaging the rest of the story? If so, delete that character.

ON YOUR OWN: Flying high, identifying the big issues

1. Reread your manuscript and make a list of changes needed.

2. Create a scene-by-scene outline using this format. Use the outline on page 203 as a guide to check the chronology and pacing of your novel; add to your list of needed revisions.

3. Selectively read through the manuscript, each time looking at a particular subplot or individual characters. Add to your list of needed revisions.

4. Prioritize revisions, starting with big issues that cut across the book, then issues that affect a single chapter or scene.

5. Revise.

CHaPtEr 24:

flying low:
polishing scenes and sentences

"I cut adjectives, adverbs, and every word which is there just to make an effect. Every sentence which is there just for the sentence."

—GEORGES SIMENON

You've made the big changes your manuscript needs. You've got a killer story. All the twists and turns in the plot are tuned to perfection. Every clue and red herring is in place. Your characters are as entertaining and interesting as you can make them. Now you're ready to fly low and examine every scene, every paragraph, every sentence, and polish that manuscript. Some final polishing can be done on screen, reading and editing directly in the electronic file. But there's no substitute for reading the printed manuscript. Somehow, errors that slip past on the computer screen seem to pop off the printed page. Expect to go through your manuscript at least three times to get the job done.

FIXING GRAMMAR, SPELLING, AND PUNCTUATION

"Don't publishers fix grammar and spelling mistakes?" an unpublished writer once asked me. Sure they do. But leave spelling and grammar errors in your manuscript, and it's an invitation for an editor to jump to the conclusion that you can't write your way out of a paper bag. Your goal should be a manuscript that's grammatically perfect and free of errors in punctuation and spelling before you send it out into the world. Here are some tasks to get you there:

• **Run the spell checker**. The electronic spell checker that comes with your word processing program will find and fix obvious typos.

• **Run the grammar checker**. I know, the grammar checker is a pain in the behind because it flags all kinds of "problems" that aren't problems at all. For instance, it'll want to fix all your sentence fragments. Dialogue is full of them, as it should be. Run the grammar checker anyway, and skip over those non-problem problems. Along the way, it'll find problems you might otherwise miss—like subject-noun agreement, missing question marks, or missing quotation marks.

• **Read and edit**. Read your manuscript carefully in order to find the errors your word processing software misses.

• **Have someone line edit for you**. If you're not great at catching spelling and grammatical errors, give the manuscript to someone who is. Have that person mark up a printout. Make the changes yourself. You'll get a lesson in spelling and grammar, and you decide which changes to make and which to leave as is.

PUMP UP THE VERBS

Throughout the manuscript, especially in suspense and action scenes, pay special attention to your verb choices.

• **Vary physical reactions**. Look out for characters who are constantly responding by smiling, frowning, nodding, or shaking their heads. The occasional smile or headshake is fine, but the rest of the time, try to come up with more telling and dramatic ways of showing a character's response. Here are three examples from Carol O'Connell's *Winter House*:

> "No." She shivered slightly, as if awakening and shaking off dreams. "No, I don't."

> "Was she *insane?*" Bitty's hand flew up to cover her mouth, as if she had just committed a social faux pas, calling attention to an infirmity in front of a cripple.

> "You what?" The vacuum cleaner switched off, and Mrs. Ortega observed a moment of silent disbelief.

• **Replace bland verbs**. Some verbs are bland and generic. Whenever you find one of them holding down a sentence, consider replacing it with a verb that more clearly shows what's happening.

Examples of bland verbs

is	make	take
get	move	watch
have	put	go
look	see	

Here is a sentence with a bland verb, and some examples of alternate versions:

Bland verb	Stronger versions
She *was* in the hall.	She *stood* in the hall.
	She *paced* in the hall.
	She *lounged* in the hall.
	She *lingered* in the hall.
	She *cooled her heels* in the hall.

• **Pick the verb that best conveys action and attitude**. Tweak the verb choice and action takes on an entirely different meaning. For example, take this sentence with generic verbs:

> He *got out* of his car and *went* to the front door.

By tweaking the verb choices, you convey an entirely different sense of what's taking place. For example, if you want to show a man on a mission:

> He *stepped* from his car and *marched* up the front walk.

If you want to show a drunk coming home from a debauched overnight:

> He *heaved* himself from his car and *stumbled* up the front walk.

On the other hand, if this is a man who's trying to beat the clock:

> He *leapt* from his car and *raced* up the front walk.

Only you know what you're trying to convey. Pick the verbs that show the action and attitude you're aiming for.

• **Don't get carried away**. A word of caution: Don't get too creative and mangle a perfectly good sentence. For example, stick with the generic *He got out of his car and went to the front door* rather than this purple alternative:

> He *exploded* from his car and *thundered* up the front walk.

"Exploded" suggests flying body parts, and "thunder" is a sound, not a quick movement. These verbs don't work in this context.

• **Ferret out -ing verbs**. Action is stronger if it's conveyed with the active form of the verb. For example:

> He was racing to the car.
> He raced to the car.

With the active verb, *raced*, the sentence feels more direct, the action more active. To find the -ing verbs in your manuscript, use the *Find* feature of your word processor. Enter "ing " (with the trailing blank space) and click Find to locate words -ing verbs in the middle of sentences. Enter "ing." (with the trailing period) to locate -ing verbs at the end of sentences. You won't want to remove every -ing verb from your manuscript. Look at each one and ask yourself: Would this sentence be stronger using the active form of the verb? If so, revise.

WEED OUT —LY ADVERBS

Writers sometimes try to pump up bland verbs with -ly adverbs (walked quickly, sat lazily, moved painstakingly). Don't. Here are two ways to revise a verb-adverb combo:
- **Replace with a verb that better conveys the action being taken**. Ambled, marched, shuffled, trundled, staggered, stumbled, goose-stepped—these can all be used to show how someone walked.
- **Replace with more descriptive action**. It takes more words, but the dramatic impact is much stronger. For example:

> **Verb-adverb combo**
> He moved painstakingly.

> **Revision with more descriptive action**
> He grimaced and held his side as he hunched forward
> and took one step, then another.

To find -ly adverbs in your manuscript, use the *Find* feature of your word processor. Enter "ly " (with the trailing blank space) and click Find to locate adverbs embedded in sentences. Enter "ly." (with the trailing period) to find -ly adverbs at the ends of sentences. As each adverb comes up, evaluate whether you want to leave it as is or revise.

PUMP UP THE DIALOGUE

Read passages of dialogue aloud to yourself to identify problem areas.
- **If it sounds wooden and artificial** . . . Revise it. Dialogue should sound like someone talking. Sentence fragments and slang belong in dialogue.
- **If it goes on for too long** . . . Cut some of the dialogue and summarize instead.
- **If characters sound alike** . . . Revise to give each character a unique voice. Shape the character's personality through careful word choice and sentence structure as well as content.
- **If it sounds flat and uninteresting** . . . Choose more appropriate words; use more physical presencing to show characters' emotions.
- **If it's unproductive** . . . Kill unnecessary chitchat. Get rid of any dialogue that doesn't serve your story.

PLAY WITH ATTRIBUTION AND ACTION
THAT ACCOMPANY DIALOGUE

Dialogue is more than the words that are in quotes. There's the attribution (he said) and the physical action that goes along with it. Here are some tips for revising those aspects of dialogue:

- **Said and asked**. These are two bland verbs that you should *not* be weeding from your manuscript. *Said* and *asked* provide invisible service to dialogue and should only occasionally be replaced with fancier verbs (exclaimed, denied, demanded, churbled) that can be intrusive.
- **"Help me," she gasped.** Verbs like gasped, hummed, or shuddered sometimes get stuck in the place of "said." The problem is, these words don't have anything to do with the act of speaking. A simple fix is to put the nontalking action in a sentence separate from the dialogue. *"Help me." She gasped.* Another fix is to relegate the action to its own phrase: *"Help me," she said, and gasped.*
- **Who's talking?** Whenever you write "he said," or "she said," it should be crystal clear to the reader who *he* or *she* is. If it isn't, then say who's talking: "I don't think so," *Linda said.* Or show who's talking with action alongside the dialogue: *Linda folded her hands.* "I don't think so."
- **Eliminate attribution wherever possible**. Once you get a back-and-forth going between two characters, you don't need *Val said/Ian said* because it's obvious to the reader that the speakers are taking turns.
- **Break up dialogue with bits of action**. You can alter the dramatic impact of dialogue by breaking it up with movement and physical detail. Below are three versions of identical content. Read them and think about which one is most powerful:

> "Are you going to leave me? Because I need to know now." She stood in the doorway, hands on her hips.

> She stood in the doorway, hands on her hips. "Are you going to leave me? Because I need to know now."

> "Are you going to leave me?" She stood in the doorway, hands on her hips. "Because I need to know now."

I think the last one is the strongest. Why? Because the reader gets a picture of this woman's stance just before she says *Because I need to know*. The placement of the action reinforces the words, pumps up the drama, and makes that final line of dialogue seem more confrontational. Play with of bits of dialogue, attribution, and physical presencing in your prose to see what arrangement works best.

NOW YOU TRY: Combine dialogue and action

Dialogue: "Don't move. If you do, I'm going to have to shoot you."

Action: The gun trembled as he gripped it with both hands.

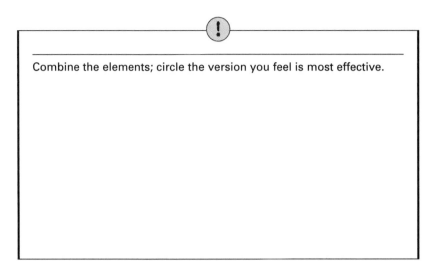

Combine the elements; circle the version you feel is most effective.

WEED OUT CLICHÉS

A cliché is a phrase that's been so overused that it feels trite. Unfortunately, even the best word processor won't find these. That's too bad, because my first drafts end up riddled with them. I'm forever having characters *batten down the hatches*, or *chomp at the bit*, or feel *cool as a cucumber*.

If you have a character who's a pompous windbag, it's fine to let him spout clichés in his dialogue. But strew them in your narrative and you're the one who comes off looking like a bag of wind.

Clichés often sneak in when you're trying to be eloquent or smart. Inspect the metaphors and similes in your writing for clichés. Then:

- **Replace clichés with fresh, new images or metaphors.** Here are three examples of some nonclichés from *Citizen Vince* by Jess Walter:

  > Game over and Vince is flush, counting a roll of bills as big as a pair of socks.

  > Vince can feel his train of thought getting away.

  > Regan's kid looks like a bookkeeper approaching middle age, just this side of respectability, even in a coat and tie.

- **Replace clichés with more descriptive terms.** Instead of telling us that a character "ate like a pig," show the gravy stains on his tie, the open-mouthed chewing, the fist-held fork. Show him hunched over the plate and grunting.

STRONG STARTS, STRONG FINISHES

Readers who skim through the middles of scenes land with a thump on the first and last sentences. Initial and final impressions matter, they linger in the reader's mind, and are worth your time to wordsmith.

Here are some places to focus your attention:

- **Page 1, paragraph 1**
  - Does your book open with a strong first line?
  - Strong first paragraph?
  - Strong first scene?

- **Start and end of each scene**
  - Does each scene start with a strong opening line and paragraph?
  - Do you establish early on in each scene where we are, when it is, and which characters are present?
  - Does each scene feel finished at the end—either with a settled or cliff-hanger ending?

- **First-time setting**
  - The first time each interior or exterior setting is used, is it described and brought to life?
  - Is the setting consistent each time your story returns there?

- **First-time character**
  - Physical presence should be established and expressed with a few telling details whenever a new character appears on the page.
  - Is that character's appearance, behavior, and dialogue consistent each time that character reappears?

- **Last page, last paragraph**
  - Does your book end with a strong final scene?
  - Strong final paragraph?
  - Strong final line?

LOOK FOR TICS

We all have images or actions that we overuse. In my prose, I tend to use the word *shrouded* whenever something in a scene is covered over or shadowy. In a novel I read not long ago, the writer described several of the female characters and a dog as *petite*.

The better, more striking, and unusual an image or turn of phrase, the more the reader will notice when you overuse it. Find your own overused words and expressions and replace them.

CONSISTENCY

It's in the details, all kind of details that cry out for consistency. Read your manuscript carefully with an eye for detail.

- **Continuity**. Does a character stand up from a chair and then, two paragraphs later, stand up again? Do two characters drink wine, and only one wine glass ends up in the sink? Does a coat that gets hung up when a character comes into a room show up folded over the back of a chair when he leaves? These kinds of details seem insignificant, but readers notice.
- **Geography**. If you're using real locations, check that the details are correct. Make sure there really is a Starbucks on the corner where your characters have coffee.
- **Time frame**. Your time frame should be logical and consistent. A scene that takes place in the morning shouldn't end with car headlights shifting across the living room window. Don't make your character drive an hour to get somewhere that's really four hours away.
- **Names**. Be consistent about what you call each character. Suppose that in scene one, you write: "Patricia opened the door." From then on, the narrative should refer to her as "Patricia"—not "Pat," "Patty," "the accountant," or "Miss Vozelle." Other characters should be consistent in how they refer to her in dialogue, too. Her son might call her "Mommy," and her mother might call her "Patty-Joe."

POINT-OF-VIEW BREACHES

If you're telling the story from your protagonist's point of view, make sure every scene is written with the protagonist as the narrator.

If you're telling the story from multiple points of view, the point-of-view character can shift from one scene to the next, but it should never slide around within a scene. Stick to a single narrator in each scene.

Look for point-of-view slips and clean them up.

ON YOUR OWN: Flying low, a checklist

Use this list when you're ready to fly low, revising the details.

WEED OUT:

- __ Spelling, grammar, punctuation errors
- __ Overused images, actions, turns of phrase, or verbs
- __ Clichés
- __ -ing verbs, -ly adverbs
- __ Wooden, artificial-sounding dialogue
- __ Over-long passages of dialogue
- __ Unnecessary chitchat
- __ Unnecessary *he said/she said*
- __ Inconsistencies in time, place, and naming
- __ Optimal placement of attribution and action with dialogue

POLISH:

___ Make each major character's dialogue distinctive.

___ Break up dialogue with bits of action.

___ Wordsmith the beginnings and endings of scenes.

___ Describe and establish each setting, the first time it appears.

___ Describe and establish each character, the first time he or she appears.

___ Keep the point of view from sliding.

CHaPtEr 25:
hearing criticism, finding your own fix

> "I hated this book! The writing is so dense it is like trying to read pea soup. The characters were confusing and undeveloped, and the plot . . . was there one?"
>
> —AN ANONYMOUS READER
> reviews a mystery novel on Barnesandnoble.com

All of us find it difficult to take criticism, especially after having labored for months and poured heart and soul into a manuscript. Give it to a reader and what you want to hear is an unqualified "Wow! Your book is more thrilling than *The Da Vinci Code* and better written than *The Maltese Falcon*." Instead you hear, "Well, I'm not too sure about the ending." Or "Why is your main character so annoying?" Or my favorite: "I don't usually read books like this, so maybe that's why I didn't get it . . . I mean, why doesn't she just call the police?"

You'll find yourself wanting to interrupt, jump up and down on the table, and explain what you were aiming for. You'll want to yank your gentle reader by the collar and say, "Yeah, right, I'd like to see you try to write a novel."

Worse still, you'll defend your book so loudly that you won't hear what this well-meaning soul, whose only major misstep in life thus far has been offering to read your manuscript, is trying to tell you. You owe it to yourself, and to anyone who's generous enough to critique your manuscript, to at least listen to and try to understand the feedback.

TIPS FOR TAKING CRITICISM

Here are some tips to help you hear what readers are telling you:
- **Don't interrupt**. To get the most out of a critique, you have to hear and understand what the person is saying. If you keep interrupting,

explaining what you were trying to do, and getting defensive, you prevent yourself from hearing the criticism. Remember, listening doesn't mean you agree or have to do everything your reader suggests. It's up to you which criticisms you decide to address. But you owe it to yourself and your reader to shut up and listen.

- **Ask clarifying questions**. If you're not sure, ask. If your reader says, "I loved the book," ask what the good parts were. If your reader says, "That character seemed flighty," ask for examples of where that character seemed flighty. If your reader says, "I didn't really understand the ending," ask the reader to summarize how your novel ended so you can see how it was misunderstood.
- **Take notes**. The mind has a wonderful ability to block out pain, so don't assume you'll remember all the comments. Taking notes has an added benefit: It gives you something to do while you're not interrupting. It's odd how comments that seem absurd or infuriating when you first hear them have a way of gaining validity when you look at them in the cool light of reason, twenty-four hours later.

WHAT TO ASK ADVANCE READERS TO LOOK FOR

You're more likely to get useful comments if you establish readers' expectations when you give them your manuscript. For instance, if you want the reader to line edit, say so. I usually tell readers not to sweat the small stuff—though most writers won't let a typo go without correcting it.

Ask your readers to put comments on the manuscript itself, and when they're done, to jot down some high level reactions, summarizing what they liked and what they didn't like. Then have a good long talk with each reader.

Here's a list of topics you might discuss with advance readers.

- **Overall reaction**: Best aspects? Weakest aspects?
- **Dramatic opening**: Did the first scene grab your attention? Make you want to keep reading? Set up the rest of the story for you?
- **Main plot**: Is it plausible? Easy to follow? Surprising? Interesting?
- **Subplots**: Are they interesting? Plausible? Easy to follow? Feel like they belong in the novel? Sufficiently resolved at the end?
- **Ending**: Is the resolution clear? Believable? Surprising?
- **Main character**: Is the main character believable? Three-dimensional? Sympathetic? Interesting?
- **Villain**: Does the villain behave logically? Seem like a worthy adversary for the main character? Is the motive for the crime(s) clear?
- **Other characters**: Do they ring true? Hold your interest?
- **Pacing**: Is it well modulated (parts that are fast-paced action and suspense alternating with others that are more leisurely story development)? Does suspense build? Does it hold your interest throughout?
- **Dialogue**: Does each character have a unique voice? Sound natural?

Don't settle for yes/no answers. Probe with follow-up questions to get specific feedback on what's working and where there are problems.

NOW YOU TRY: Get feedback on a chapter you've written

1. Add your own concerns to the list of questions below.

   QUESTIONS
   a. What did you like or dislike?
   b. Is the story holding your interest or does it bog down in places?
   c. Is the story easy to follow or confusing?
   d. Were there any parts that seemed implausible? What doesn't make sense?
   e. Are there aspects of any of these characters that you especially like or don't like?
   f. Were there any characters who didn't ring true? Which ones, and how did they seem artificial?
   g. Does the story so far seem predictable or surprising?

   YOUR ADDITIONAL QUESTIONS
   a.
   b.
   c.
   d.
   e.

2. Give the questions and the chapter to a trusted friend or fellow writer. Invite that person to read the material, write their reactions on the manuscript, and think about the questions.

3. Sit down and discuss the chapter with your reader. Go through the questions. While you're listening, jot down notes about the person's comments along with notes about your own reactions that you're not sharing.

Notes on the critique:

Notes on your reaction to the critique:

4. Assess both the critique and your own reactions. Next time, try to consciously adjust anything you are doing or feeling that might prevent you from getting the most out of a critique.

TRANSLATING COMMENTS INTO FIXES

Okay, now you've heard the critique. You've got it all written down so you can consider it rationally. How do you decide what to fix and what to ignore?

There's a scene in one of my all-time favorite mystery novels, *Gaudy Night* by Dorothy L. Sayers, which dramatizes this issue. Harriet Vane has asked Lord Peter Wimsey to read a mystery novel she's writing. She knows something is wrong, but she doesn't know exactly what it is. Peter poses the question she's been dreading:

> "If you ask me," said Wimsey, "it's Wilfrid. I know he marries the girl—but must he be such a mutt? Why does he go and pocket the evidence and tell all those unnecessary lies?"

Harriet defends her hero but is open to discussion with Peter:

> "I admit that Wilfrid is the world's worst goop. But if he doesn't conceal the handkerchief, where's my plot?"
>
> "Couldn't you make Wilfrid one of those morbidly conscientious people, who have been brought up to think that anything pleasant must be wrong—so that, if he *wants* to believe the girl an angel of light she is, all the more likely to be guilty. Give him a puritanical father and a hell-fire religion."
>
> "Peter, that's an idea."
>
> "He has, you see, a gloomy conviction that love is sinful in itself, and that he can only purge himself by taking the young woman's sins upon him and wallowing in vicarious suffering . . . He'd still be a goop, and a pathological goop, but he would be a bit more consistent."
>
> "Yes—he'd be interesting. But if I give Wilfrid all those violent and lifelike feelings, he'll throw the whole book out of balance."
>
> "You would have to abandon the jigsaw kind of story and write a book about human beings for a change."

This illustrates one of the most difficult questions a reader can ask: why a major character does something that's critical to your plot. It's a groaner, because you realize that the "fix" involves altering the character's underlying personality, reworking his entire backstory, and integrating the changes into the plot. The revision will cut a huge swath through your book. How can you tell if this is an issue you need to address?

Look for corroboration. If you agree with a criticism, of course you need to address it. If more than one person who read your manuscript mention the same problem, it should go on your to-do list. If two readers disagree with each other, ask each one to elaborate; the more information you have, the easier it will be to decide whether to address the concern or ignore it.

Next, translate problems into solutions. Here are some examples:

The reader said:	The fix is:
Chapter three ends rather abruptly.	Decide whether chapter three should have a cliffhanger or settled ending; then revise the ending so the chapter doesn't feel unfinished.
I knew who did it—I realized Charlie was guilty in the birthday scene.	Revise the birthday scene. Tone down the clues or eliminate. Check the rest of the manuscript to be sure you're not telegraphing the villain's identity.
I couldn't tell where this scene takes place.	Establish the setting at the start of the scene.
The wife seemed over the top; no one's that evil.	Shade the wife; check her dialogue, clothing, mannerisms, etc. to make her more believable *everywhere* she appears.
Why is your protagonist chasing after the child molester instead of calling the cops?	Establish motivation earlier; add flashbacks showing aspects of Bob's own experience being molested; establish his distrust of the police; show his growing determination to bring the villain to justice.

Carefully consider all the comments you get from readers, but a little red flag should go up whenever someone tells you how to fix your novel. Don't ignore the comment; try to understand where it's coming from. Ask follow-up questions, and repeat after me: *This is my novel.* You want to know what's working and what's not, and then decide yourself how to revise it.

NOW YOU TRY: Find your own fix

Return to the comments you captured when you did the last exercise and had someone critique a chapter or two of your book. In the table below, note the reader's main criticisms or suggestions on the left, and note the changes you're going to make on the right.

The reader said:	The fix is:

WHAT MAKES A GOOD ADVANCE READER?

Who should you ask to read your manuscript? Freelance editor Lorraine Bodger gives this advice:

> Protect your work. Of course you protect your work by
> backing up and having extra copies of the manuscript
> tucked away somewhere safe, but that's not the kind of
> protection I mean. You're going to want feedback on your
> work, and your instinct will be to give the manuscript to
> your friends, family members, and (worst of all) your mate
> to read. *Don't do it.* Friends, family members, and mates
> are unreliable readers and critics. Their feelings about
> you will influence what they say about your work—and
> they may love you too much or not enough, be afraid of
> hurting you, feel threatened, feel competitive, or even se-
> cretly wish you ill. You cannot trust them *where your work
> is concerned.* Only an objective, uninvolved reader can
> give you feedback that's really useful, and even then you
> must be cautious about whom you choose.

A capable reader is someone who's smart, kind, clear thinking, and articulate; someone who reads good literature and isn't afraid to tell you the truth. If you're in a good writing group, you're fortunate to have capable readers ready and waiting.

Give your manuscript to someone who is an avid reader and you're more likely to get a good overall picture of what's working and what's not. A fellow writer can often frame the strengths and weaknesses of the manuscript in more "writerly" terms. For example, if the narration is weak, a writer might explain it as a point-of-view issue, whereas the average reader may only be able to tell you that your writing seems tepid.

If you want someone who will catch all your spelling, grammar, and continuity errors, give your manuscript to a nitpicker.

You need a sufficient number of readers so you can judge whether one reader's reaction is an aberration. On the other hand, you don't want so many that you're overwhelmed with conflicting opinions. I suggest you give your work to at least three readers, but not more than six.

A WORD ABOUT BOOK DOCTORS
AND FREELANCE EDITORS

It is very difficult to get the perspective you need to edit your first novel. If you're in a good writing group, or taking a top-notch fiction writing class, you may be able to get all the critical feedback and advice necessary in order to turn out a salable manuscript.

Many writers wonder if it's worthwhile to hire and pay an outside professional editor to bring their books up to snuff. Here are some of the terms you might hear:

- **Book doctor**. An independent (freelance) editor who reads your novel and edits it thoroughly for structure, plot, character development, style, continuity, and so forth.
- **Manuscript evaluation**. The editor reads your entire manuscript and gives you feedback that usually includes strengths, weaknesses, and general suggestions for change.
- **Developmental (content) edit**. The editor reads your novel, notes problems such as structure, pacing, character development, and style; the editor may make revisions or provide you with detailed guidance on how to make the fixes.
- **Copyedit**. The editor corrects grammar, spelling, punctuation, usage, and so on; also catches logical inconsistencies and continuity problems.
- **Line edit**. The editor focuses on the sentences and words, fixing grammar, word choice, punctuation, usage, and spelling.

If you decide to hire someone to help with your book, buyer beware. There are scam artists out there, happy to take your money with promises of guaranteed success (you know, there is no such thing).

I recommend you think long and hard about the decision to hire a freelance editor. It's an expensive proposition—from hundreds of dollars for a basic copyedit to several thousand for a thorough developmental edit from an experienced freelance editor. If you go for it, get your money's worth by hiring someone with solid credentials:

- **Ask for a résumé.** Look for professional editing and/or writing experience.
- **Ask for references, authors the editor has worked with.** Call up a few and chat about their experience with this editor.
- **Ask for titles of published books the person has edited.** Check out the books to see if the editor is thanked on the acknowledgments page.
- **Ask to see a sample critique the editor has written.** Try to imagine you were the author and consider whether these comments would be helpful to you.
- **Meet the freelance editor face-to-face, preferably in his office.** Second best, have an extended telephone conversation. Be sure this is someone with whom you feel comfortable.
- **Check for reported problems with this editor.** You can check Web sites that report complaints—Preditors & Editors (www.anotherealm .com/prededitors) and Writer Beware (www.sfwa.org/beware).

If the editor checks out, be sure you define exactly what you want the editor to do and put it in writing. A reputable freelance editor will provide you with a contract that specifies the work she will do, the time frame, and the cost.

ON YOUR OWN: Hearing criticism; finding your own fix

1. Give your manuscript to three to six trusted readers.

2. Take notes on their suggestions for changes.

3. Try to hear past their suggested "fixes" and decide what you think needs to be changed.

4. Sift, prioritize, and make a list of potential revisions.

PaRt 4:
selling your
mystery novel

Introduction

> "Closely akin to the popular delusion . . . that the construction of the detective story is child's play, is an equally unfounded, general belief that the form is a literary gold mine, with financial rewards to the author out of all proportion to the amount of labor involved."
>
> —HOWARD HAYCRAFT
> *Murder for Pleasure: The Life and Times of the Detective Story* (1941)

And you thought writing the book was hard. For most of us, selling it to a publisher is an endurance test. The race goes not to the clever or swift but the bullheaded and persistent who don't know enough to give up.

I know one writer whose manuscript was rejected by forty-five literary agents before one picked her up; a few months later, she had a two-book contract with a major publishing house.

Here are the basic ways to sell your book:

- A literary agent, who represents you, shops your manuscript to publishers, and negotiates a contract on your behalf; this is the best way to sell your novel to a major publishing house.
- You or your agent queries small presses; if an editor is interested, you or your agent sends your manuscript; you or your agent negotiates the deal.
- You win a contest. There are reputable contests for first mystery novels; winning can open the door to representation with a great agent. A few contests sponsored by major publishers have a book contract as the prize. Visit Writer Beware (www.sfwa.org/beware) and become informed about the fake contests out there. See the Appendix for more information about contests.

There are entire books written on how to sell a novel. One I recommend is the annually updated *Novel & Short Story Writer's Market* published by Writer's Digest Books.

The chapters in this section provide tips for selling a mystery novel, including how to pick agents and publishers to query, how to put together a query packet that makes an editor or agent want to read your novel, and that miserable process of sending out queries and handling rejections.

CHaPtEr 26:
targeting agents

> "Finding the right agent is as hard as finding the right spouse. You are looking for the person who loves your work because it takes that kind of passion to steer a book, and a writer, through this prickly and demanding marketplace."
>
> —LAURA LIPPMAN

Honesty, integrity, chutzpa, smarts, and an insider's knowledge of the book business—those are the basic ingredients of a competent literary agent. There are many out there, some with formidable track records; others are just starting out and hungry to prove themselves.

Finding the right agent is a little bit like finding a soul mate, though the match should be between *your writing* and *the agent's taste*. In short, the right agent for you is one who is competent and loves your writing. Unvarnished enthusiasm for your work combined with the knowledge of which editors will share that enthusiasm—that's the ticket.

DO YOU NEED AN AGENT?

You need a literary agent if you want your book to be considered by any of the major mystery publishers. St. Martin's Minotaur, Berkley Prime Crime, HarperCollins, Ballantine Books, Warner Books, and all the biggies each publish a few unpublished authors each year and nearly always pick them from manuscripts submitted by literary agents.

You don't need an agent to sell your novel to a small press. It is standard practice at most small presses to be queried directly by the author. Most small presses can offer only a modest advance to a new writer, rendering the potential agent's commission miniscule. Most small presses have their submission guidelines on their Web sites.

WHAT A LITERARY AGENT DOES FOR YOU

A literary agent submits your book to editors. A good agent knows which editors at which publishing houses are likely to respond to your writing and keeps after the editors to make sure your manuscript doesn't get lost. The better your agent's reputation, the more quickly your manuscript will rise to the top of an editor's slush pile and get read.

An agent keeps you informed. If your book is getting rejected, your agent will tell you the reasons given and forward rejection letters. Your agent will call you the moment you get a nibble. An agent will try to get an auction going—a bidding war between publishing houses for your novel—and negotiate all the contract details with your interests in mind. A good agency has an attorney who reviews all contracts. Many agents sell and negotiate foreign rights; some get involved in selling subsidiary rights, as well—an audiobook or a movie option, for example.

All reputable literary agents work strictly on commission. That's the built-in incentive—your agent doesn't get paid until your book sells. You don't get paid until your agent does. Your publisher sends your advance and royalties to your agent; your agent takes out agreed-upon commission and expenses and cuts you a check for the remainder.

WHAT A REPUTABLE LITERARY AGENT SHOULD *NOT* DO

An agent who charges you for services prior to selling your novel is violating accepted industry practices. Some agents charge for expenses such as photocopying. This is fine if it's been documented and agreed upon, up front. But beyond that, if you're being charged for services before you get a book contract—whether it's called a reading fee, marketing fee, retainer, or other euphemism—something's fishy.

FINDING AN AGENT WHO'S RIGHT FOR YOU

You may need to query many agents before you find one who agrees to represent you. Agents who belong to The Association of Authors' Representatives (AAR) have agreed adhere to industry standards. When I last checked their online database (www.aar-online.org), there were 356 literary agents listed.

Target agents who are open to representing genre fiction, ideally those who represent successful mystery writers. I'm biased in favor of agents headquartered in New York City, the home of America's publishing industry.

Here are some ways to identify agents to query:

• **Get referrals from friends and fellow writers.** A referral from a friend or colleague, ideally a published author or editor whose opinion the agent respects, is hands-down the best way to get your work considered. Ask everyone you know—you'll be surprised to discover that you know people who know literary agents. Network with published writers you meet at mystery conferences, or join the local chapter of Mystery Writers of America, Sisters in Crime, or the National Writers Union. I have found that most published mystery authors are happy to share their experiences with agents, and you might even get a referral.

• **Meet agents at writing conferences and workshops.** Agents teach, speak on panels, critique manuscripts, and listen to pitches from writers at many writing conferences and workshops. For instance, twenty-six literary agents attended Bouchercon 2004, the largest annual crime fiction conference. They spoke on panels and schmoozed at cocktail parties. Most were looking for new talent. You could have walked up and introduced yourself. There are mystery conferences like the New England Crime Bake, an annual mystery conference sponsored by the New England chapters of Sisters in Crime and Mystery Writers of America, at which you can sign up for an appointment to pitch your novel to an editor or agent. Find out about conferences focusing on crime fiction from the *Deadly Directory* (www.cluelass.com/ddo). Find out about writing conferences and workshops at ShawGuides (http://writing.shawguides.com).

• **Check out "acknowledgments" in published books.** Go to the mystery section of a bookstore and pull out every recently published mystery novel that reminds you of your own, or by any author whom you admire. Read the "acknowledgments" page. Most writers thank their agents. Make a list of which agent represents which author. It's a good bet that any of those agents are worth querying.

• **Read about the latest hot deals.** Find out which agents are bringing home the bacon. Read *Publishers Weekly*, or get a free subscription to the online newsletter *Publishers Lunch* (www.caderbooks.com) and read the weekly Deal Lunch that reports on recent agent/publisher deals.

CHECKING REPUTATIONS, GETTING CONTACT INFORMATION

To find out more about a particular agent, consult a recent guide to literary agents. *Guide to Literary Agents* (Writer's Digest Books) is updated annually and publishes information provided by agents themselves. I found that book invaluable when I was querying agents for my first novel.

Here's the kind of information you can expect to find:
• name of the agency
• whether they are a member of AAR
• contact names
• how to contact
• how long in business
• number of clients

- recent deals
- whether they are taking new clients
- whether they represent unpublished authors
- whether they handle fiction in general, mystery fiction in particular
- terms (percent commission on domestic/foreign sales)
- recent sales
- tips (for example, "Obtains new clients through recommendations or upon occasion, a really good letter.")

ON YOUR OWN: An action plan for targeting agents

1. Compile a list of ten to thirty potential agents to target, including the specific reason you picked each agent.
   a. name of the friend, relative, colleague, or other writer who referred you
   b. date and event where you met the agent
   c. published mystery author this agent represents
   d. the great deal this agent recently negotiated

2. First cut: Eliminate any agency known to have had complaints against it, for example, for charging fees or providing poor contracts. Web sites with useful information for identifying disreputable agents include Preditors & Editors. (www.anotherealm.com/prededitors) and Writer Beware (www.sfwa.org/beware).

3. Second cut: Look up each agent in the current volume of a guide to agents such as *Guide to Literary Agents* (Writer's Digest Books). Read the entry to see how large the agency is, whether they are accepting new clients, and if they represent genre/mystery fiction. Based on what you glean, add this agent's contact information or eliminate the agent from your list.

4. Check to see if the agent is a member of the Association of Authors' Representatives (www.aar-online.org). While there are reputable agents who are not AAR members, you might want to give higher priority to one who is.

5. Sort: Prioritize your list, from the agent you see as most desirable to least.

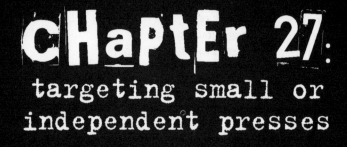

CHaPtEr 27:
targeting small or independent presses

> "When I'm reading manuscripts, I think, 'Would my customers like this book?'"
>
> —KATE MATTES
> owner of Kate's Mystery Books and acquiring editor
> for Kate's Mystery Books (Justin, Charles & Co.)

"Small press" is an elastic term that can refer to a mom-and-pop operation working out of a garage, a small publisher whose print runs rarely exceed five thousand and publishes ten or so titles a year, or a university press that publishes a handful of fiction titles each year. There are many reputable small presses. Some specialize in crime fiction, including Justin, Charles & Co. with its Kate's Mystery Books imprint, and Poisoned Pen Press.

Most small presses consider submissions directly from the author. But don't go this route just to avoid finding an agent. The best small presses are overwhelmed with submissions and can afford to be picky.

Many small presses post their submission guidelines on their Web sites.

WHAT A REPUTABLE SMALL PRESS DOES FOR YOU

Just like any major publishing house, a small press enters into a contract with you, pays you an advance and royalties, edits, and publishes your book. Generally speaking, small presses offer smaller advances and have smaller print runs than major publishing houses.

It will be easier to get your book into bookstores if the small press sells its books through a major distributor such as Ingram Book Group or Baker & Taylor, Inc. in the United States. You don't want to be selling books out of the trunk of your car.

If you sell your manuscript to a small press without the help of a literary agent, I strongly recommend you hire a knowledgeable attorney to review the contract before you sign. You want to be sure your best interests are represented across the range of important issues, including how royalties are computed and reversion of rights (what happens when your book goes out of print or the small press goes belly-up).

WHAT A REPUTABLE SMALL PRESS DOES *NOT* DO

A reputable small publisher does not charge the author anything for publishing the book—no "marketing fee," no "editing fee," no "expense charges," no nothing.

FINDING A SMALL PRESS THAT'S RIGHT FOR YOU

To find a small press that's a good fit for your novel, you need to do some research. Here are some suggestions:

• **Refer to these information sources.** These sources maintain lists of small publishers that handle mystery fiction:

- *Deadly Directory*—last I checked, this online directory (www.cluelass.com/ddo) listed eighty-six small presses that publish crime fiction.
- Mystery Writers of America—look for mystery fiction links to publishers under Resources on their Web site (www.mysterywriters.org).
- *Novel & Short Story Writer's Market* (Writer's Digest Books)—lists small presses, contact information, and other information provided by each publisher.
- *Literary Market Place* (Information Today, Inc.)—also known as LMP, this enormous, two-volume reference is available in public libraries. It lists publishers along with the genres they represent, the number of books they published the previous year, contact names, and how to get in touch with them.

• **Browse in a mystery bookstore or big-box bookstore.** If you're lucky enough to live near an independent mystery bookstore, go in browse the shelves; chat with the owner or sales staff and ask which small presses have impressed them with the quality of their offerings. If not, visit one of the big-box stores and browse current mystery fiction. Look for books that appeal to you that are published by small presses. At home, you can search the Internet for small presses or use the "advanced search" feature of one of the online bookstores to see what other books that small press has published. Look at how these books are selling and if they are getting reviewed in *Kirkus Reviews*, *Publishers Weekly*, *Library Journal*, or any of the major newspapers.

• **Meet small press editors at mystery and writing conferences.** Editors from small presses often speak at conferences where they can showcase and sell their latest books. Some conferences offer the opportunity to pitch your ideas to an editor at a small press or get your manuscript critiqued. See the Appendix for more information about conferences.

• **Meet small publishers at a regional booksellers' association conference.** Attend the annual conference of your regional retail booksellers association. Each area of the country has one—in New England, it's the New England Booksellers Association (NEBA). Check out the booths of small presses, looking for publishers that may be interested in mysteries with a regional flair. Talk to the folks manning the booth. This is not the time to pitch your novel, but find out if they are looking for new authors. Examine the books they have on display and the way they are marketing them to see if your work would fit in.

CHECK THE REPUTATION OF THE SMALL PRESSES

Before you query a small press, check out its reputation. Ask any published authors you know. Web sites with useful information about publishers include Preditors & Editors (www.anotherealm.com/prededitors) and Writer Beware (www.sfwa.org/beware). Go to a bookstore and check that books from the small press are represented among the mysteries. Leaf through some of their mysteries. Are the book cover, binding, paper quality, page formatting, and editing up to your own standards?

ON YOUR OWN: Gearing up to approach small presses

1. Decide if you want to be published by a small press.

2. Compile a list of small presses to target:

Small press	Reason you picked this publisher	Checks out in *Novel & Short Story Writer's Market*?	Checks out in Preditors & Editors?	Contact information

Small press	Reason you picked this publisher	Checks out in *Novel & Short Story Writer's Market?*	Checks out in Preditors & Editors?	Contact information

3. Check the reputation of each publisher on your list by consulting the Preditors & Editors Web site (www.anotherealm.com/prededitors). Eliminate any that have had problems reported.

4. Check out each publisher on your list in *Novel & Short Story Writer's Market*. Based on what you glean, add this publisher's contact information or eliminate it from the list.

5. Sort. Prioritize your list, from the small presses and independent publishers you see as most desirable to least.

CHaPtEr 28:
putting together
a query packet

> "Do not be intimidated by the legendary volume of agents' query mail, the so-called 'slush pile.' (My office receives several hundred letters a week.) A well-written letter and a solid premise always stand out."
>
> —DONALD MAASS
> literary agent, *Writing the Breakout Novel*

Wouldn't it be nice if you could just throw copies of your manuscript into envelopes along with your business card and mail them out? Unfortunately, the publishing world doesn't work that way. Agents and editors like to be queried first—which is a fancy way of saying they want to see the two-minute version of your novel so they can decide if they want to read it. Never send out your entire manuscript unless an editor or agent has specifically asked for it.

That brings us to the all-important query packet. This is a few pages that you put together that convey your novel in such an enticing manner that every agent or small press editor you send it to will immediately pick up the phone or e-mail you, asking you to send your manuscript, post haste.

The query packet is 100 percent marketing, somewhat like a book jacket, and its only purpose is to make an agent or editor want to read your book.

A typical query packet includes:
- a query letter, custom written for each submission
- a synopsis
- a self-addressed, stamped envelope

When I submitted our first book to prospective agents, I included the opening chapter. Since then, I've heard agents say emphatically that they do not want to be sent an unsolicited chapter. To be on the safe side, check the agency or publisher submission guidelines.

THE QUERY LETTER

The query letter should be short, no more than one page. Agents tell me they prefer letters that are businesslike and to the point. (For specific help in formatting your query letter or any other part of your submission packet, see *Formatting & Submitting Your Manuscript* by Cynthia Laufenberg and the Editors of Writer's Digest Books.) See page 236 for an example of a cover letter to an agent.

Here's some extra ammunition to use, if you've got it:

- If an author, editor, or other mutual acquaintance suggested you send your manuscript to this person, say so.
- If you have anything in common with this person—went to the same college, grew up in the same small town in Minnesota—say so.
- If you met this person at a conference, or bookstore, or party, or wherever, say where and when.
- If you heard this person speak somewhere, or read something this person wrote, mention that, and comment on some idea you took away from their remarks.
- If any established, respected writers or media personalities have read and liked your manuscript, and agreed that you can quote them, by all means include the quote.

Finally, make sure your query is letter-perfect—no spelling, grammar, or punctuation errors; no clunky sentences or awkward transitions.

THE SYNOPSIS

The synopsis for querying agents and editors is much shorter and less detailed than the before-the-fact synopsis you may have written when you were planning your novel.

Some writers, me included, find this synopsis harder to write than the novel. You have only a few pages to get it right, and the future of your manuscript hangs in the balance, because unless you write a compelling synopsis, agents and editors won't read it. The synopsis has to be informative but it cannot be boring. It has to make your novel sound fabulous, but it can't make you sound puffed up with self-praise.

Keep saying to yourself: *It's a marketing pitch.* Remember, this is *not* a blueprint of the book or a summary of everything in it.

To get a flavor of how to write a synopsis that pitches your mystery novel, visit an online bookstore and read publishers' descriptions of mystery novels. These usually start with a strong overview of the book. Here are some examples from publishers' descriptions of mystery novels:

❶ Siegfried Shazam
23 Piltdown Lane
Paramus, New Jersey 03333
Phone: 002-444-5555
Email: SShazam@isp-server.com

L.A. Jones
Jones Literary Agency, Ltd.
4 Fifth Ave., Suite 206
New York, NY 10011

March 9, 2005

Dear Mr. Jones:

❷ I am enclosing a synopsis of *Jiggery Pokery*, a mystery novel I recently finished, in the hope that you will want to see the manuscript and help me find a publisher for it.

❸ *Jiggery Pokery* is a suspense-thriller that takes place in Las Vegas and features Melinda Starr, private investigator. Starr is the daughter of a master magician, and uses the skills she learned as her father's assistant to hunt down a serial killer who picks his victims with the help of a roulette wheel.

❹ I know you have represented Max Flash, whose mystery novels I admire. This book, too, takes readers to the world of the professional magician, and though it is more hard-boiled and less occult, it should appeal to a similar audience.

❺ I am a professional magician with a considerable following in the North America and in Europe. I have written more than a dozen non-fiction articles on magic, and have a monthly column in *Magic*, the magazine for professional magicians. This is my first novel.

❻ Please let me know if I can send you the manuscript to evaluate. Contact me by phone or email, or use the enclosed SASE.

❼ Sincerely,

....

❶ *Your contact information, front and center.* ❷ *Get right down to business and say why you are writing.* ❸ *Include a one-paragraph mini-synopsis.* ❹ *Explain why you think this particular literary agent is the right one for your novel. Tell what kind of mystery you've written, and the target audience.* ❺ *Highlight any aspects of your personal background that are relevant, and will help sell the book.* ❻ *Ask if you can send your manuscript.* ❼ *State how you can be contacted.*

The secrets of a group of childhood friends unravel in this haunting thriller . . . (Delacorte Press, *Absent Friends*, S.J. Rozan)

A series of apparently motiveless murders disrupts the lives of some very different people in darkly atmospheric London. (Crown Publishers, *The Rottweiler*, Ruth Rendell)

Indigo Tea Shop owner Theodosia Browning is catering a Charleston benefit, a "Ghost Crawl" through Jasmine Cemetery. But the organizer, Dr. Davis, won't get to enjoy the festivities: During the Crawl's theatrical number, he drops dead. (The Berkley Publishing Group, *Jasmine Moon Murder*, Laura Childs)

A synopsis should continue for one to four pages, summarizing your story, including your opening gambit and all the major plot twists. A one-page synopsis can be single-spaced. A four-page synopsis should be double-spaced.

The example below is the first half of the synopsis of our novel, *Delusion*.

In the eerie pre-dawn mist, a backyard pool in a wealthy Boston suburb is transformed into a brutal bloodbath. The floating corpse is the young wife of a computer games wizard, Nick Babikian. Riddled by paranoia, Nick can provide no alibi and no potential witness other than his own mentally ill mother, whose tortured mind is permanently entrenched in her own past—her parents were Armenian Holocaust survivors. He is arrested for the crime.

Nick's attorney, Chip Ferguson, asks neuropsychologist Dr. Peter Zak to evaluate Nick. Dr. Zak runs a unit at the prestigious Pearce Psychiatric Institute and is an experienced expert witness.

Despite overwhelming circumstantial evidence of Nick's guilt, instinct and experience tell Dr. Zak that there's more to the crime than meets the eye. Dr. Zak meets with Nick in jail, and later in the prison hospital. He finds a brilliant man, haunted by the certainty that people are out to get him, convinced that his wife had a secret lover who was the father of her unborn child.

Is Nick paranoid, or is he surrounded by assassins? In an effort to tease apart reality from delusion, Dr. Zak administers a battery of psychological tests. He interviews the therapist Nick and Lisa saw for marriage counseling.

The case takes a twist when police find the remains of Lisa's unborn child buried in her therapist's garden.

To everyone's surprise, DNA results determine that Nick is the father. Nick is furious and accuses police of tampering with the lab results.

Nick's paranoia seems to be seeping into Peter's world. Is it Peter's imagination, or did he see his wife's killer, Ralston Bridges, peering in through the window at the jail? Is Bridges behind the disturbing packages Peter's mother has been receiving? The box of dead cockroaches wasn't sent by a well-wisher. Does Bridges have anything to do with the depraved advertisements someone is posting in local bars, urging patrons to call PI Annie Squires? Or is Peter's paranoia trying to connect the dots?

Either his imagination is feeding off his Nick's delusion, or somebody really is lurking in the shadows, watching his every move. Somebody who knows Peter's darkest secrets—and most crippling fears . . .

Here are some techniques to borrow from this example for your synopsis:
- Write in the present tense.
- Summarize your main characters.
- Tell the setting and context.
- For once, it's okay to tell and not show.
- Summarize the plot, hitting the major plot twists.
- Communicate your protagonist's motivation and key challenges.
- Don't try to explain every character and plot point.

SENDING OUT QUERIES

Sending out queries and waiting for responses can be difficult. Try to disconnect from the whole process emotionally. Think of it as a marketing campaign, and you're the hired help—because as surely as there is death and taxes, you will get rejections. Do not become discouraged. Remember, a successful literary agent gets hundreds of queries each year and takes on only a handful of new clients. This race goes to the persistent.

Make multiple copies of your query packet with pre-addressed envelopes, ready to go. Twenty or so, to start. Send out a batch, five or so, to the top agents or small presses on your list. Follow up by phone or e-mail only after the response time that the publisher states in its guidelines has passed. And even then, wait another week or so.

Every time you get a rejection, send out the next query packet. If an agent or editor wants to see your manuscript, send it immediately.

SUBMITTING A PROFESSIONAL MANUSCRIPT

To make the best impression, your manuscripts should be formatted the way agents and editors expect. Here's a checklist to ensure that you are following marketing standards:

___ 8.5" x 11" paper (copy paper is fine)

___ No holes punched

___ Loose pages; no folder, staples, or binding

___ Print one-sided

___ Black ink only

___ Title page with the title of your book, your name, and your contact information

---

Murder by the Book

by Victor Yablonsky

Victor Yablonsky
33 Elm st., Oadale, ILL
011-822-3344–VictorY@email.net

— Double-spaced text, left justified
— Paragraphs: Indent the first line five spaces
— Margins: 1″ to 1.25″ all around
— Font: Courier 10 or 12 point; or Times New Roman 12 point
— Headers on each page: flush left: your name and the title of the book; flush right: page number

— Number pages consecutively, not by chapter
— No footers
— No copyright notice is necessary; editors and agents know your story is copyrighted because U.S. an International Copyright Laws say so

ABOUT REJECTION

Expect rejection. You'll have agents who say "no thank you" to your query letter; you'll have agents who ask to see a chapter (shout for joy!), then ask for the manuscript (cross all fingers and toes), and then send you a "Dear Author" letter saying sorry. An editor may even hold on to your book for months as your hopes mount, only to reject it.

Remind yourself how competitive this business is. A good agent already has a full plate of clients vying for attention. Each editor has slots for only a few unpublished authors in a given year. With each rejection, feel your skin thickening as your ego grows calluses—you'll need them.

Each time a rejection arrives, pick yourself up, dust yourself off, and send out the next query packet. Remember, it could be the next one that clicks.

Most often, the rejection letters say something general, as in these examples from my very own pile of agent rejections:

> "I am sorry to say that I don't have the requisite enthusiasm to take on the project and represent it properly."

> "The market is very tight right now, and I am being highly selective about the new properties which I am taking on."

> "I'm afraid I don't think I'd be able to sell it. The writing is good, but the story line didn't work for me."

But you may also get rejection letters that go into some detail about your novel's weaknesses. Cherish these, because agents and editors rarely take time to critique material unless they see potential. If you start to see a pattern—for example, if several rejection letters say your main character isn't strong enough, or if more than one point to the same weakness in your plot—you might want to stop, consider the criticism, and decide whether to revise your book before continuing to send it out.

Few editors make go/no-go decisions by themselves. The editor who loves your book has to convince his peers, and also sales and marketing, that not only is your book terrific, but there's a strong market for it. Remember, book publishing is a business. A decision to publish a book is not a reward for literary quality; it's a gamble for financial gain.

You may get rejected for reasons totally beyond your control. I cursed and screamed when I read this in a rejection letter our agent forwarded to us:

> "The authors have done a splendid job in setting up an intriguing mystery: My problem is that I've just acquired a series by a forensic psychiatrist and starring a forensic psychiatrist, so this came in, alas, about a month too late."

A FINAL WORD

If your mystery novel is a good one, it will find an agent. If it's good *and* luck is with you, it will find a publisher. When that happens, break out the champagne. Celebrate!

Then start writing the next book before you get sucked into the vortex of promoting the one you just sold.

ON YOUR OWN: Putting together a query packet

1. Write tailored query letters for each agent or small press. Use this checklist to guide you:

   — Put your contact information front and center.

   — Say why you are writing.

   — Provide a mini-synopsis of the novel.

   — Say why you think *this particular literary agent or small press* is the right one for your book.

   — Describe the kind of mystery you've written, and the audience for your novel.

   — Highlight any aspects of your personal background that are relevant and will help sell the book.

   — Ask: Can I send you my manuscript?

   — If it applies, include: a reminder of where you met this agent or editor; who referred you; praise for your work from a published writer who has agreed to let you use the quote; and anything else you share in common with this agent or editor.

   — State how you can be contacted.

   — Check spelling, grammar, punctuation errors; revise clunky sentences and awkward transitions.

   — Include an SASE.

2. Write a synopsis that pitches your novel:
   a. One page, single-spaced, double-spaced between paragraphs; or two to four pages, double-spaced, indent paragraphs.
   b. Start with a strong overview of your book.
   c. Summarize the plot story in a compelling, present-tense narrative.
   d. Don't try to explain every character and plot point; cover the major plot twists.
   e. Summarize the main characters and their challenges.
   f. Make it informative but not boring.

3. Revise your query packet to the professional standards that editors and agents expect, using the checklist provided in this chapter.

Appendix of Resources for Mystery Writers

GROUPS

Here are some organizations that can be helpful to budding mystery writers:

Sisters in Crime (SinC) www.sistersincrime.org

Sisters in Crime is a supportive organization for published and unpublished mystery writers with chapters worldwide. Its mission is "To combat discrimination against women in the mystery field, educate publishers and the general public as to inequities in the treatment of female authors, raise the level of awareness of their contributions to the field, and promote the professional advancement of women who write mysteries." SinC has a special chapter for unpublished writers (GUPPIES), an Internet chapter, and local chapters.

Mystery Writers of America (MWA) www.mysterywriters.org

Mystery Writers of America is a nonprofit, professional organization of mystery and crime writers. MWA gives out the annual Edgars, the "Academy Awards" for mystery fiction. Unpublished authors can join as Affiliate Members. MWA sponsors an annual meeting in New York City with informative panels for mystery writers; there are local chapters that hold regular meetings. There is also an e-mail discussion group (EMWA) that provides an online community for members. They use this moderated e-mail discussion list to get answers to questions about anything from guns, to forensics, to writing, to finding an agent. Participants generously share a wide range of skills and knowledge. It's a supportive group and tolerant of newbies as long as you follow the rules and stay on topic.

DorothyL www.dorothyl.com

This online e-mail discussion list is a virtual community for lovers of the mystery genre. Scores of messages are posted daily. Anyone can sign up to participate.

National Writers Union www.nwu.org

NWU is a writers organization and a labor union that represents freelance writers in all genres. One of its services is a network of contract advisors who assist members in reviewing contracts. NWU maintains an agents database.

GUIDES TO ALL THINGS MYSTERIOUS

Here are two useful compendiums of information about mystery fiction:

Deadly Directory www.cluelass.com/ddo

This invaluable online directory is updated annually and includes information about mystery booksellers, organizations, events, periodicals, independent publishers, information resources, and awards.

MysteryNet.com www.mysterynet.com

One of the best all-around sites for mystery writers and readers. The "Resources" section contains essays about mystery writing, plus information about mystery awards, events, organizations, and bookstores.

CONFERENCES

There are nearly two dozen conferences that focus on mystery fiction held each year. Visit *The Mysterious Home Page (www.cluelass.com)* to find Web links. Here are a few noteworthy examples:

Bouchercon

This annual fall conference is the largest mystery event for fans and authors in the United States. It shifts location each year. Buchercon can be a bit overwhelming, but it's a great place to get an overview of the industry and to meet established writers, publishers, and agents.

Book Passage Mystery Writers Conference

In July, this intimate and intensive four-day program is sponsored by California's premier independent bookstore, Book Passage, in Corte Madera. It's pricey, but the faculty is primo.

Left Coast Crime

This annual West coast conference is smaller than Bouchercon but still attracts the *crème de la crème* of mystery writing. Scheduled in February/March, it shifts location each year.

Malice Domestic®

This conference takes place in the spring in or near Washington, D.C., and focuses on "traditional mysteries." There is even a hat contest (and parade).

MARKET RESOURCES

Here are some sources for sleuthing out the track records and reputations of literary agents and publishers:

Association of Authors' Representatives (AAR)

AAR is a nonprofit professional organization for agents. The Web site posts the ethical standards by which members agree to abide. Check their online database (www.aar-online.org) to see if an agent belongs.

Guide to Literary Agents (Writer's Digest Books)

This annually updated volume provides a comprehensive listing of literary agents, with specific information provided by the agencies themselves on what they want and how they want it. It also includes useful tips and interviews with insiders.

Literary Market Place (Information Today, Inc.)

This two-volume reference is available in public libraries. It lists publishers along with the genres they represent, the number of books they published the previous year, contact names, and how to get in touch with them.

Novel & Short Story Writer's Market (Writer's Digest Books)

Find the latest information about the market for mystery fiction in this annually updated volume. Find out which book publishers are looking for mystery fiction, including major houses as well as small and independent presses.

Preditors & Editors www.anotherealm.com/prededitors

This independent Web site provides all kinds of information for authors. Dishonest agents, shoddy publishing practices, contest scams, book doctors who fleece unwitting authors, and poorly run writing workshops are exposed.

Publishers Lunch/Deal Lunch www.caderbooks.com

Subscriptions are free to this online newsletter reporting the latest news in the publishing business. The weekly Deal Lunch reports on recent agent/publisher deals.

Writer Beware www.sfwa.org/beware

This is part of the Science Fiction and Fantasy Writers of America's Web site and provides information about fraudulent agents, scams, writer alerts, copyright, electronic rights, and so on.

Writer's Market www.writersmarket.com

Subscribe to this comprehensive, online resource for writers and get access to a searchable database of writing markets, or find much of this information in the annually updated book, *Writer's Market* (Writer's Digest Books).

CONTESTS

Here are some of the best contests for unpublished mystery writers:

St. Martin's Press/Malice Domestic Contest for the Best First Traditional Mystery Novel

This contest is open to authors who have never published traditional mystery. The prize is a book contract with St. Martin's Minotaur.

Best Private Eye Novel Contest Sponsored by the Private Eye Writers of America (PWA) and St. Martin's Press

The contest is open to authors who have never published a "private eye" mystery. The prize is a book contract with St. Martin's Minotaur.

Sara Ann Freed Memorial Award for a First Mystery

The contest is open to writers who have never been published in the mystery genre and considers straight mysteries, noir, police procedurals, or historicals with a male or female protagonist who is an amateur or professional detective. The prize is a book contract with Mysterious Press/Warner Books.

The Crime Writers' Association (CWA) Debut Dagger Award

The contest is open to anyone who has not had a novel published, commercially, in any genre. It is sponsored by Britain's club for crime writers and awards a cash prize; winning is prestigious and often leads to publication.

index

Act, 75
Action sequence, 171-178
  believable, 175-177
  speeding up and slowing down, 175
  visualization in advance, 173-174
Adjectives, describing setting, 146
Advance readers, 216-218, 221
Adverbs
  describing setting, 146
  -ly, 209
Agent, 226-229
Aha! moment, 179, 180, 182
Attribution, 210

Backstory, 186-193
  in dialogue, 188-189
  in extended flashback, 191-192
  in fictional documents, 189-190
  first-person narrator and, 187
  memories and, 190
  third-person narrator and,
    187-188
Blueprint for planning, 86-91
Book doctors, 221-222

Caper, 3
Chapter, 75
Chapter transitions, 124-125
Characters
  adversary, 53-54
  details about, 108-110
  dynamics between, in Q&A,
    154-156
  innocent suspects, 45-49
  introducing, 108-110
  major, 108, 110-114
  minor, 108, 115-116

mystery sleuth, 18-35. *See also*
  Mystery sleuth
  picking point-of-view, 133
  presencing, 143
  read through by, 205
  researching, 20-21
  revising, 202
  sidekick, 50-52
  supporting, 54-56
  victim, 36-38
  villain, 40-44
  walk-ons, 108, 116-117
Clichés, 211
Climax
  dramatic, 74
  final, 74-75
Clues, 153, 157-159
Coda, 194-197
Coincidence, 161-162
Conferences, 243
Conflict
  adversary and, 53
  reflection and, 183-184
Contests, 244
Cozy, 3
Criticism
  asking for, 216-218
  tips for taking, 215-216
  translating comments into fixes,
    218-219
Current events, 58-59

Dialogue
  action/prop for, 143
  authentic-sounding, 141-142
  backstory in, 188-189
  convincing, 139-141

dialect, 140
internal. *See* Internal dialogue
    investigation and, 153
    point of view and, 134
    referring to characters in, 118
    reflection in, 180-181
    revising, 209
    showing emotion in, 143
    summarizing vs. 144
Dramatic action, 93-94
Dramatic opening, 71-73, 96-102
    analyzing, 96-97
    beginning, 100-101
    ending, 101
    sketching out, 99-100
    writing, 101

Editors, freelance, 221-222

Fem-jep subgenre, 4
First draft, 93-95
Flashback, extended, 191-192
Forensic subgenre, 4
Foreshadowing, 166-167

Genre busters, 4
Genre fiction, 3
Grammar
    in dialogue, 140
    revising, 206-207

Historical mystery, 4
Hook, 5-6, 72

Ideas, 14-17
Internal dialogue, 179
    characters' differing, 134-135
    introspection and, 172
    reflection in, 182
Investigation, 93
    clues vs. red herrings, 157-159
    coincidence and, 161-162
    confusion and, 161
    interrogating, 152-157
    observing, 152-154
    withholding information from
        reader about, 159-161

Legal subgenre, 4
Libel, 111
Literary agent, 226-229

Manuscript
    format for, 239
    length of, 95

Modus operandi, 43
Mystery fiction
    components of, 93-94
    popular, 5-6
    series and standalones, 4-5
    subgenres, 3-4
    what is?,2
Mystery sleuth, 18-35
    appearance of, 22-24
    background of, 25-26
    dark past of, 19
    disequilibrium and, 24-25
    importance of crime to, 38-39
    naming, 32-35
    personality of, 28-29
    profession of, 19-21
    talents and skills of, 27
    tastes and preferences of, 30-32
    under duress, 29-30
    See also Protagonist

Naming characters, 117-118
    sleuth, 32-35, 110
    supporting characters, 55-56

Opening scene. *See* Dramatic opening
Organizations, 242
Outline, 78-79. *See also*
    Scene-by-scene outline

Pacing, 125
Payoff, 75, 122-123, 167-168
Place
    creating sense of, 145-151
    See also Setting
Planning, blueprint for, 86-91
Planning process, 12-91
Plot, 69-81
    before-the-fact synopsis, 79-81
    dramatic opening (setup), 71-73
    final climax, 74-75
    outlining, 78-79
    revising, 202
    shape of mystery, 70
    sleuth's quest and, 70-71
    structure, 75-77
    subplot, 77-78, 205
    twists and dramatic climaxes,
        73-74
Point of view, 126-138
    first-person, 126-127, 187
    multiple-third-person, 127-129
    omniscient, 127, 129-130
    picking characters, 133
    revising, 202

revising breaches in, 213
sliding, 130-133
story and changing, 133-135
strong narrator, 135-138
third-person, 187-188
third-person-limited, 126, 128
Police procedural subgenre, 3, 64
Premise, 14-17
Private investigator (PI) subgenre, 3
Protagonist
home or office of, 62
introducing, 103-107
ways to plague, 70-71
See also Mystery sleuth
Psychological suspense, 4

Q&A. *See* Interrogation
Query packet, 234-241
query letter, 235
sending out, 238
synopsis, 235, 237-238

Reading list, 7-8
Red herrings, clues vs., 157-159
Reference books, 9
Reflection, 93-94, 179-185
conflict and, 183-184
in dialogue, 180-181
in internal dialogue, 182
Rejection, 239-240
Resources, 242-245
Revising
attributions, 210
author tics, 212
chronology check, 203
clichés, 211
for consistency, 213
dialogue, 209
grammar, spelling, and punctuation, 206-207
main character, 202
pacing check, 204
plot, 202
point of view, 202
point-of-view breaches, 213
process, 198-223
selective read-throughs, 205
starts and finishes, 212
strategy for, 199-200
techniques for, 201

Scene, 75
descriptions, 119-122
final. *See* Coda
pacing, 125
payoff in, 122-123
setting, 145-147
starting new, 123-124
Scene-by-scene outline
chronology check using, 203-204
pacing check using, 204
Schedule, writing, 8-9
Selling your novel, 224-241
Setting, 57-68
context, 63-65
creating vivid, 145-147
details of, 149
finding information about, 66-67
realistic, 65-67
uses of, 147-149
when, 57-60
where, 60-62
Sleuth. *See* Mystery sleuth
Small press, 230-233
Subgenres, 3-4
Suspects, innocent, 45-49
Suspense, 93-94
ending with payoff, 167-168
foreshadowing vs. telegraphing,
166-167
modulating, 165-166
sensory detail and, 163-165
slowing down time and, 165
Synopsis
before-the-fact, 79-81
in query packet, 235, 237-238

Telegraphing, 166-167
Title, 82-85
Tone, dialogue and, 140

Verbs
action, 172
describing setting, 146-147
revising verb choices, 207-209
Victim, 36-38
Villain, 40-44, 202
Violence, villain and, 44

Word choice, dialogue and, 140
Writing process, 10-11, 92-197
Writing space, 8-9